Deprivation of Liberty: A Handbook

Her Honour Nazreen Pearce

District Judge Sue Jackson
Nominated Judge of the Court of Protection

JORDAN
PUBLISHING

Published by Jordan Publishing Limited
21 St Thomas Street
Bristol BS1 6JS

Whilst the publishers and the author have taken every care in preparing the material included in this work, any statements made as to the legal or other implications of particular transactions are made in good faith purely for general guidance and cannot be regarded as a substitute for professional advice. Consequently, no liability can be accepted for loss or expense incurred as a result of relying in particular circumstances on statements made in this work.

British Library Cataloguing-in-Publication Data

A catalogue record for this book is available from the British Library.

ISBN 978 1 78473 011 6

Typeset by Letterpart Limited, Caterham on the Hill, Surrey CR3 5XL

Printed in Great Britain by Hobbs the Printers Limited, Totton, Hampshire SO40 3WX

Deprivation of Liberty:
A Handbook

PREFACE

'1 Everyone has the right to liberty and security of person. No one shall be deprived of his liberty save in the following cases and in accordance with a procedure prescribed by law ... the lawful detention of persons for the prevention of the spreading of infectious diseases, of *persons of unsound mind*, alcoholics or drug addicts or vagrants ...

4 Everyone who is deprived of his liberty by arrest or detention shall be entitled to take proceedings by which the lawfulness of his detention shall be decided speedily by a court and his release ordered if the detention is not lawful.

5 Everyone who has been the victim of arrest or detention in contravention of the provisions of this Article shall have an enforceable right to compensation.'

(Art 5, European Convention for the Protection of Human Rights and Fundamental Freedoms)

The European Convention for the Protection of Human Rights and Fundamental Freedoms (ECHR) was incorporated into UK law in October 2000. The government of the day was justly proud of the rights it enshrined. However, for those lacking capacity to make decisions for themselves, no framework was available for the right to liberty to be upheld when cared for by the State. As a consequence, the UK government was criticised in the leading case of *R v Bournewood Community Mental Health NHS Trust ex parte L (Secretary of State for Health and others intervening)* [1998] 3 All ER 289 HL cited on appeal to ECtHR as *HL v United Kingdom (Bournewood)* [2004] 40 EHRR 761. The government attempted to bridge the gaps highlighted by ECtHR by amendments to the Mental Capacity Act 2005 which provided an administrative regime of deprivation of liberty safeguards to authorise and review care provided to those in residential/hospital accommodation. The new regime was deficient in two important areas because it failed to give a definition of what might amount to a deprivation of liberty and because it provided no protection for those who were provided with services by the State outside the residential sector, but where the services were such that they amounted to a deprivation of liberty.

In *P v Cheshire West and Chester County Council and Another; P and Q v Surrey County Council* [2013] UKSC 19, [2014] COPLR 313, SC (referred to as *Cheshire West* and *MIG and MEG*) the Supreme Court addressed these issues by devising a test for when there may be a deprivation of liberty and confirming that a whole range of provision by the State from high-end secure residential care to domiciliary packages of support can operate as a deprivation of liberty for which safeguards need to be in place. In consequence of this decision various attempts have been made to provide a procedure for the wide range of situations that now come within the test suggested by the Supreme Court in the *Cheshire West* case, including rule changes, and the validity of the test has been criticised. Whilst jurists, academician, lawyers, judges and the Law Commission argue about how best to protect the most vulnerable in our society within the framework of the European Convention the reality is that, in the absence of a statutory framework for anything other than residential care, the responsibility for safeguarding liberty lies with the Court of Protection

This Handbook is therefore designed to assist legal, medical and social work practitioners to navigate the law, practice and procedure as it currently stands relating to this sensitive and complex area, so as to provide the best possible protection for some of the most vulnerable in society.

Nasreen Pearce
Sue Jackson
September 2015

CONTENTS

TABLE OF CASES

References are to paragraph numbers.

TABLE OF STATUTES

References are to paragraph numbers.

TABLE OF STATUTORY INSTRUMENTS

References are to paragraph numbers.

CHAPTER 1

INTRODUCTION

1.1 BACKGROUND

> A person lacks capacity in relation to a matter if he is not able to make decisions
> for himself in relation to a specific matter because of impairment of or disturbance
> in the functioning of his mind or brain.[1]

Those who lack capacity may not be able to decide upon nor give consent to,
care and/or accommodation provided for them by a public body. This may
include hospital or other institutional admissions for care and treatment or
placements in sheltered accommodation, supported lodgings or with adult
carers provided for them by local authorities. Depending on the nature and
extent of these arrangements and their circumstances, the provision of the
placement and the care may result in a deprivation of liberty. Similarly, those
receiving extensive support and monitored care provision from health and local
authorities in their own homes to which they cannot give agreement because of
a lack of capacity may also be deprived of their liberty.

Historically, it was assumed that persons of unsound mind should be kept in
some form of confinement but during the nineteenth century the risk of
unjustified confinement began to be recognised. Statutory provisions contained
in the Mental Deficiency Act of 1913 and 1927 provided for the care of those
who fell within this category. However there was no protection for those who
lacked capacity to give consent for reasons other than for medical attention. A
paternalistic approach to the care of those who lacked capacity and who
needed state provision gave rise to the notion that, so long as an adult was
compliant with care, he or she was taken not to object to the arrangements
made on their behalf. The care of the mentally disordered and mentally
impaired by the state underwent much needed modernisation during the second
half of the twentieth century. Since the 1950s mental health legislation has
transformed previous brutal and harsh remedial strategies into the concept of
treatment and care within the community. For those suffering mental disorder,
the Mental Health Act 1959 introduced a statutory framework for compulsory
detention and treatment with a right to seek review of the need for detention
before a Mental Health Review Tribunal. These provisions did not include
those who lacked capacity for reasons other than mental disorder and thus, as
before, this group fell outside the statutory framework of protection. However

---

[1] MCA 2005, s 2.

in adopting a medical approach, emphasis was placed upon the idea of voluntary acceptance of intervention either in the form of treatment in the community or by way of admission to hospital. The concept of informal admission under s 5 of the Mental Health Act 1959 meant that a person could be admitted to hospital with their consent and without the provider using statutory powers of detention as had been necessary in the past. Moreover, informal admission was also intended to apply to those with mental impairment placed in hospitals and residential care, who lacked capacity to consent to their placement and who were not actually resisting. So by the end of the twentieth century, most people admitted to care and who lacked capacity were regarded as being admitted and detained 'informally', notwithstanding the absence of consent for which we now know, there was no basis in law. This was confirmed by the House of Lords in *Re F (Mental Patient: Sterilisation)*[2] when it decided that no one was authorised by law to consent to treatment on behalf of an adult who lacked capacity to consent; nor could the court give such consent, but it was lawful for the person who lacked capacity to be given treatment and care as was necessary in his own best interests. This principle has come to be known as the 'necessity principle'. If, however, there was any doubt or dispute in relation to such treatment or care the High Court had jurisdiction to declare whether or not the proposed action was lawful. This principle was subsequently included in the Mental Capacity Act 2005 (MCA 2005), s 5. The Act as originally drafted also included a provision in s 6(5) (now deleted), which made it clear that any action taken against a person lacking capacity which is more than merely to restrain P and deprives P of his liberty within the meaning of Art 5(1) of the European Convention for the Protection of Human Rights and Fundamental Freedoms 1950 (ECHR) (whether or not is a public authority) is not permitted.

The main categories of people who lack capacity to consent to provision by the state include: the elderly who with the onset of advancing years develop dementing illness; victims of strokes or accidents causing brain injury; the mentally ill; or those with learning disabilities. Further examples are set out in the *Mental Capacity Act 2005 Code of Practice*, para 4.12. The vast majority of people who live in residential or nursing homes or hospitals will be older people who lack capacity at the time of admission or who lose capacity during their residence in care. Most institutions, for understandable safety and security reasons, have barriers preventing them from leaving or a regime where life is constantly under the control of the management and staff. In more extreme cases of violent behaviour they maybe the subject of non-consensual physical restraint. It is unlikely that many would actively resist their detention. No less important is the provision of care in a domestic setting where in reality P may live within a regime imposed by carers.

The approach of public bodies to the care and treatment of those lacking capacity to decide for themselves was regarded as falling within the 'principle of necessity'. How far these principles were compliant within Art 5 of the ECHR remained untested. Those lacking capacity had no mechanism to challenge

---

[2]   [1990] 2 AC 1, [1991] UKHL 1.

provision amounting to a deprivation of their liberty, for instance by way of the tribunal regime created for mentally ill people under the Mental Health legislation.

1.2 CONVENTION RIGHTS

The European Convention for the Protection of Human Rights and Fundamental Freedoms 1950 (ECHR) aimed to secure the universal and effective recognition and observance of certain rights which were embodied in the Convention and, provided a procedure for an individual to have access to an international court to challenge the law of a state or the decision of the domestic court on the basis that it was not compliant with Convention rights. The Human Rights Act 1998 incorporated the ECHR into our domestic law by providing that domestic law should be enacted, interpreted and applied so that it is compatible with the Convention. The ECHR operates to protect the rights of citizens against unlawful actions of the state. Article 5 guarantees a right to liberty and security. It provides:

> 5(1) 'Everyone has the right to liberty and security of person. No one shall be deprived of his liberty save in the following cases and in accordance with a procedure prescribed by law ...
>
> (e)   the lawful detention of persons for the prevention of the spreading of infectious diseases, **of persons of unsound mind**, alcoholics or drug addicts or vagrants.
>
> 5(4) Everyone who is deprived of his liberty by arrest or detention shall be entitled to take proceedings by which the lawfulness of his detention shall be decided speedily by a court and his release ordered if the detention is not lawful'
>
> 5(5) Everyone who has been the victim of arrest or detention in contravention of the provisions of this Article shall have an enforceable right to compensation.

1.3 THE *BOURNEWOOD* GAP

The leading case of *R v Bournewood Community Mental Health NHS Trust ex parte L (Secretary of State for Health and others intervening)*[3] cited on appeal to the European Court of Human Rights (ECtHR) as *HL v United Kingdom (Bournewood)*,[4] highlighted the absence of any available procedure to safeguard the rights of those lacking capacity who are detained or restrained or restricted to a degree that could be interpreted as a deprivation of their liberty.

HL was a mentally incapacitated man who was detained in hospital against the wishes of his carers and without being sectioned under Mental Health Act 1983 (MHA 1983). There was no statutory authority for his detention. He was regarded as being admitted informally. Since he did not resist admission nor did he attempt to leave, he was taken to have consented. Judicial review proceedings were brought to challenge the decision to detain him. The House of

---

[3]   [1998] 3 All ER 289, HL.
[4]   [2004] 40 EHRR 761.

Lords held that there was a common law power under the doctrine of necessity to detain those who lack capacity, if it is in their best interests. Thus HL's detention was lawful and he had not been deprived of his liberty unlawfully.

The decision of the House of Lords was challenged before the ECtHR. The European Court decided that HL had been deprived of his liberty in contravention of Art 5(1) of the ECHR, as it did not provide a procedure prescribed by law to challenge the actions taken by the public body and, in contravention of Art 5(4) for failure to provide a speedy access to a court. The following (*Bournewood*) gaps in UK legislation for those who lack capacity to consent and for whom the state needs to provide a placement were noted inter alia:

- No fixed procedural rules for admission and detention of a compliant incapacitated person.
- No requirement to specify the need for detention.
- No requirement to specify the purpose of detention.
- No method of nominating a particular person as a representative to support P and to represent P's interests, wishes and feelings.
- No procedure available for a continuing assessment and review of the proposed provision of care and detention.
- No procedure available for the person detained or a representative on his behalf to have the decision reviewed or challenged either on merit or in breach of his Art 5 rights before an independent tribunal.

Although the MCA 2005 had dealt with some of these concerns the specific gaps identified by the ECtHR were not bridged and it was necessary for the government to respond to the problem.

1.4 DEPRIVATION OF LIBERTY SAFEGUARDS

The Deprivation of Liberty Safeguards (DoLS) were introduced in 2009 by way of amendment to the recently introduced Mental Capacity Act 2005. This was the government's attempt to address the shortcomings of domestic law as it related to the detention and restraint of those lacking capacity, where that amounts to a deprivation of liberty. The Mental Capacity Act had been in force only a short time and had revolutionised the approach of the law to those lacking in capacity generally. It created a revamped Court of Protection and a framework of dedicated rules and allied Code of Practice. The government therefore saw this legislation as the appropriate vehicle to carry the new safeguards for those who lacked capacity to make decisions, who were detained in hospitals or care homes, but who were deprived of their liberty, otherwise than under the Mental Health Act 1983.

The challenge was to create a regime which authorised detention where it was found to exist and provide rights of redress. DoLS created a two-fold scheme for this:

- an administrative process, now contained in Sch A1 to the Mental Capacity Act whereby a hospital or care home detaining those lacking capacity (P) has to seek authorisation for accommodation amounting to a deprivation of liberty and, enabling challenge to the granting of the authorisation either by using the administrative appeal procedure or, by way of application to the Court of Protection;

- a power for CoP to authorise and review P's deprivation of liberty where the authorisation regime does not apply (s 4A) and to authorise a deprivation of liberty for life sustaining treatment (s 4B).

What the legislators avoided was an accompanying statutory definition of what amounts to a deprivation of liberty. This has led to misunderstanding and confusion about what amounts to a deprivation of liberty and how and when safeguards are to be applied. In particular arrangements made in P's best interests where there is no alternative were not regarded as requiring authorisation. Neither residential placements out with the Sch A1 regime were considered to deprive liberty, nor were placements other than residential placements ie adult foster care. In those situations P was prevented from accessing the safeguards and the protection was diluted.

Two cases which were decided by the Supreme Court in 2014, *P v Cheshire West and Cheshire County Council* and *P and Q v Surrey County Council*,[5] colloquially known as *Cheshire West* and *MIG & MEG* crystallised jurisprudence in this respect. The approach is encapsulated in the phrase of Lady Hale: 'A gilded cage is still a cage'. The effect of these decisions is to bring within the DoLS regime of authorisation, either under Sch A1 or by the court, all those who lack capacity, and who receive any accommodation arranged by the state or a high level of domiciliary service from the state. Health and local authorities have a responsibility to identify those concerned and obtain authorisation. The numbers involved are huge and apply to a wide range of circumstances.

1.5 POST-*CHESHIRE WEST* DEVELOPMENTS

A week before the Supreme Court's judgment the House of Lords Select Committee on the MCA 2005 was critical of the DoLS. Lady Hale in her judgment referred to the safeguards as having the appearance of 'bewildering complexity (para 9). On 3 April 2014 the Department of Health published guidance *Positive and Pro-active Care: Reducing Restrictive Intervention*, for adult health and care staff to develop a culture so that physical restraint and other restrictive practices are only used as an option of last resort.

In June 2014 the Government published its response to the Select Committee's report in which it set out a number of steps that it proposes to take (which includes commissioning up to date guidance on DoLs to be published by the end of 2014; a project to consider the current forms and redraft or create new

---

[5]   [2014] UKSC 19.

forms that are more user friendly by the end of November 2014; and producing a revised Code of Practice to deal with the interface between the MCA 2005 and the Mental Health Act 1983) for consultation. It has also asked the Law Commission to undertake a review of the DoLS procedures; to consult on and then to draft a new legal framework to allow for the authorisation of best interests deprivation of liberty in supported living arrangements.

In the meantime in *Re X and Others (Deprivation of Liberty)*,[6] the President of the Family Division Sir James Munby gave guidance on how the government needed to respond, and devised a 'streamlined' procedure setting out how DoLS cases which fall outside the Sch A1 regime should be dealt with to steer these authorisations through the court. In brief the President distilled the following principles:

- Authorisations made by the court must be ordered by a judge and not by way of an administrative procedure.

- Some authorisations may be considered on the papers without the need for an oral hearing in straightforward cases.

- Triggers for an oral hearing include authorisations where capacity is at issue, where the parties are in dispute, where P needs to be made a party or objects.

- Authorisations must be reviewed annually by a judge but can be done on the papers unless issues such as those listed above apply (see further under Chapter 4).

The new process was put into effect on a pilot basis in November 2014. The process was subsequently given formal approval by a new Practice Direction, PD10AA accompanied by a new form and a model form of order. The MOJ developed a dedicated procedure for these applications.

Alongside the introduction of the 'streamlined process' two of the parties in *Re X* appealed against the President's ruling that it is not necessary for P to join as a party to proceedings which seek to deprive him of his liberty. The Court of Appeal handed down its judgment on 16 April 2015. The Court held that it had no jurisdiction to hear the appeals because the first decision at first instance did not affect the appellants directly and secondly because the President had not made any decisions that related to any of the parties before him but was based on hypothetical situations. The Court, however, ruled that:

'The particular course he [the President] adopted was not one that was open to him ...[7]

He engaged in an illegitimate approach to the determination of what he and all legal representatives regarded as generic academic issues without any, or any proper, identification of the particular issues which arose in the specific cases

---

[6]   [2014] EWCOP 25.
[7]   Black LJ at [58].

before him, he had no jurisdiction to make the determinations which he did. In consequence and, with respect, what are merely his opinions in relation to those matters …'[8]

and that:

'… involved an inappropriate use of the court's process … It was in substance a consultative exercise intended to promote the development of new rules of procedure and for that reason it was not … one which the court was entitled to undertake.'[9]

The MOJ has respected the decision and for the time being has suspended use of the streamline procedure, pending consideration of an alternative way forward possibly involving a rule change.

In any event, in March 2015 the Court of Protection Rules 2007 were amended by the Court of Protection (Amendment) Rules 2015.[10] Of particular relevance to this publication is the insertion of the new r 3A which makes provision for P's participation in proceedings. This rule and how it impacts on the CA's ruling in *Re X* on P's party status is discussed in Chapter 6.

The development of the law practice and procedure is currently being driven by force of circumstances, on a piecemeal trial and error fashion which has not assisted those who are affected by it or those who have the responsibility to provide care, treatment, security and protection for them.

The Law Commission report with a draft bill has been brought forward to 2016. The consultation paper was published on 7 July 2015. It acknowledges the complexities of the current regime, which should be simplified. It considers a different approach to safeguards in different settings. Further, it suggests avoiding the current narrow focus on Art 5 of the ECHR to allow new legislation to incorporate compatibility with the provisions of Art 8 and UN Convention on the Rights of Persons with Disabilities. When the process is completed it may bring some clarity in the future.

Currently the law, practice and procedure is stated at September 2015.

---

[8]   Gloster LJ at [127].
[9]   Moore-Bick LJ at [146].
[10]   SI 2015/548.

CHAPTER 2

WHAT IS DEPRIVATION OF LIBERTY?

2.1 INTRODUCTION AND LEGISLATIVE GUIDANCE

Chapter 1 briefly dealt with the transformation during the twentieth century of the approach towards the treatment and care of the mentally ill and those who lack mental capacity to make decisions for themselves. In particular, the recognition of the need to protect and respect the ECHR rights of liberty and security under Art 5 of the Convention led to the Deprivation of Liberty Safeguards (DoLS).

DoLS provisions (for details see Chapter 3) were introduced into the Mental Capacity Act 2005 (MCA 2005) to address the shortcomings in relation to the detention and restraint of those lacking capacity (P) where that amounts to deprivation of liberty. However, the legislators did not provide a clear definition of deprivation of liberty or the factors which would constitute a deprivation of liberty. The only reference to the meaning of deprivation of liberty in the MCA 2005 is set out in the interpretation clause – s 64(5) which provides that:

> In this Act, references to deprivation of a person's liberty have the same meaning as in Article 5(1) of the Human Rights Convention.

In all cases a distinction needs to be made between circumstances which would constitute deprivation of liberty as opposed to mere restraint. The issue of restraint is dealt with in Chapter 5.

2.2 GUIDANCE UNDER THE DOLS CODE OF PRACTICE

The *Deprivation of Liberty Safeguards Code of Practice* (DoLS Code of Practice) in Chapter 2 provides some guidance for institutions on how to assess whether the particular steps that they are taking or proposing to take might amount to a deprivation of liberty. This guidance is based on case-law which existed when the DoLS Code of Practice was drawn up. It also considers what other factors may be taken into account when considering the issue of deprivation of liberty. Finally, a summary of the decisions of European Court of Human Rights and domestic courts cases is set out in the DoLS Code of Practice as a guide to enable practitioners to identify how the courts have approached this issue.

The cases referred to in the DoLS Code of Practice must be considered in the light of decisions which post-date the 2009 amendments to MCA 2005 up to 2014, when the Supreme Court's opinion in *P v Cheshire West and Chester Council and P and Q v Surrey County Council*[1] was handed down, and the current thinking about its impact.

As the guidance clearly points out, there is no simple definition of deprivation of liberty. Whether the characteristics of a particular regime amount to deprivation of liberty is a legal question to be determined by the courts.

The factors which the DoLS Code of Practice recommends should be taken into account in determining whether deprivation of liberty has occurred or is likely to occur and the steps that can be taken to reduce the risk of deprivation of liberty occurring are set out at paras 2.6 and 2.7 of the Code of Practice. These are referred to in the next chapter under **3.2** and **3.3**.

2.3   LEADING CASE-LAW ON MEANING OF DEPRIVATION OF LIBERTY BEFORE 2009

In *Guzardi v Italy*[2] Judge Matcher said (rather unhelpfully, but probably accurately) that deprivation of liberty was 'a concept of some complexity, having a core which cannot be the subject of argument but which is surrounded by a "grey zone" where it is difficult to draw the line'. It is those 'grey zones' with which the court and decision makers have to grapple. The case was instrumental in confirming that deprivation of liberty was not limited to restrictions of movement and that in order to determine whether someone has been deprived of his liberty within the meaning of Art 5 'the starting point must be his concrete situation and account must be taken of whole range of criteria such as type, duration, effects and manner of implementation of the measure(s) in question'.

In *Storck v Germany*,[3] three elements were identified as amounting to deprivation of liberty:

(1)   an objective view of confinement for not a negligible length of time;

(2)   subjective assessment of the validity of consent; and

(3)   that the deprivation of liberty must be one for which the state is responsible.

In *JE v DE (By the Official Solicitor) Surrey County Council and EW*[4] Munby J (as he then was) in determining the issue of whether P had been deprived of his liberty referred to the above three elements, and when considering the objective element he stated that:[5]

---

[1]   [2014] UKSC 19.
[2]   (1980)3 EHHR 333.
[3]   [2005] ECHR 406.
[4]   [2006] EWHC 3459 (Fam), [2007] 2 FLR 1150.
[5]   At para 115.

'The fundamental issue in this case is whether DE was deprived of his liberty to leave the X home and whether DE has been and is deprived of his liberty to leave the Y home. And when I refer to leaving the X home and the Y home, I do not mean leaving for the purpose of some trip or outing approved by SCC or by those managing the institution; I mean leaving in the sense of removing himself permanently in order to live where and with whom he chooses, specially removing himself to live at home with JE.'

In *Secretary of State for the Home Department v JJ and Others*[6] (a case concerning control orders) Lady Hale stated:[7]

'What does it mean to be deprived of one's liberty? Not, we are all agreed, to be deprived of the freedom to live one's life as one pleases. It means to be deprived of one's physical liberty: *Engel v The Netherlands (No 1) (1976)* 1 EHRR 647, para 58. And what does this mean? It must mean being forced or obliged to be at a particular place where one does not choose to be: eg *X v Austria* (1979) 18 DR 154. But even that is not always enough, because merely being required to live at a particular address or to keep within a particular geographical area does not, without more, amount to a deprivation of liberty. There must be a greater degree of control over one's physical liberty than that. But how much? As the Judge said, the Strasbourg jurisprudence does not enable us to narrow the gap between "24-hour house arrest seven days per week (equals deprivation of liberty) and a curfew/house arrest of up to 12 hours per day on weekdays and for the whole of the weekend (equals restriction on movement)".'

The court thus emphasised that the line between restriction and deprivation remains indistinct. The starting point must be P's concrete situation and account must be taken of a range of criteria such as type, duration, effects and manner of implementation of the measure in question (see para 58).

And again in *Secretary of State for the Home Department v E and Others*[8] Lady Hale said:[9]

'The starting point in any consideration of deprivation of liberty is the "core element" of confinement. The length of the curfew in this case is within the range which Strasbourg has accepted as merely restricting liberty. Nor is there anything to make it more severe: the appellant is confined to his own home with his wife and children; other family members and the children's friends were allowed to visit. These factors greatly reduce the extent to which he is cut off from society even during the curfew hours. Outside those hours, he is not subject to any geographical restriction and can attend the mosque of his choice. He does have to get Home Office approval for visitors to his home and for pre-arranged meetings outside it and his home is subject to intrusive searches at any time. These may call in question certain other convention rights but do not, on their own, turn his "concrete situation" into one in which he is deprived of his liberty.'

---

[6] [2007] UKHL 45, [2007] 3 WLR 720.
[7] See para 57.
[8] [2007] UKHL 47.
[9] At para 25.

So merely being required to live at a particular address does not without other restriction amount to a deprivation of liberty. There must be a greater degree of control over one's physical liberty than that. Similarly, in *HL v United Kingdom (Bournewood)*[10] it was recognised that locked doors and wards were not a determinative factor. Some factors the court considered were important in finding that HL's detention amounted to deprivation of liberty were:

- arbitrary detention;
- complete and effective control over care and movement;
- continuous supervision and control with no freedom to leave;
- a regime of enforced medication and restraint; and
- P being unable to maintain social contact because of the restriction placed on access such that it mounted to loss of autonomy.

Other factors that were considered as relevant in cases decided before 2009 were:

- Restrictions which had been placed for the benefit of P (see eg *HM v Switzerland*):[11] but in *JE v DE and Surrey County Council*[12] Munby J (as he then was) observed that it was an error to confuse the question of deprivation of liberty with whether it had been justified in the interests of the person concerned). Much will depend on the facts of the individual case. That P was compliant was regarded as relevant in *HM v Switzerland* (see above). The issue of whether there was consent however could be established by evidence of P's behaviour and actions in relation to his placement and confinement, e g where P had attempted to leave her placement on numerous occasions and was restrained from so doing by chaining her to a radiator; or in *JE v DE and Surrey County Council* (above) where P had expressed his wish without any prompting that he wished to live with his wife.

- Freedom to leave: whether P was free to leave or not was considered to be a relevant factor in *JE v DE (above)* but see the observations of Lady Hale in *Secretary of State for the Home Department v JJ and Others* (above) where there were geographical restrictions placed on JJ.

2.4   THE LAW POST-2009 AND THE INTRODUCTION OF DOLS

The introduction of the Sch A1 DoLS regime into the MCA 2005 and the accompanying DoLS Code of Practice was intended to make provision of care and treatment of those who lacked capacity ECHR compliant, but this regime is limited to those in hospitals and residential care provided by or through the state. In applying this regime the issue which has confounded the providers has been whether the purpose of the arrangement, such as the 'normality of the arrangement for P; the protective environment provided for P; that P was thriving in the placement and that the arrangement made was in P's best

---

[10]   [2004] 40 EHRR 761.
[11]   [2002] 38 EHRR 314.
[12]   [2006] EWHC 3459 (Fam).

interests, was relevant in determining whether P had been deprived of his liberty. Principles established by earlier case-law were that:

- P's concrete situation is the starting point;
- the test as to deprivation of liberty is objective;
- the test as to consent is subjective but that happiness and purpose of the placement was not significant;
- control of lifestyle and contact with others were relevant factors;
- the lack of freedom to leave and live where P chose was a significant factor;
- the lack of objection on P's part was an issue which was taken account in the greater scheme provided for P;
- requirement that P should live at a specific address was not considered as an indicator of deprivation of liberty;
- the normality of the arrangement was a relevant factor.

2.4.1 Factors referred to in the DoLS Code of Practice

The DoLS Code of Practice sets out a non-exhaustive list of examples where ECtHR and domestic courts have determined as potentially giving rise to a deprivation of liberty. These include:[13]

- where restraint is used including sedation to admit P to an institution when P is resisting admission;
- where staff exercise complete and effective control of a person for a significant period;
- where staff exercise control over assessments, treatment, contact and residence;
- where decision is taken by the institution that P will not be released into the care of others, or permitted to live elsewhere, unless the staff in the institution consider it appropriate;
- where a request by possible carers for P to be discharged into their care is refused;
- where the restrictions are placed on P's ability to maintain social contact with others or to have access to other people;
- where P loses autonomy because he/she is under continuous supervision and control.

The DoLS Code of Practice also sets out in para 2.7 some directions regarding the process which should be followed to avoid depriving P of his liberty. These are set out in **3.3**. The effect of this multi-factorial approach led to uncertainty and difficulty in assessing and identifying situations which would amount to deprivation of liberty. The result often was that the issue was very much dependent on the judgment of one person who undertook the assessment and made the decision. This applied also to decisions made by the court where a

---

[13] DoLS Code of Practice, para 2.5.

judge in the High Court may take one view but on appeal the Court of Appeal took a different approach as occurred in the *Cheshire West* and *MIG and MEG* cases (see below). There was also confusion amongst professionals on the implications of Arts 5 and 12 of the Convention on the Rights of Persons with Disabilities. Article 5 of this Convention provides that all persons are equal before and under the law and are entitled without any discrimination to the equal protection and equal benefit of the law. Article 12 provides that:

> 1. States Parties reaffirm that persons with disabilities have the right to recognition everywhere as persons before the law.
>
> 2. States Parties shall recognize that persons with disabilities enjoy legal capacity on an equal basis with others in all aspects of life.
>
> 3. States Parties shall take appropriate measures to provide access by persons with disabilities to the support they may require in exercising their legal capacity.
>
> 4. States Parties shall ensure that all measures that relate to the exercise of legal capacity provide for appropriate and effective safeguards to prevent abuse in accordance with international human rights law. Such safeguards shall ensure that measures relating to the exercise of legal capacity respect the rights, will and preferences of the person, are free of conflict of interest and undue influence, are proportional and tailored to the person's circumstances, apply for the shortest time possible and are subject to regular review by a competent, independent and impartial authority or judicial body. The safeguards shall be proportional to the degree to which such measures affect the person's rights and interests.

Consequently, it created further uncertainty on whether in all cases P should be treated as lacking capacity.

The difficulties that arise can best be illustrated by the facts in the *Cheshire West* and *MIG and MEG* cases which were finally decided in the Supreme Court.

2.4.2   The facts in *Cheshire West*

P was a 39-year-old man who was born with cerebral palsy and Down's Syndrome and had a history of cerebral vascular accidents. He lacked capacity, had significant physical and learning disabilities and his behaviour was challenging. He lived with his mother from birth until 2009. From December 2008, her health began to deteriorate to the point where the local authority concluded that she was no longer able to care for her son. Following interim proceedings P was placed at Z House, where he remained. Although cosy and homely, P had no choice about his placement. He was unable to leave and had no control over his treatment and care. P needed care of the most intimate nature. He was incontinent and required help with toileting, incontinence and personal hygiene generally. P could be resistant to intervention. A particularly worrying feature of his behaviour was the chewing of his incontinence pads sometimes including fecal matter. Staff were required to carry out a finger sweep of his mouth to check for and/ or remove debris to avoid choking. In addition physical restraint was sometimes necessary to prevent aggressive attacks on staff. The extent of P's impairment was huge and difficult for staff to manage without intrusive interventions. Therefore it was not surprising that at first instance Baker J reached the conclusion that P was being deprived of his liberty at Z House. On appeal ([2011] EWCA Civ 1257) Munby LJ (as he then was) disagreed. His analysis drew the following conclusions by way of guidance:

(1) The starting point is the 'concrete situation', taking account of a whole range of criteria such as the 'type, duration, effects and manner of implementation' of the measure in question. The difference between deprivation of and restriction upon liberty is merely one of degree or intensity, not nature or substance.

(2) Deprivation of liberty must be distinguished from restraint. Restraint by itself is not deprivation of liberty.

(3) Account must be taken of the individual's whole situation.

(4) The context is crucial.

(5) Mere lack of capacity to consent to living arrangements cannot in itself create a deprivation of liberty.

(6) In determining whether or not there is a deprivation of liberty, it is legitimate to have regard both to the objective 'reason' why someone is placed and treated as they are and also to the objective 'purpose' (or 'aim') of the placement.

(7) Subjective motives or intentions, on the other hand, have only limited relevance. An improper motive or intention may have the effect that what would otherwise not be a deprivation of liberty is in fact, and for that very reason, a deprivation. But a good motive or intention cannot render innocuous what would otherwise be a deprivation of liberty. Good intentions are essentially neutral. At most they merely negative the existence of any improper purpose or of any malign, base or improper motive that might, if present, turn what would otherwise be innocuous into a deprivation of liberty. Thus the test is essentially an objective one.

(8) In determining whether or not there is a deprivation of liberty, it is always relevant to evaluate and assess the 'relative normality' (or otherwise) of the concrete situation.

(9) But the assessment must take account of the particular capabilities of the person concerned. What may be a deprivation of liberty for one person may not be for another.

(10) The comparator is the ordinary adult going about the kind of life which the able-bodied man or woman on the Clapham omnibus would normally expect to lead.

(11) But not in the kind of cases that come before the Family Division or the Court of Protection. A child is not an adult. Some adults are inherently restricted by their circumstances. The Court of Protection is dealing with adults with disabilities, in most contexts (as, for example, in the control order cases) the relevant often, as in the present case, adults with

significant physical and learning disabilities, whose lives are dictated by their own cognitive and other limitations.

(12) In such cases the contrast is not with the previous life led by X (nor with some future life that X might lead), nor with the life of the able-bodied man or woman on the Clapham omnibus. The contrast is with the kind of lives that people like X would normally expect to lead. The comparator is an adult of similar age with the same capabilities as X, affected by the same condition or suffering the same inherent mental and physical disabilities and limitations as X. Likewise, in the case of a child the comparator is a child of the same age and development as X.

The downside of this approach to the definition is an over reliance upon the 'no realistic alternative' interpretation in difficult cases. So where P may object to living in a particular care home, find supervision intrusive and security unacceptably restrictive, providers may nonetheless conclude that P has not been deprived of his liberty, because there is no realistic alternative. This of course means P will have no recourse to the Deprivation of Liberty Safeguards for challenging a placement, nor will there be in place legal obligations requiring the authorities to assess and review placement and/or treatment. Review by the Court of Protection is also excluded where there is no deprivation of liberty. The decision was appealed, the underlying concern being that emphasis should surely be upon bringing P within the DoLS framework, not excluding him from protection.

2.4.3   The facts in *MIG and MEG*

The appellants were two young women with learning difficulties who had been abused by their mother and stepfather as children. Both were the subject of care orders. MIG was accommodated in an adult foster placement by the local authority and MEG in a small group residential home for learning disabled adolescents with complex needs. Both placements were provided and paid for by the local authority. Both placements used restrictive measures to control the young women's independence. For example in MIG's case her foster mother did not allow her out alone and always accompanied her. She never attempted to leave but had she done so she would have been restrained from leaving. In MEG's case the same applied but in addition she was also subjected to a regime of physical restraint because of her challenging behaviour and received tranquillising medication. In the Court of Appeal Wilson LJ considered that neither of the young women were being deprived of their liberty by reason of the nature of the placements. In MIG's case this was because she was living in 'an ordinary family home' where she was attached to the carer and in MEG's case because she was living in a small group home, had access to the outside world through education and a full social life and was happy. Both the trial judge and the Court of Appeal held that the sisters' living arrangements were in their best interests and that they did not amount to deprivation of liberty.

These cases illustrate the anomaly which arises in treating placements differently because of their nature. If they are organised by the state reviewed by the state and paid for by the state, it is difficult to see why P should be excluded from the benefits of the deprivation of liberty safeguards. Similarly, that P presents as happy and contented in placement this should not be conflated with consent, an approach criticised in *Bournewood*.

For those reasons inter alia there was an appeal in both cases to the Supreme Court.

2.5 DEPRIVATION OF LIBERY POST-UKSC'S DECISION IN *CHESHIRE WEST* AND *MIG AND MEG*

The Supreme Court in the leading case of *P v Cheshire West and Chester Council and Another; P and Q v Surrey County Council*[14] (referred to as *Cheshire West* and *MIG and MEG*) has brought some clarity to when and in what circumstances living arrangements organised by the state for those who lack mental capacity to decide for themselves amounts to deprivation of liberty. It also provides guidance on the factors which are relevant and those which are not in defining deprivation of liberty. In the *Cheshire West* case the Supreme Court unanimously allowed the appeal. In *MIG and MEG* the appeal was allowed by a majority of 4/3.

2.5.1 What is deprivation of liberty – Art 5 and the 'universality test'

Lady Hale, who gave the leading judgment while accepting that European jurisprudence had to be applied to find out what is meant by deprivation of liberty, distinguished these appeals on the basis that none of the European cases concerned the type of placements in which the appellants had been situated. The thrust of Lady Hale's opinion was that in assessing whether the action taken or proposed to be taken amounts to deprivation of liberty, people with disabilities, both mental and physical, have the same human rights as the rest of the human race. She concluded:[15]

> 'it is axiomatic that people with disabilities, both mental and physical have the same human rights as the rest of the human race. It may be that those rights have sometimes to be limited or restricted because of their disabilities, but the starting point should be the same for everyone else. This flows inexorably from the universal character of human rights, founded on the inherent dignity of all human beings, and is confirmed in the United Nations Convention on the Rights of Person with Disabilities. Far from disability entitling the state to deny such people human rights: rather it places upon the state (and upon others) the duty to make reasonable accommodation to cater for the special needs of those with disabilities.'

And:[16]

---

[14] [2014] UKSC 19, [2014] COPLR 313.
[15] At para 45.
[16] At para 46.

'what it means to be deprived of liberty must be the same for everyone, whether or not they have physical or mental disabilities. If it would amount to deprivation of my liberty to be obliged to live in a particular place, subject to constant monitoring and control, only allowed out with close supervision, and unable to move away without permission of a person with capacity then it must also be a deprivation of liberty of a disabled person. The fact that my living arrangements are comfortable, and indeed make my life as enjoyable as it could possibly be, should make no difference. A gilded cage is still a cage.'

In their dissenting judgments Lord Carnwath and Lord Hodge, whilst agreeing that 'the comparator should in principle be a person with unimpaired health and capacity' (para 88) and the attraction of a universal test, applicable to all regardless of any physical or mental disabilities, took the view that it was not a concept which as reflected in the Strasbourg cases. They placed greater significance on European jurisprudence as the authoritative interpreter of the Convention because in providing the definition in s 64(5) Parliament had 'decided that it is to the Strasbourg jurisprudence that we must turn to find out what is meant by deprivation of liberty' (paras 91 and 94).

2.5.2   What is not relevant?

- The fact that P is complacent or is not objecting to his placement.
- The 'relative normality' of P's placement (an approach adopted by the Court of Appeal in MIG and MEG's case), 'not in a hospital or social care which is as close as possible to "normal" home life'.
- Reasons for and/or purpose behind the placement although it may seem both sensible and humane because the lives they were leading were not the same as those which would be led by other teenagers (para 47).
- The initial authorisation of that placement by a court as being in the best interests of P (see paras 32 and 50). The fact that the living arrangements are comfortable and enjoyable should make no difference. 'A gilded cage is still a cage'.

In his judgment Lord Neuberger stated:

- In relation to absence of objection that 'it would be inappropriate to hold that, if certain conditions amounted to deprivation of liberty in the case of a person who had the capacity to object, they may, or – even worse – would not do so in the cases of a person who lacked capacity to object ... That cannot possibly be right. Alternatively, there would be a different test for those who were unable to object and those who could not do so. That would be a recipe for uncertainty'. Additionally he stated that 'the notion that the absence of objection can justify what would otherwise amount to deprivation of liberty is contrary to principle' and 'it involves turning that principle on its head to say that the absence of objection will justify that would otherwise be a deprivation of liberty' (paras 67 and 68). Furthermore, relying on European jurisprudence he stated that if this factor was valid 'it would undermine the universality of human rights' (para 69).

- On the issue of 'relative normality' Lord Neuberger pointed out that the Strasbourg court has never had to consider a case where a person was confined within an ordinary home he could not 'see any good reason why the fact a person is confined to a domestic home as opposed to a hospital or other institution, should prevent her from contending that she has been deprived of her liberty' (the facts and decision in *Guzardi v Italy*[17] relied on). However, Lord Neuberger also pointed out that this would not arise in the case of children; the restrictions would not infringe Art 5 because they would not be imposed by the State. While this would also apply to adoptive parents he doubted whether it would include foster parents. He went on to state that:[18]

   'in the great majority of cases of people other than young children living in ordinary domestic circumstances the degree of supervision and control and the freedom to leave would take the situation out of Art 5.4. And where Art 5.4 did apply, no doubt the benignly intimate circumstances of a domestic home would frequently help to render any deprivation of liberty easier to justify.'

- In relation to criteria of the regime being no more intrusive or confining than is required for the protection of P (ie purpose) Lord Neuberger, relying on the decision in *Austin v United Kingdom*[19] and in *Creango v Romania*,[20] stated that the fact that 'the object is to protect or treat or care in some way for the person taken into confinement' has 'no bearing on the question that person has been deprived of his liberty although it may be relevant to the subsequent inquiry whether the deprivation of liberty is justified'; and that 'the purpose of measures by the authorities depriving applicants of their liberty no longer appears decisive for the court's assessment of whether there has in fact been deprivation of liberty' (see para 66).

- As to the 'best interests' test Lord Neuberger was unimpressed. He stated:[21]

   'The court's involvement in cases such as those to which these appeals relate is not equivalent to that of a court sentencing a criminal to a specific term of imprisonment. It is deciding that the circumstances of an innocent and vulnerable person, suffering from disability, are such that there must be an interference with his liberty. If that interference would otherwise amount to deprivation of liberty, I find it hard to understand why it should be otherwise simply because the court has approved it. The court's approval will almost always justify the deprivation from its inception, but again, it is hard to see why i should continue to justify it for a potentially unlimited future. The only reason which can be advanced to justify such a conclusion is, as I see it,

---

[17] (1980) 3 EHRR 333.
[18] At para 72.
[19] [2012] 55 EHRR 14.
[20] [2013] 56 EHRR 11.
[21] See para 70.

based on the purpose of the interference with liberty which brings one back
to the observations in the Grand Chamber referred to in para 8 above.'

2.5.3   Is there an 'acid test'?

Lady Hale did not set out any prescriptive list of criteria which should be
applied. The answer she said lay in those features that have been applied
consistently in European jurisprudence. These consist of two components:

(1)   was P under continuous supervision and control? and

(2)   was P free to leave?

Both the above conditions must be satisfied to amount to deprivation of liberty
(para 49).

2.5.3.1   *Continuous supervision and control – what does this entail?*

A distinction must be drawn between those cases where the constraints are
imposed by the state to which Art 5 applies from those imposed by parents in
the exercise of their parental responsibility where similar constraints would not
necessarily amount to a deprivation of liberty (para 54).

In relation to P in *Cheshire West* and *MIG and MEG*, the court found that they
were under continuous supervision. In *Cheshire West* because P's life was
completely under the control and supervision of the staff both during the day
and night and he needed to be restrained. In MEG's case the staff controlled
every aspect of her life. Sometimes she had to be physically restrained and she
received tranquillising medication for her anxiety and had to be sedated. In
MIG's case, although she was living in an ordinary family home, going out to
attend an educational unit and enjoyed good family contact with a foster
parent, her foster mother and others responsible for her care exercised complete
control over every aspect of her life. In all three cases the supervision and
control was 'continuous' because they did not go out alone and their activities
were controlled.

When providing for the needs of those who lack capacity the details of the
arrangements made will necessarily have to take into account the nature of
support and the extent of the supervision provided because it will always be
questionable when support crosses the line and may be regarded not as support
but supervision. This is a grey area with which the courts and all professionals
will have to grapple in future.

2.5.3.2   *Free to leave*

In *JE v DE*[22] Munby LJ (as he then was) stated that 'free to leave' did not mean
being allowed to leave for the purposes of some trip or outing approved by the
local authority or by those managing the institution. It meant leaving in the

---

[22]   [2007] 2 FLR 1150.

sense of removing oneself permanently in order to live where and with whom he chooses. Similar situations were also considered in *Stanev v Bulgaria*,[23] where absences from the care home required permission and was frequently denied and P was liable to be arrested if he overstayed. In *DD v Lithuania* (Application No 13469/06) the care home in which the applicant was placed had complete control over her movements. She was not fee to leave without permission and was brought back by the police when she tried to leave. In *Kedsior v Poland* (Application No 4502/07) the applicant was not allowed to leave without the permission of the management of the care home he was thus not free to leave. The frequency of outings or the duration of the time out is therefore not relevant.

Applying these principles the court held that, although P was able to go out, these outings were supported; he was not able to go out on his own, and if he had wished to go out he would have been prevented from so doing. Similarly in MIG and MEG's case their 'freedom to leave' their respective placements were restricted to that which was approved and permitted. Freedom therefore means free from external constraints which a person of the same age and full capacity would have.

Lords Carnwath and Hodge however took the view that the European Court had applied a case-specific test and had adopted a multi-factorial approach. While the court had attached weight to the factor of whether P was free to leave without permission it was not 'treated as conclusive in itself; it was only one of a number of factors leading to the overall assessment', and that the fact that a person lacks capacity does not necessarily mean that he is unable to comprehend his situation. Lord Clarke took a similar view, indicating that the question is very much fact specific and that the ECtHR 'has not held that there is only one question (or acid) test namely whether the individual concerned is free to leave. Its approach is more nuanced than that'. In relation to MIG and MEG's case he took the view that since it is a question of fact and degree involving balancing different considerations the decision of the trial judge should not be interfered with by an appellate court unless it concludes that the judge has erred in principle or that the judge was wrong. Having considered Parker J's judgment in detail Lord Clarke took the view that MIG and MEG's liberty had been interfered with but they had been deprived of their liberty; that Parker J had rightly undertaken an objective assessment of the various criteria in arriving at her conclusion. He disagreed that this is a comparative exercise with other people in different situations. It was an assessment of the individual on the facts of their particular case (para [109]).

It will thus be necessary in each case to consider first whether the deprivation of liberty is likely to last only for a short period. The Supreme Court did not indicate the length of time. Although it pre-dates the Supreme Court's decision the Court of Appeal in *Commissioner of Police for the Metropolis v ZH*[24] that the initial restraint applied on ZH for a period of 15 minutes and his placement

---

[23] [2012] 55 EHRR 22.
[24] [2013] EWCA Civ 69.

in a cage in the back of a police van for 25 minutes making a period in total of 40 minutes constituted a deprivation of his liberty. The first instant judge on the particular facts of the case had made an assessment of the type, duration, effects and manner of implementation of the measure in question in reaching his conclusion. In *Gillian v UK*[25] a detention of less than 30 minutes was considered as not breaching Art 5. If in doubt, it is best to err on the side of caution and take immediate steps by way of an emergency application, by telephone if needs be, and seek authorisation from the court.

2.5.4   Does the test comprise an objective and/or subjective element?

The Supreme Court confirmed that deprivation of liberty comprises both an objective and subjective element. Lord Neuberger stated that the 'question whether there has been deprivation should be answered primarily by reference to an objective standard and that the subjective element of the test is confined to the issue of whether there has been a valid and effective consent' (para 87). Lord Kerr in his judgment dealt with this issue in some detail. He stated:[26]

> 'While there is a subjective element in ascertaining whether one's liberty has been restricted, this is primarily to be determined on an objective basis. Restriction or deprivation of liberty is not solely dependent on the reaction or acquiescence of the person whose liberty has been curtailed. Her or his contentment with the conditions in which she finds herself does not determine whether she is restricted in her liberty ...
>
> The question of whether one is restricted (as a matter of actuality) is determined by comparing the extent of your actual freedom with someone of your age and station whose freedom is not limited ...'

Applying the comparator principle of a person of similar age, unimpaired health and full capacity to MIG and MEG's situation, Lord Kerr concluded that it was clear that their liberty '*is in fact* circumscribed. They may not be conscious, much less resentful, of the constraint but, objectively, limitations on their freedom are in place' (paras 76-77).

The subjective element is the absence of valid consent to the constraints (see paras 31 and 81 and the cases cited). A person's right to liberty cannot be lost simply because P has given himself up, especially where he is legally incapable of consenting to or disagreeing with it (see *Stanev v Bulgaria* above).

2.6   TO WHOM DOES ART 5 NOW APPLY?

The Deprivation of Liberty Safeguards set out in Sch A1 of MCA 2005 apply only to those who lack capacity and who are detained in hospital or in a state provided residential institution. The Supreme Court's decision means that deprivation of liberty extends to other kinds of provision in respect of which P's

---

[25]   (2010) EHRR 45.
[26]   See paras 76 and 77.

Art 3 rights require protection. Lady Hale's observation in para [52] indicates that Art 5 applies in every case where the state is involved in providing care and support. It will thus apply to the following categories of people:

2.6.1   Those in residential care

Of those who are in residential care it is not known how many suffer from dementing illnesses either at the point of admission or during their stay. On the basis of the Supreme Court's decision this category of persons will now be included and their detention in their accommodation considered to be potentially unlawful. They must now be brought into some safeguarding provision for the state to guarantee their Art 5 rights.

2.6.2   Domiciliary care

State funded community care available to support adults lacking capacity is wide ranging and can extend from sheltered accommodation to a package of care help and support in P's own home. All these interventions may bear the hallmarks of a deprivation of liberty and have to be considered on the facts.

2.6.3   Adults in foster care

Adult foster placements of those lacking mental capacity will now be included as those whose rights need to be protected. Article 5 will also include those who remain at home and are cared for by their parents/relatives with local authority's input in providing supervision support, funding, especially where restraint has to be applied physically or by medication.

2.6.4   Children

Lord Neuberger indicated in his judgment that the infringement of Art 5 would not apply in the case of children living at home because it will not have been imposed by the state (para [72]) but by someone with parental responsibility for the child. However, he also stated that it would apply to foster parents unless perhaps they had the benefit of a care arrangement order which provided for the child to reside with them. It is likely also to apply to a child who is a subject of a care order irrespective of whether the child is placed in foster care or residential care.

2.6.5   Hospitals

It is likely that many patients regarded as informally admitted for psychiatric care and treatment will fall within either the Mental Health Act 1983 regime or the DoLS regime in which case the placements will require authorisation, if the two elements set out in the acid test are met. This creates an overlap between the protection provided by mental health legislation and mental capacity legislation. In the case of someone lacking capacity who needs long term care, for example in a rehabilitation unit where his stay is structured and visits from or to family members are restricted, the acid test would suggest that P is deprived of his liberty. Depending on the basis of the admission and the circumstances of the individual he may be entitled to the Mental Health Act safeguards or the DoLS. Other situations within a hospital setting may include those who are unconscious or in a PVS/MCS state. If this amounted to a mental disorder then authorisation under Sch A1 should be requested. If it is not, s 4B of the MCA 2005 permits deprivation of P's liberty where it is wholly or partly for the purposes of giving life sustaining treatment or doing any vital act or consists of wholly or partly of giving life sustaining treatment or to do any vital act. If in doubt or where there are or likely to be family objections authorisation should be sought from the Court of Protection. In all other cases a decision should be sought from the court under s 16(2)(a).

In the case of child lacking mental capacity who is 16 or over the MCA 2005 applies. However, the Sch A1 DoLS provisions apply only to those aged 18 or over and therefore authorisation under the DoLS regime cannot be granted. In such cases authorisation should be sought from the court either under the MCA or in the High Court under the inherent jurisdiction. It is a moot point whether in such cases consent given by a parent(s) or someone exercising parental responsibility would take the case out of the deprivation of liberty provisions.

2.7   ARE THE FACTORS IDENTIFIED BY THE EUROPEAN COURT STILL RELEVANT?

In applying the acid test and the guidance given in the DoLS Code of Practice although the emphasis will be on supervision and control and freedom to leave, the various factors identified by the European Court such as type, duration effect etc will continue to be relevant considerations. In many cases there will need to be careful liaison between local authorities care homes and hospitals than has hitherto been the case. In this respect it is relevant that the Department of Health's guidance *Positive Care: Reducing Restrictive Intervention* published on 3 April 2014 not only refers to the relevant provisions of the MCA on this issue but specifically and comprehensively deals with restraint and deprivation of liberty and the DoLS. Of particular relevance is the guidance that sets out in para 98 some of the factors which may amount to deprivation of liberty. These include:

- staff having complete control over a person's care or movements for a long time;
- staff making all decisions about a person including choices about assessments, treatment and visitors and controlling where they can go and when;
- staff refusing to allow a patient to leave for example with a carer or family member;
- staff restricting a person's access to their friends or family.

Of relevance also is content of para 99 of the guidance which incorporates the 'acid test'.

2.8 PERIODIC REVIEWS

Lady Hale suggested that because of the extreme vulnerability of people like P, MIG and MEG she believed that one should err on the side of caution in deciding what constitutes deprivation of liberty in such cases bringing those lacking capacity within the scheme of authorisation so they can benefit from safeguards protecting their Art 5 rights. Periodic independent checks on whether the arrangements made for them are in their best interests were necessary but such checks 'need not be as elaborate as those currently provided for in the Court of Protection or the DoLS and which could in due course be simplified and extended to placements outside hospitals and care homes' (para 57). Lords Carnwath and Hodge also favoured a policy of periodic supervision of arrangements made under the Act and agreed with Lady Hale that there were legitimate concerns about the potential bureaucracy of the statutory procedures.

In *Re X and Others (Deprivation of Liberty)*[27] the President, after considering previous authorities held that annual review by a judge would be the norm unless circumstances required a shorter period. Upholding earlier decisions in *Re GJ, NJ and BJ (Incapacitated Adults)*[28] and *Re BJ (Incapacitated Adult)*[29] the President held that an oral hearing is not required in every case and that a review can take place on the papers. Chapter 4 deals with the up to date position as to the current process.

2.9 APPROACH OF THE COURTS POST-*CHESHIRE WEST*

The underlying philosophy of *Cheshire West* was that the application of safeguards for those who are deprived of their liberty is a beneficial and protective measure. This is illustrated in particular by the Supreme Court's opinion that a whole raft of provision by the state may amount to a deprivation of liberty extending the ambit to supported lodgings, adult foster care placements and domiciliary care packages all of which would require authorisation. The philosophy was confirmed by Court of Appeal in *Re X*. This was an appeal from a decision of the President on procedural matters arising out of the *Cheshire West* decision. The inclusion of a huge variety of provision was thought likely to swamp the Court of Protection with applications from public bodies for authorisation. This is dealt with in more detail in Chapter 4, but the relevance here is that the Court of Appeal dismissed the notion that P's participation in the court authorisation process should not be diluted. The

---

[27]   [2014] EWCOP 25.
[28]   [2008] EWHC 1097 (Fam), [2008] 2 FLR 1295.
[29]   [2009] EWHC 3310 (Fam), [2010] 1 FLR 1373.

Court of Appeal endorsed the approach that deprivation of liberty safeguards are fundamental to domestic and European law in which P should be included rather than excluded.

Some attempt to diminish the *Cheshire West* effect can be seen in the decisions of Mostyn J in *Rochdale Metropolitan Borough Council v KW*;[30] *Rochdale MBC v KW (by her litgation friend)) Note*;[31] *London Borough of Tower Hamlets v TB (By Her Litigation Friend the Official Solicitor) and SA*[32] and *Bournemouth City Council v PS & DS*.[33]

The agenda in these decisions seems to be that the idea of P being regarded as deprived of his/her liberty is somehow negative and stigmatising so that a narrow approach to the definition is to be preferred excluding P from the definition where possible.

In the *Rochdale* case a middle-aged woman who lacked capacity because of a serious brain injury was confined to her own home because of her disabilities. She was supported by an extensive care package from her local authority 24/7, carers attended her every need. Mostyn J described the arrangement thus:

> 'I find it impossible to conceive that the best interests arrangement for Katherine, *in her own home*, provided by an independent contractor, but devised and paid for by Rochdale and CCG, amounts to a deprivation of liberty within Article 5.'

And:

> 'I am of the view that the matter should be reconsidered by the Supreme Court.'

In *Tower Hamlets* Mostyn J equated a deprivation of liberty with '*state detention*'.

The *Bournemouth* case was about a 28-year-old man who lacked capacity in all respects because of autism and learning difficulties. He lived in his own home staffed 24/7 by carers. He was not locked in but sensors would be set to go off to alert staff if he tried to leave. About the arrangements Mostyn J said:

> 'I cannot say that I know that B is being detained by the state when I look at his position. Far from it. I agree with Mr Mullins that he is not. First, he is not under continuous supervision. He is afforded appreciable privacy. Second, he is free to leave. Were he to do so his carers would seek to persuade him to return but such persuasion would not cross the line into coercion. The deprivation of liberty line would only be crossed if and when the police exercised powers under the Mental Health Act. Were that to happen then a range of reviews and safeguards would

---

become operative. But up to that point B is a free man. In my judgment, on the specific facts in play here, the acid test is not met. B is not living in a cage, gilded or otherwise.'

These decisions do not concur with the opinion of the Supreme Court in *Cheshire West* which has received the whole-hearted approval of the Court of Appeal in *Re X*. The alternative view can no longer be reasonably sustained. The emphasis is to include P within the regime so that s/he may benefit from the safeguards.

That is not to say that the court does not have a discretion in scrutinising the arrangements within the *Cheshire West* context. In *W City Council v Mrs L*,[34] Bodey J decided that arrangements for an elderly woman living in her own home but with access to her garden, as arranged by her family, receiving visits from carers did not amount to a deprivation of her liberty but rather a restriction on her liberty. Further the arrangement was not imputed to the state but instead to the family.

Each situation will turn on its facts and the messages must be:

(1) If in doubt, apply to the court for a decision as to whether arrangements amount to a deprivation of liberty.

(2) DoLS are of benefit to P as affording welcome protection from arbitrary decision making by the state.

---

[34] [2015] EWCOP 20.

CHAPTER 3

THE DEPRIVATION OF LIBERTY SAFEGUARDS – THE SCHEDULE A1 REGIME FOR AUTHORISATION

3.1 INTRODUCTION

The administrative regime in Sch A1 to the MCA 2005 only applies to those admitted to hospitals or resident in care homes. The procedure is unaffected by the changes in relation to judicial authorisations. It imposes a duty on providers to protect the Art 5 rights of those they look after and incorporates the following safeguards for the authorisation of deprivation of liberty:

- duty to identify any deprivation of liberty;
- creation of a body with administrative responsibility for authorisations;
- assessments requirements;
- appointment of representatives;
- procedure for authorisation;
- procedure for monitoring and review;
- procedure for challenge either to the supervisory body or the Court of Protection;
- administrative requirements, eg for record keeping and or decision making.

There are considerable benefits to P where the Sch A1 regime applies by reason of the checks and balances it imposes in scrutinising P's placement and care. There is also an obligation on decision makers to have regard to the wishes and feelings of P and his family so P's Art 8 rights are also protected.

3.2 FACTORS TO BE TAKEN INTO ACCOUNT TO IDENTIFY DEPRIVATION OF LIBERTY

Guidance in *Deprivation of Liberty Safeguards Code of Practice* (DoLS Code of Practice), para 2.6 refers to some relevant cases to identify examples of the factors that should in general be considered by the decision maker in considering whether an act done or proposed to be undertaken may amount to a deprivation of liberty. These are:

- All the circumstances of each and every case.

- What measures are being taken in relation to the individual? When are they required? For what period do they endure? What are the effects of any restraints or restrictions on the individual? Why are they necessary? What aim do they seek to meet?

- What are the views of the relevant person, their family or carers? Do any of them object to the measures?

- How are any restraints or restrictions implemented? Do any of the constraints on the individual's personal freedom go beyond 'restraint' or 'restriction' to the extent that they constitute a deprivation of liberty?

- Are there any less restrictive options for delivering care and treatment that avoid deprivation of liberty altogether?

- Does the cumulative effect of all the restrictions imposed on the person amount to a deprivation of liberty, even if individually they would not?

3.3   STEPS TO BE TAKEN TO REDUCE THE RISK OF DEPRIVATION OF LIBERTY

The Code also sets out the steps which should be taken to reduce the risk of deprivation (para 2.7).

- Make sure that all decisions are taken (and reviewed) in a structured way and reasons for the decision recorded.

- Follow established good practice for care planning.

- Make proper assessment of whether the person lacks capacity to decide whether or not to accept the treatment proposed, in line with the principles of the Act.

- Before admitting a person to hospital or residential care in circumstances that amount to deprivation of liberty consider whether the person's needs could be met in a less restrictive way. Any restrictions placed on the person while in hospital or in a care home must be kept to the minimum necessary, and should be in place for the shortest period.

- Take proper steps to help P to retain contact with family, friends and carers. Where local advocacy services are available, their involvement should be encouraged to support P and his family friends and carers.

- Review the care plans on an ongoing basis. It may be helpful to include an independent element, possibly via an advocacy service in the review.

3.4   AUTHORISATION OF DEPRIVATION OF LIBERTY UNDER THE SCH A1 REGIME

Provisions contained in Sch A1 of the Act, (inserted by the Mental Health Act 2007), which came into force on 1 April 2009, permit a managing authority of a hospital or care home to deprive a person lacking capacity of his/her liberty (P) by detaining him/her provided three conditions are satisfied. These are that:

(1)   P is detained in hospital or care home for the purpose of being given care or treatment;

(2)   a standard or urgent authorisation is in force;

(3)   the standard or urgent authorisation relates to the incapacitated person and the hospital or care home in which that person is detained.[1]

A person who carries out any act in pursuance of giving care or treatment or an authorisation is excluded from liability, and is placed in the same position as if the person lacking capacity had had capacity to consent in relation to the doing of the act and had consented to his/her detention;[2] but it does not absolve the person from civil or criminal liability for negligent acts committed when giving the authorised care or treatment. Any act done must be done for the purpose of the standard or urgent authorisation and where a standard authorisation is in force it does not authorise a person to do anything else which does not comply with the conditions (if any) included in the authorisation.[3]

A standard authorisation is usually requested by the managers of the hospital or care home where the person lacking capacity (P) is, or is likely to be deprived of his liberty. The managing authority should make the request for standard authorisation when it appears likely that, either currently or within the next 28 days, P will be accommodated within a situation which amounts to a deprivation of liberty or there is or is likely to be a change in the place of P's detention.[4] The request is made to the supervisory authority which will grant or refuse authorisation depending on the outcome of assessments of P's qualifying requirements (see below).

3.5   THE RESPONSIBILITIES AND DECISION MAKING PROCESS OF THE MANAGING AUTHORITY

In order to obtain the authorisation the managing authority should ensure that the qualifying requirements set out in Sch A1, Part 3, para 12 are met as the supervisory authority will arrange for assessments to be carried out to determine whether these requirements are met. The managing authority should have a procedure in place that identifies:[5]

• whether deprivation of liberty is or may be necessary in a particular case;

• what steps they should take to assess whether to seek authorisation;

• whether they have taken all practical and reasonable steps to avoid a deprivation of liberty;

• what action they should take if they need to request an authorisation;

• how they should review cases where authorisation is or may be necessary; and

---

[1]   MCA 2005, Sch A1, Part 1, paras 1 and 2.
[2]   MCA 2005, Sch A1, Part 1, para 3.
[3]   MCA 2005, Sch A1, Part 1, para 4.
[4]   MCA 2005, Sch A1, Part 4, para 24.
[5]   DoL Code of Practice, para 3.6.

- who should take the necessary action.

The supervisory body for both hospitals and care homes is the local authority for the area where P is ordinarily resident or, if the person is not resident in the area of any local authority, the supervisory body will be the local authority for the area in which the hospital or care home is situated.[6] If P's residence remains unclear the local authority which received the application should deal with it (see Mental Capacity (Deprivation of Liberty: Standard Authorisations and Assessments and Ordinary Residence) Regulations 2008, SI 2008/1858, set out in **Appendix 4**).

3.6   THE QUALIFYING REQUIREMENTS

The following are the qualifying requirements which must be met before a standard authorisation is granted:

(1)   the age requirement;

(2)   the mental health requirement;

(3)   the mental capacity requirement;

(4)   the best interests requirement;

(5)   the eligibility requirement;

(6)   the no refusals requirement.

3.6.1   The age requirement

P must be 18 (for those under 18 a different safeguards regime applies). A birth certificate will be considered sufficient evidence of age. If there is doubt and no other document to establish P's age, eg a paperless asylum seeker, an age assessment may be required. A paediatric assessment may indicate P's age but a local authority may assess the age of P by relying on the assessment of experienced social workers. The assessment in such a case should be by way of interviews and observations of at least two experienced social workers over a period of time (see *B v London Borough of Merton;*[7] *A v LB Croydon and SS for the Home Department (Interested Party); WK v SS for Home Department & Kent CC*[8]). Where there are two conflicting age assessments it may be necessary for a fact finding hearing before a court to determine P's age (*R (CJ) v Cardiff County Council*[9]).

3.6.2   The mental health requirement

P must be suffering from a mental disorder within the meaning of the Mental Health Act 1983 as amended ie 'any disorder or disability of mind, but including for these purposes a person with learning difficulties whether or not

---

[6]   DoL Code of Practice, paras 3.1–3.3.
[7]   [2003] EWHC 1689 (Admin), [2003] 2 FLR 888.
[8]   [2009] EWHC 939(Admin), [2010] 1 FLR 193.
[9]   [2011] EWHC 23 (Admin), [2011] 2 FLR 90.

associated with abnormally aggressive behaviour or seriously irresponsible conduct'.[10] The mental health assessment must be carried out by a doctor approved under s 12 of the Mental Health Act 1983 (see also DoLS Code of Practice, paras 4.35–4.39), or who has at least 3 years' special experience in the diagnosis and treatment of mental disorder and have completed the relevant training (see Mental Capacity (Deprivation of Liberty: Standard Authorisations, Assessments and Ordinary Residence) Regulations 2008 as amended by SI 2009/827, reg 4 at **Appendix 4**).

3.6.3   The mental capacity requirement

P must lack capacity to decide whether or not he/she should be accommodated in the relevant hospital or care home for the purpose of being given the relevant care or treatment. The key principles set out in s 1 of the Act and the provisions of ss 2, 3 and 4 of the Act must be applied when assessing whether the person lacks capacity. The assessment must be carried out by people who are qualified to carry out a mental health assessment (reg 6 and see above) or a best interests assessment (reg 6 – see below).

3.6.4   The best interests requirement

Four conditions must be met to satisfy this requirement. These are:
(1)   the person is, or is to be, a detained resident;
(2)   the person's detention is in his/her best interests;
(3)   the detention is necessary to prevent harm to the person; and
(4)   the detention is a proportionate response to the likelihood of the person suffering harm and the seriousness of that harm.

Best interests assessments must only be carried out by mental health practitioners approved under Mental Health Act 1983, s 114(1) (approved mental health professionals appointed under the MHA 1983 by a local social services authority) or certain health practitioners (nurses, occupational therapists or psychologists) with all the relevant skills and specialism, or social workers, all of whom must have had at least 2 years' post-registration experience, and have completed the required training (reg 7). Assessors must be independent of the local authority, hospital and care home. They should seek the views of anyone who has been named as someone P would want to be consulted, anyone caring for P, anyone interested in P's welfare (eg family member or friend) and any attorney or deputy who represents P and record their names addresses and views. Assessor must consult the managing authority and have regard to the conclusions of the mental health assessor on the impact or likely impact of detention on P's mental health, any relevant needs assessment and care plan. If the report is positive, it must state the maximum authorisation period (which should not exceed 12 months), and may provide for different periods to apply in relation to different kinds of standard

---

[10]   MCA 2005, Sch A1, Part 3, para 14.

authorisations. Assessors may also recommend conditions to attach to the authorisation. If the conclusion is that deprivation of liberty is not in P's best interests or that there is or has been an unauthorised deprivation of liberty this must be stated in the assessment.

3.6.5   The eligibility requirement

A person is ineligible if already detained in a hospital under the Mental Health Act 1983 (MHA 1983), or meets the criteria for detention but is objecting to being detained or to some or all of the treatment proposed. In those circumstances detention will be authorised under MHA 1983. A person would also be ineligible if on leave of absence, or subject to a guardianship, or a community treatment regime, or conditional discharge and subject to a measure which would be inconsistent with an authorisation if granted. Similarly if the authorisation granted would be for deprivation of liberty in a hospital for the purpose of treatment for mental disorder. This assessment must be carried out by a mental health assessor who is a doctor approved under s 12 of the Mental Health Act 1983 or a best interests assessor who is also an approved mental health professional. For those who come within the 1983 Act the process set out in that Act will apply.

In *GJ v Foundation Trust PCT v Secretary of State for Health*,[11] Charles J considered the application of the eligibility criteria in relation to a challenge by P to his detention under DoLS. Three important areas were highlighted. Where the person detained comes within the scope of MHA 1983, this takes primacy regardless of there being alternative solutions under MCA 2005. Medical practitioners and decision makers could not choose between the two statutory regimes on the basis that they considered one to be preferable for P. The focus should be on the reason why P should be deprived of his liberty. If the reason for the detention is for psychiatric treatment the MHA 1983 provisions would apply. The fact that P may also have other physical illness for which he/she requires treatment does not make it lawful for him to be made the subject of authorisation under MCA 2005. If the detention is for the purpose of physical treatment only, then the person detained is not authorised as a mental health patient. In considering eligibility, there must be reference to the reality of the purpose of detention and the court must focus upon the position as it is when the case falls to be decided and, not what it may have been at the time authorisation was granted. This approach was adopted by Baker J in *BB v AM*.[12] He determined the issue relating to BB's circumstances by asking (a) whether the criteria under ss 2 and 3 of MHA 1983 had been met ie is she suffering from mental disorder for which needs to be assessed or receive medical treatment. If the answer was yes, then she would be ineligible to be deprived of her liberty. If the MHA 1983 conditions were not met then (b) do the circumstances of her detention amount to a deprivation of liberty as set out in the DoLS Code of Practice (see above).

---

[11]   [2009] EWHC 2972 (Fam), [2009] COPLR Con Vol 567.
[12]   [2010] EWHC1916 (Fam).

3.6.6 The no refusals requirement

A person meets this requirement unless he/she has made a valid advance decision refusing some or all of the treatment in question. A valid refusal, which is within the scope of his authority, may be given by a donee of a lasting power of attorney or deputy.

3.7 STANDARD AUTHORISATION

3.7.1 When to apply

The managing authority must request a standard authorisation where:

(1) it is proposing to detain in a relevant hospital or care home, or is likely to do so within the next 28 days, someone who meets the requirements; or

(2) where it appears to the managing authority that someone already accommodated in the relevant hospital or care home is likely at sometime within the next 28 days to be detained or who, within the next 28 days, will meet all the qualifying requirements; or

(3) where a detained resident in the relevant hospital or care home meets all the qualifying requirements or is likely to do so at some time within the next 8 days; or

(4) if there is, or is likely to be a change in the place of detention provided that a standard authorisation has been given and remains in force (the managing authority will then become the managing authority of the new placement).

Before a standard authorisation is given, the supervisory authority must secure an assessment of all the qualifying requirements and be satisfied that these requirements are met. The Mental Capacity (Deprivation of Liberty: Standard Authorisations, Assessments and Ordinary Residence) Regulations 2008 (see **Appendix 4**) provide for who should carry out the assessments, the professional skills and training which the assessors must have and the timeframe within which the assessments must be completed (see above).

3.7.2 How to obtain a standard authorisation

A request must be made in writing to the supervisory body. A prescribed form for making the application for standard authorisation is not provided in the Act or the COP Rules but pursuant to the DoLS Code of Practice, para 3.7 the Department of Health has developed standard forms for the assessments and the application. In England the request must include:

• the name and gender of P;

• the age of P or where this is not known whether the managing authority reasonably believes that P is a person aged 18 or over;

- the address at which P is currently located and the telephone number of the managing authority who is dealing with the request;
- the purpose of the authorisation requested;
- the date from which the authorisation is sought; and
- whether the managing authority has given an urgent authorisation and if so the date on which it expires.
- the request must also include if it is available or could reasonably be obtained:
- any medical information relating to P's health that the managing authority considers to be relevant to the proposed restrictions of P's liberty;
- the diagnosis of the mental disorder (within the meaning of MHA 1983 but disregarding any exclusion for persons with learning disabilities) from which P is suffering;
- any care plans and need assessments;
- P's racial ethnic or national origins;
- whether P has any special communication needs;
- details of the proposed restriction on P's liberty;
- whether it is necessary for an Independent Mental Capacity Advocate (IMCA) to be instructed;
- where the authorisation is required to give treatment; whether P has made an advance decision that may be valid and applicable to some or all of that treatment;
- whether there is an existing standard authorisation in relation to P and if so the date when it will expire;
- whether P is subject to the requirements of the MHA 1983 and the name address and telephone number of any person named by P as someone to be consulted about his/her welfare; anyone engaged in caring for the P or interested in P's welfare; any donee of LPA granted by P or any deputy appointed for P by the court and any IMCA who has already been instructed (DoLS Code of Practice, paras 3.8 and 3.9).

The managing authority must also inform P's family, friends, carers and any IMCA already appointed that a request has been made unless it is impractical or impossible to do so, or undesirable in terms of the interests of P's health or safety. Anyone engaged in P's care or interested in his/her welfare or anyone who has been named as a person to consult must be given an opportunity to input their views on whether a deprivation of liberty is in P's best interests as part of the best interests assessment. If P has expressed views about who should be informed and consulted those views should be taken into account.[13] The importance of taking account of P's wishes and feelings was highlighted in *Stanev v Bulgaria*.[14]

---

[13] DoL Code of Practice, para 3.15.
[14] (Application No 36760/06) a decision of the Grand Chamber of 17 January 2012.

In order to obtain authorisation the managing authority will have to ensure that P meets the qualifying requirements (see above), because before authorisation is granted the supervisory authority will arrange for assessments to be carried to determine whether these requirements are met. It is best, therefore, to be prepared in advance to avoid any delay in providing the appropriate care and treatment plan for P and avoid the need for an urgent authorisation.

3.8   THE SUPERVISORY BODY – ITS RESPONSIBILITIES AND DECISION-MAKING POWERS

Upon receipt of the request, the supervisory body must, as soon as practical and possible, consider whether the request is appropriate, valid, complete and should be pursued. Any information that it requires from the managing authority to help with the decision should be sought. If the supervisory body has any doubts about proceeding with the request, it should seek to resolve the issue with the managing authority. Where the local authority is both the managing body and the supervisory body it should ensure that the 'tail' of the service provision did not wag the 'dog' of welfare planning (see *London Borough of Hillingdon v Steven Neary (By the Official Solicitor) and Others* below). The supervisory body should also consider whether P has somebody who is not engaged in providing care or treatment in a professional capacity or for remuneration to support P. If there is no such appropriate person who may be consulted, the supervisory body must immediately instruct an IMCA to represent P. This is of even greater importance if an urgent authorisation has been given to ensure that there is someone to make any input on behalf of P. Guidance is set out in Chapter 10 of the Code of Practice in identifying an IMCA who is suitably qualified to represent P.[15]

3.8.1   Appointment of assessors and content of assessments

The supervisory body must appoint assessors to assess the six qualifying requirements. The supervisory has a legal duty to ensure that the assessors selected are both suitable and eligible to undertake the assessments.[16] The Deprivation of Liberty: Standard Authorisations Assessments and Ordinary Residence) Regulations 2008 (see **Appendix 4**) set out the qualifications, skills and training needed by the person who carries out the assessments and the time frame within which the assessments must be completed. There must be a minimum of two assessors. The mental health and best interests assessments must be undertaken by different assessors. The best interests assessors may be an employee of the supervisory body or the managing authority provided that the person is not involved in the care or treatment of P or in the decisions about P's care. An assessor must not be a relative of the person being assessed nor of a person with a financial interest in the person's care (DoLS Code of Practice, para 4.13). The best interests assessment is not a routine piece of work. It is the

---

[15]   DOL Code of Practice, paras 3.22–3.23.
[16]   Code of Practice, para 4.4.

cornerstone of the DoL safeguarding regime. Its purpose is to ensure that P is deprived of his liberty only where he is eligible and it is in his best interests, and is necessary and proportionate in relation to the likelihood and seriousness of the harm that he might otherwise suffer. The assessor should consider, compare and contrast all viable options. If the assessor fails to do so and, the supervisory body does not question the omissions, the assessment will be flawed (see *A County Council v MB, JB and A Residential Home*[17]). If an IMCA has been appointed any information given by the IMCA should be taken into account when assessing the best interests requirement. The supervisory authority has a duty to scrutinize the assessments and to grant the authorisation only when it is satisfied that the best interests deals with all the relevant issues thoroughly.

3.8.2   Time limit for completion of assessments

The assessments must be completed with 21 days from the date the supervisory body received the request. If an urgent authorisation has been granted the assessment must be completed within the period of the urgent authorisation including any extension granted by the supervisory body.[18]

If any of the assessments is negative, the supervisory body must refuse the authorisation and notify the managing authority, P, any IMCA and every interested person consulted by the best interests assessor. The supervisory body may review a standard authorisation at any time and must do so, if requested by P or his/her representative or the managing authority. If a request for review is made, the supervisory body must decide whether review of any of the qualifying requirements is needed and if so, commission review assessments. To ensure the authorisation process proceeds smoothly the supervisory body should have in place a procedure to identify the actions they should take, who should take it and within what time scale, communicated to local managing authorities. The flow chart set out in Annex 3 of the DoLS Code of Practice summarises the process that a supervisory body should follow.

3.8.3   Protection of P's human rights

The supervisory body must ensure that P's rights enshrined under Art 8 of the European Convention are respected. Failure to take these matters into consideration risks actions taken under any authorisation granted to be deemed unlawful. In *London Borough of Hillingdon v Steven Neary (By the Official Solicitor) and Others*[19] P, who was 20, suffered from autism and severe learning difficulties and lived with his father. Support from the local authority included respite care at a support unit from which he was not returned home. The local authority initially detained him under an urgent authorisation and subsequently made three requests for standard authorisation to the supervisory body, unfortunately chaired by the team manager who was responsible for the

---

[17] [2010] EWHC 2508 (COP), [2010] COPLR Con Vol 65.
[18] DoL Code of Practice, para 4.1.
[19] [2011] EWHC 1377 (COP), [2011] COPLR Con Vol 632, [2012 1 FLR 72.

support services team. The father and the Official Solicitor on behalf of P challenged the authorisation on the ground that their action had been unlawful and had deprived P of his liberty. Jackson J concluded that: (a) P had been deprived of his liberty throughout the relevant period; (b) the authorisations relied upon by the local authority were flawed and even if they had been valid they did not in the circumstances of the case amount to lawful authority for keeping P at the support unit; (c) the mere belief that the local authority was acting in the best interests of P was not relevant. It had acted as if it had the right to make decisions about P, and by a combination of turning a deaf ear and force majeure, it had tried to wear down the father's resistance. It had thus failed to activate the statutory safeguards. Consequently, the local authority had breached P's rights to family life and deprived him of his liberty in contravention of Arts 8 and 5 of the ECHR.

3.8.4   Guidance on practice issues

The *Steven Neary* case also provides useful guidance on number of practice issues of which three were specifically referred to. These are:

(1)   *The purpose of DoL authorisations and of the Court of Protection.* Significant welfare issues that cannot be resolved by discussion should be placed before the Court of Protection, where decisions can be taken as a matter of urgency where necessary. The DoLS scheme is an important safeguard against arbitrary detention. Where stringent conditions are met, it allows a managing authority to deprive a person of liberty at a particular place. It is <u>not</u> to be used by a local authority as a means of getting its own way on the question of whether it is in the person's best interests to be in the place at all. Using the DoLS regime in that way turns the spirit of the Mental Capacity Act 2005 on its head, with a code designed to protect the liberty of vulnerable people being used instead as an instrument of confinement. In this case, far from being a safeguard, the way in which the DoL process was used masked the real deprivation of liberty, which was the refusal to allow Steven to go home.

(2)   *Decision-making.* Poor decision-making processes often lead to bad decisions. Where a local authority wears a number of hats, it should be clear about who is responsible for its direction. Where one sub-department of the local authority's adult social services provides social work support and another is responsible for running facilities such as the support unit and, at the same time, senior social workers represent the supervisory body that determines whether or not a DoL authorisation should be granted, welfare planning should be directed by the team to which the allocated social worker belongs, although there will of course be the closest liaison with those who run the support facilities. The tail of service provision, however expert and specialised, should not wag the dog of welfare planning.

(3)   *The responsibilities of the supervisory body.* The granting of DoL standard authorisations is a matter for the local authority in its role as a supervisory body. The responsibilities of a supervisory body, correctly

understood, require it to scrutinise the assessment it receives with independence and a degree of care that is appropriate to the seriousness of the decision and to the circumstances of the individual case that are or should be known to it. Where a supervisory body grants authorisations on the basis of perfunctory scrutiny of superficial best interests assessments, it cannot expect the authorisations to be legally valid.

3.9   FURTHER ASSESSMENTS

A supervisory body is not obliged to obtain further assessments if:

(1)   it has a written copy of an existing assessment whether or not such an assessment was carried out in connection with a request for a standard authorisation or for some other purpose;

(2)   the assessment complies with all the required requirements under Sch A1;

(3)   the existing assessments were carried out within the last 12 months; and

(4)   it is satisfied that there is no reason why the existing assessment may no longer be accurate.

3.10   THE AUTHORISATION – FORM AND CONTENT

The supervisory body must grant a standard authorisation if all the assessments are positive and it has written copies of the assessments. All assessments are positive if each assessment concludes that the relevant person meets the qualifying requirements to which the assessment relates.[20] It must be in writing.

The authorisation must set out the period during which the authorisation is to be in force but the period must not exceed the maximum period recommended in the best interests assessment. The commencement date of the period may be a date after the authorisation is given. The authorisation must be in writing and must name the relevant person, the hospital or care home, the period during which the authorisation is to be in force, the purpose for which it is given, any conditions which may apply and the reasons why the qualifying requirements are met. Copies must be provided to all involved.

3.11   REVIEW OF STANDARD AUTHORISATION

The supervisory body may review a standard authorisation at any time and must do so if requested by the person detained under its provision, his/her representative or the managing authority. If a request is made, the supervisory body must decide whether any of the qualifying requirements appear to need a review and if so commission review assessments.

---

[20]   MCA 2005, Sch A1, Part 4, para 50.

Managing authorities must comply with any conditions attached to the authorisation, and must request a review in the event of any material change in circumstances.

3.12 DECISION ON UNAUTHORISED DETENTION UNDER SCH A1 REGIME

3.12.1 Who may apply?

An eligible third party may request the supervisory body to decide whether or not there is an unauthorised deprivation of liberty, provided the following conditions are met:

(1) the eligible person must have notified the managing authority that it appears that there is an unauthorised deprivation of liberty;

(2) the eligible person must have asked the managing authority to request a standard authorisation;

(3) the managing authority has failed to make a request for standard authorisation within a reasonable period of the request having been made.

3.12.2 What the supervisory body must do

Where a request is made by an eligible third party the supervisory body must select and appoint a person to carry out an assessment of whether or not the person to whom the request relates is a detained resident unless it appears to the supervisory body that the request is frivolous or vexatious, or where the issue has already been decided and since that decision there has been no change of circumstances which would merit the question being decided again. The supervisory body's decision must be notified to the eligible person, the person to whom the request relates, the managing authority and any IMCA.[21]

3.13 URGENT AUTHORISATION

3.13.1 When and by whom can it be granted?

The managing authority of a relevant hospital or care home may give an urgent authorisation to provide a lawful basis for deprivation of liberty before a request for a standard authorisation is made, if it is required to make a request for a standard authorisation and they believe that the need for the relevant person to be a detained resident is so urgent that it is appropriate for the detention to begin before they make the request, or where they have made the request for a standard authorisation and they believe that the need for the relevant person to be a detained resident is so urgent that it is appropriate for the detention to begin before the request is disposed of.

---

[21] MCA 2005, Sch A1, Part 4, paras 67–69.

3.13.2   Form and content and processing of an urgent authorisation

If the managing authority decide to give an urgent authorisation it must:[22]

- Specify the period during which the authorisation is to be in force not exceeding 7 days.

- Give the urgent authorisation in writing.

- State the name of the relevant person, the name of the relevant hospital or care home, the period of authorisation and the purpose for which the authorisation is given.

- Keep a written record of why they have given the urgent authorisation.

- As soon as practicable after giving the authorisation, give a copy of the authorisation to the relevant person and any s 39A IMCA.

- Take such steps as are practicable to ensure that the relevant person understands the effect of the authorisation and the right to make an application to the Court to exercise its jurisdiction under s 21A and give the appropriate information both orally and in writing.

3.13.3   Extension of duration of urgent authorisation

The managing authority may seek an extension of the duration of the urgent authorisation but must keep a written record of the reasons for the request and give the relevant person notice of the request for an extension. The supervisory body may on request grant an extension of the period of urgent authorisation only if they are satisfied that a request for a standard authorisation has been made; that there are exceptional reasons why it has not yet been possible for the request to be disposed of, and that it is essential for the existing detention to continue until the request is disposed. The extension must not exceed 7 days. If an extension is granted the supervisory body must notify the managing authority stating the period of the extension, keep a written record of the outcome of the request and the period of the extension.

3.14   APPOINTMENT OF RELEVANT PERSON'S REPRESENTATIVE

The provisions, for the appointment of a representative to a person in respect of whom a standard authorisation has been issued, are set out in the Act at Sch A1, paras 139–140. It provides that the supervisory body must appoint a person to be the relevant person's representative (RPR) and that person must, if appointed, maintain, represent and support the relevant person in matters relating to or connected with his/her deprivation of liberty. The functions of a representative are in addition to and do not affect the authority of any donee, the powers of a deputy or any powers of the Court.[23] The Mental Capacity (Deprivation of Liberty: Appointment of Relevant Person's Representative)

---

[22]   MCA 2005, Sch A1, Part 5, paras 77–83.
[23]   MCA 2005, Sch A1, Part 10, para 141(1) and (2).

Regulations 2008, as amended by SI 2008/2368 (Part 2, regs 10-14, see **Appendix 5** and see also Chapter 6), provide for the selection and termination of appointment of a representative, and the formalities of the appointment and termination of a representative's appointment.

3.14.1   Who may be appointed?

A person can only be selected to be a representative if they are:[24]

(1)   18 years of age or over;

(2)   able to keep in contact with the relevant person;

(3)   willing to be the relevant person's representative;

(4)   not financially interested in the relevant person's managing authority;

(5)   not a relative of a person who is financially interested in the managing authority;

(6)   not employed by, or providing services to, the relevant person's managing authority, where the relevant person's managing authority is a care home;

(7)   not employed to work in the relevant person's managing authority in a role that is, or could be, related to the relevant person's case, where the relevant person's managing authority is a hospital; and

(8)   not employed to work in the supervisory body that is appointing the representative in a role that is, or could be, related to the relevant person's case.

3.14.2   Selection process

It will be for the best interests assessor to determine whether P has the capacity to select a representative to act on his behalf. Where the best interests assessor determines that the relevant person has capacity, the relevant person may select a family member, friend or carer. Where the relevant person does not wish to make a selection the best interests assessor may make the selection under the provisions of reg 8 (reg 5). A donee of a LPA/EPA or a deputy appointed by the Court of Protection may select themselves or a family member, friend or carer to be the representative where the scope of their appointment permits it (reg 6). The best interests assessor determines whether the person selected by P or a donee or deputy is eligible and, if so, to recommend that appointment (reg 7). Where no selection has been made the best interests assessor is given power to select a P's family member friend or carer. The supervisory body is also empowered to select and pay for a person in a professional capacity to be a representative (regs 9 and 15). The process of appointing a representative begins as soon as a best interests assessor is selected upon a request for a standard authorisation or, as soon as an existing representative's appointment is about to terminate (reg 10).

---

[24]   Regulation 3.

The role of the RPR is key to P having a voice in the authorisation process. It is therefore essential for an independent person who is appropriate for the role be appointed. The case of In the matter of the Mental Capacity Act 2005 and in the matter of *AJ (Deprivation of Liberty Safeguards)* [2015] EWCOP 6 is a classic example of the consequences of selecting the wrong person as RPR. AJ was an 88-year-old lady who had lived in an annex to the home of her niece and her husband, Mr and Mrs C for some years. They were also her attorneys under a registered lasting power. Over time Mrs C found the caring role increasingly difficult and needed in the short term respite care so she and Mr C could go on holiday and in the long term a full time placement for AJ in residential care. A respite placement was identified and Mr and Mrs C both hoped that if AJ settled there she could become a permanent resident. AJ angrily objected to the placement and expressed vigorously her desire to return home. Mr and Mrs C upon their return from holiday expressed their view that residential care was the best option. Despite this conflict Mr C was appointed AJ's RPR. There was delay in appointing an IMCA who had little communication with Mr C. So although AJ's opposition to the placement was known no legal challenge was made for several months. In his judgment Baker J considered that Mr C ought never to have been appointed because, although he fulfilled the criteria for appointment contained in Sch A1 and the accompanying regulations, he was actually ineligible under para 140. This demands that a person is not selected to be an RPR unless s/he would represent P in matters under the Schedule. Clearly Mr C could not do that by reason of the conflict of interest between them.

Regulations 12–14 deal with the formalities of appointment and termination of a representative.

3.15   CHALLENGING AUTHORISATION

The DoLS provide a regime for appropriate assessments to be carried out in relation to P which operate to justify P's detention. However, the regime would be inadequate unless there is available to the person detained, the right to challenge the authorisation together with a system of monitoring. The ECtHR has emphasised the need for P to have access to reviews even where the detention has been authorised by judicial authority and Art 5(4) of the ECHR provides that everyone who is deprived of his liberty by arrest or detention shall be entitled to take proceedings by which the lawfulness of his detention shall be decided speedily by a court and his release ordered if the detention is not lawful. The need for periodic checks on whether the arrangements made are in P's best interests was also emphasised by Lady Hale in the *Cheshire West* case (para 57). The amendments made to the MCA 2005 provide two routes of challenge to the grant of authorisations; first by an application to the supervisory body for review and secondly, on an application for review to the Court of Protection.

3.15.1   Review by the supervisory body

Part 8 of Sch A1 provides for a built in monitoring and review procedure where standard authorisations have been given and which remain in force. Monitoring provides an opportunity for quality control in addition to safeguarding the detention. The review process focuses upon the validity of the qualifying requirements and thus the eligibility of P to be subject to the regime. It does not however apply to urgent authorisations.

Paragraph 102(1) of Sch A1 to the MCA 2005 imposes a monitoring responsibility upon the supervisory body to carry out its own review. Whilst this not compulsory, it is unlikely that the supervisory bodies will fail to build into their individual policies on deprivation of liberty safeguards, their own review mechanism particularly having regard to the view expressed by the ECtHR. Failure to do so would inevitably lead to challenge through the courts. If the supervisory body is required to carry out a review by an eligible person the supervisory body must do so (para 102(2)). Those eligible to seek a review are defined as P, P's representative, or the manager of the relevant hospital or care home. The purpose is to provide access for the decision to be reconsidered.

The grounds for review are set out in paras 105–107. In summary, the grounds for review are that: (a) P does not meet the qualification requirements; (b) P is ineligible under Sch A1 (if P is ineligible by reason of being a mental health patient; (c) where the reason for the initial authorisation has changed; or (d) where conditions need to be reconsidered or varied.

The power of the supervisory body in this context is either to terminate the standard authorisation or vary the conditions. Discretion is limited. So for instance where review assessments are carried out and reach a negative conclusion the supervisory body must terminate the authorisation.

It is suggested that any request for a review should be made in writing although there is no specific stipulation for this and no pro forma for the application. The process of review is detailed and mandatory. There is no scope for misunderstandings. The supervisory body must:

- Give notice of the review, decide which of the requirements is reviewable, and where there is more than one, ensure they are subject to separate assessments.
- Secure separate review assessments where necessary, eg best interest requirements are non-assessable if a variation of conditions only is sought or there has been no significant change.
- Complete the review by deciding whether or not the requirements are reviewable and if so whether or not to terminate or vary the authorisation.
- Give notice stating the outcome and any variation of terms of authorisation. The notice must be made in writing.
- Keep records of their reviews and outcomes.

Paragraph 118 of Sch A1 provides that according to the outcome of the individual reviewable assessments the overall review of the standard authorisation is complete at a variety of different stages. For instance the review will be complete if the supervisory body decides that none of the qualifying requirements are reviewable (para 110). In those circumstances the supervisory body need go no further save to report the outcome. Where one or more of the review assessments reach a negative conclusion the supervisory body must terminate the authorisation (for full details see the MCA Sch A1 in **Appendix 1** and Annex 4 of the *Deprivation of Liberty Code of Practice* which sets out a flow chart).

3.15.2 The Court's powers in relation to standard and urgent authorisation under Sch A1

Section 4A of the MCA 2005 clarifies that the legislation does not authorise deprivation of liberty except by way of court order or authorisation under Sch A1.

The Court of Protection has jurisdiction to ensure that Art 5(4) of the ECHR is complied with by reviewing the lawfulness of the detention of anyone for whom authorisation has been granted to provide care or treatment. The application for a review may be made by the person who has been deprived of his/her liberty or a representative for that person.

Section 21A of the Act provides that where a standard authorisation has been made the Court may determine any questions relating to:

(1) whether the relevant person meets one or more of the qualifying requirements;

(2) the period during which the standard authorisation is to be in force;

(3) the purpose for which the standard authorisation is given;

(4) the conditions subject to which the standard authorisation is given,

and may make an order varying or terminating the standard authorisation or directing the supervisory body to vary or terminate the standard authorisation.[25]

Where an urgent authorisation has been given, the Court may determine any question relating to:

(1) whether the urgent authorisation should have been given;

(2) the period during which the urgent authorisation is to be in force;

(3) the purpose for which the urgent authorisation is given,

---

[25] MCA 2005, s 21A(2) and (3).

and may make an order varying or terminating the urgent authorisation or directing the managing authority of the relevant hospital or care home to vary or terminate the urgent authorisation.[26]

A court may, in relation to either of the above applications, consider a person's liability for any act done in connection with the standard or urgent authorisation before its variation or termination, and make an order excluding a person from liability.[27]

The legislation is comprehensive and self-explanatory. In summary, in the case of an application relating to an urgent authorisation, the court can determine whether the authorisation should have been given, the period for which it remain in force and its purpose. In the case of a standard authorisation, the court can determine whether the qualifying requirements are met, the period purpose and conditions of the authorisation.

3.16 PRACTICE AND PROCEDURE IN RELATION TO DOL APPLICATIONS UNDER S 21A RELATING TO STANDARD OR URGENT AUTHORISATION UNDER SCH A1

The practice and procedure in relation to deprivation of liberty applications are set out in Part 10A of the Court of Protection Rules 2007 and related Practice Directions. Deprivation of Liberty (DoL) applications means applications for orders under s 21A of the Act relating to standard or urgent authorisation under Sch A1 of the Act. It is acknowledged that by their nature such applications are of special urgency. The procedure set out hereunder relates to only such applications. They do not apply to applications concerning other matters, which may also raise issues relating to deprivation of liberty and require urgent attention. This should be explained to the DoL team at the court so that the applications are handled appropriately.

The Practice Direction relating to applications for a deprivation of liberty identifies the key features of the special DoL procedure as follows:

(1) special DoL forms ensure that DoL court papers stand out as such and receive special handling by the Court office;

(2) the application is placed before a judge as soon as possible – if necessary before the application is issued – for directions to be given as to the steps to be taken in the application and who is to take each step and by when;

(3) the usual COP Rules will apply only so far as consistent with the judicial directions given for the particular case;

(4) a dedicated team in the court office (the DoL team) will deal with such applications at all stages including liaison with would be applicants/other parties;

---

[26]   MCA 2005, s 21A(4) and (5).
[27]   MCA 2005, s 21A(6) and (7).

(5) the progress of each DoL case will be monitored by a judge assigned to that case, assisted by the DoL team.

3.16.1   When should an application be made?

Section 21A sets out the circumstances in which an application may be made to the Court. In summary the application can be made:

- before standard authorisation is given;
- after a standard authorisation is given;
- where an urgent authorisation is given.

3.16.2   Who may apply?

The following person can apply without permission:[28]

- P;
- a donor of a Lasting Power of Attorney to whom an application relates or their donee;
- a deputy who has been appointed by the Court to act for the person concerned;
- a person named in an existing order;
- P's RPR;
- the Official Solicitor in certain circumstances;
- the Public Guardian;
- any other person where the application is made under s 21A of the Act.

3.16.3   How and where and when should the application be made?

The applicant must contact the Deprivation of Liberty Team (DoL team) at the earliest opportunity before making the application to inform the team that the application is to be made and how quickly the court's decision is required on the merits of the application and when the application is likely to be lodged. Where this is not possible, the applicant should liaise with the DoL team either by telephone or fax at the time when the application is lodged. The information that the DoL team will need in advance is:

(1) that the DoL application is to be made;

(2) how urgent the application is (by when should the court's decision, or interim decision on the merits be given); and

(3) when the court will receive the application papers.

Prescribed forms must be used.

---

[28] COP Rules 2007, as amended, r 51.

In very urgent cases arrangements can be made by the team for directions to be given or an interim order to be obtained by telephone conference before the application is issued. In such cases the court will require brief details including the following:

(1) the parties' details and where they live;

(2) the issue to be decided;

(3) the date of the urgent or standard authorisation;

(4) the date of effective detention;

(5) the parties' legal representatives;

(6) details of any family members or other interested parties, who are involved; and

(7) whether there have been any previous proceedings relating to the parties and, if so, details of the same.

The DoL team should be contacted at:

PO BOX 70185
The Court of Protection
First Avenue House
42-49 High Holborn
London WC1A 9JA
DX: 160013 Kingsway 7
Enquiries: 0300 456 4600

The public counter is open between 9.30 am to 4.30 pm on working days. The DoL team can receive telephone calls and faxes between 9.00 am and 5.00 pm. Faxes transmitted after 4.30 pm will be dealt with the next working day.

In cases of emergency, where it is necessary to make an application out of office hours, the security office at the RCJ should be contacted on 020 7947 6000. The security officer should be informed of the nature of the case. In the Family Division the procedure involves the judge being contacted through the Family Division Duty Officer, and the RCJ security officer will need to contact the duty officer and not the judge's clerk.[29]

3.16.4   Issuing the application

To issue a DOL application the following forms should be filed at court:[30]

(1) form DLA: Deprivation of Liberty Application Form;

(2) form DLB: Request for Urgent Consideration. If the application is urgent, the reasons for the application and the urgency and the timetable the applicant wishes the case to follow and any interim relief sought (plus draft order);

---

[29]   COP Rules 2007, PD10A, paras 3–7.
[30]   COP Rules 2007, PD10A, paras 10–12.

(3) the appropriate court fee of £400;

(4) if possible an electronic version of the draft order on disc should be lodged;

(5) where an application is made out of hours an undertaking will be required that the DLA form will be filed and the court fee paid unless an exemption applies.

3.16.5 The Court office

As soon as the DoL team is notified of the application the team will ensure that the application is placed before a judge nominated to hear Court of Protection cases and DoL applications. During office hours the application will be placed before a judge at the Court of Protection. During out of office hours the application will be placed before the judge who is most immediately available. Initially the application will be dealt with by the judge and any orders made without attendance of the applicant or his representatives.[31]

3.16.6 Possible directions which the court may make

(a) Upon whom, by when and how service of the application should be effected;

(b) dispensing with acknowledgement of service of the application or allowing a short period of time for so doing, which in some cases may amount to a few hours only;

(c) whether further lay or expert evidence should be obtained;

(d) whether P/the detained person should be a party and represented by the Official Solicitor and whether any other person should be a party;

(e) whether any family members should be formally notified of the application and of any hearing and joined as parties;

(f) fixing a date for a First Hearing and giving a time estimate;

(g) fixing a trial window for any final hearing and giving a time estimate;

(h) the level of judge appropriate to hear the case;

(i) whether the case is such that it should be immediately transferred to the High Court for a High Court Judge to give directions;

(j) provision for a bundle for the judge at the First Hearing.

As soon as the order is made the DoL team will notify the applicant of the order and carry out any other directions given by the judge and make arrangements for any transfer of the case to another court and for a hearing.[32]

---

[31] COP Rules 2007, PD10A, paras 19–20.
[32] COP Rules 2007, PD10A para 17.

3.16.7   After issue/directions given

After issue and any directions given, the applicant or his legal representatives must:[33]

(1)   ensure that any directions given by the judge are complied with;

(2)   ensure that the application, any orders made and the acknowledgement of service in Form DLE are served on the respondents to the application;

(3)   form DLD – Deprivation of Liberty Certificate of Service/Non-service and Certificate of Notification/Non-notification is filed;

(4)   prepare an indexed and paginated bundle of documents which should include a case summary, skeleton arguments and draft order for the hearing on notice; and

(5)   serve an index of the bundle on all parties to the application and, where a party appears in person, serve a copy of the bundle on that person.

3.16.8   The first hearing

The first hearing will be listed for the Court to fix a date and or give directions, make an interim order or final order if appropriate or make such other orders as the appropriate in the case. Section 21A MCA 2005 provides that the Court may determine questions relating to standard authorisation. The Court must determine how it approaches that task; it is not compelled to carry out a full inquiry regardless of the merit. The fact that P's deprivation was to be reviewed is a factor which it will take into consideration. Furthermore, in order to deal with an appeal and give it due consideration, 'may not require any lengthy consideration. A full hearing is not necessarily a lengthy, time consuming or expensive hearing' (Moses LJ at para 75 in *TA v AA*[34]). The hearing is as a general rule held in private.[35] The Court may direct that the hearing takes place in public if the criteria in r 93 apply.[36]

3.16.9   Orders the Court can make

The Court may make any appropriate orders, grant an injunction and give directions. These will include:

(1)   a declaration whether or not the person who is the subject of the proceedings lacks capacity;

(2)   a declaration whether the act done or proposed to be done is lawful or in the best interests of the person who lacks capacity;

(3)   authorising acts which deprive a person of his liberty;

(4)   authorising appropriate restraint to be used;

(5)   orders varying or terminating the standard or urgent authorisation;

---

[33]   COP Rules 2007, PD10A, paras 20–22.
[34]   [2013] EWCA Civ 1661.
[35]   COP Rules 2007, r 90 and PD13A.
[36]   COP Rules 2007, PD10A, paras 23–25.

(6)   orders directing the managing authority or supervisory body to comply
      with any directions the Court gives; and

(7)   prohibiting a person from doing certain acts.

The general rule in all cases concerning health and welfare is that there will be
no order as to costs of the proceedings.[37] This also applies to DoL applications.

3.17   APPEALS

Part 20 of the COP Rules applies to appeals from the Court's decision.
Permission to appeal will be required[38] (for the consequences of failure to apply
to the trial court for permission to appeal see *TA v AA and Knowsley
Metropolitan Borough Council*[39]). Permission will only be granted if the Court
considers that the appeal would have a real prospect of success or there is some
other compelling reason why the appeal should be heard.[40]

3.18   PRACTICE IN RELATION TO WITHOUT NOTICE
APPLICATIONS

Concerns have been expressed by the Court that practitioners too regularly do
not follow the guidance on the information to be provided and the procedure to
be followed in seeking without notice relief and that such failure shows an
insufficient appreciation of the exceptional nature of without notice relief and
the impact it has or could have on the rights, life and emotions of the person
concerned in relation to whom and others against whom the order is made. It is
only in exceptional circumstances and in accordance with the guidance set out
in the relevant case-law and practice guidance should without notice
applications be made (*B Borough Council v S (By the Official Solicitor)*[41]). It is
therefore important to ensure that the evidence in support of an application for
deprivation of liberty gives a balanced, fair and particularised account of the
events leading up to the application and the facts upon which it is based. Where
possible it should include what the applicant thinks the respondent's case is or
is likely to be. It should also include an account of the steps the applicant
proposes concerning services, the giving of explanation of the order and the
implementation of the order. This is of particular importance where emotional
issues are involved and family members of a person who lacks capacity are the
subject of injunctions and orders. In such cases information of the applicant's
intentions is likely to inform issues as to the need, form and the proportionality
of the relief sought and granted (*LLBC v TG, JG and KR*[42]).

---

[37]   COP Rules 2007, r 157.
[38]   COP Rules 2007, r 172.
[39]   [2013] EWCA Civ 1661.
[40]   COP Rules 2007, r 173.
[41]   [2006] EWHC 2584 (Fam), [2007] 1 FLR 1600.
[42]   [2007] EWHC 2640 (Fam), [2009] 1 FLR 414.

Where an order is obtained on a without notice application the term 'liberty to apply' should be replaced with the terms:

'If any person served with this order disagrees with any part of this order and wishes to seek to set aside or vary it, they should make an application to this court to set it aside or vary it within 21 days of service of it upon them.'

This suggestion endorses the observation made in *B Borough Council v S (By the Official Solicitor)*[43] by Charles J in relation to without notice applications:

'There is a natural temptation for applicants to seek, and the Court to grant, relief to protect vulnerable persons whether they are children or vulnerable adults. In my view this can lead (and experience as the applications judge confirms that it does lead) to practitioners making without notice applications which are not necessary or appropriate, or which are not properly supported by appropriate evidence. Also there is in my view a general practice of asking the Court to grant without notice orders over fairly extended period with expression permission to apply to vary or discharge on an inappropriately long period of notice (often 48 hours). It seems to me that on occasions this practice pays insufficient regard to the interests of both the person in respect of whom and against whom the orders are made, and that therefore on every occasion without notice relief is sought and granted the choice of the return date and the provisions as to permission to apply should be addressed with care by both applicants and the court. Factors in that consideration will be an estimation of the effect on the person against whom the order is made of service of the order and how that is to be carried out.'

3.19   PRECEDENT AND PROCEDURAL GUIDE FOR APPLICATION FOR DEPRIVATION OF LIBERTY ORDER

3.19.1   Draft order

(1)   The first respondent ... is eligible to be deprived of his/her liberty at V pursuant to an authority under section 4A of the Mental Capacity Act 2005.

(2)   Notwithstanding ... P's inability to consent, it shall be lawful and in his/her best interests for his/her clinicians and care workers including the applicant's and the ... respondents employees servants or agents to:

(a)   admit the first respondent ... to units provided by ... At either the A care home or the B Care home for the purpose of caring for his/her welfare and providing him/her with psychological, behavioural and psychiatric treatment.

(b)   Provide him/her with psychological, behavioural and psychiatric treatment in accordance with the care plans provided by ...

(c)   Use such reasonable restraint as may be necessary in conveying the First Respondent ... to and preventing him/her from leaving the unit, including measures that may amount to the deprivation of liberty for the purpose of caring for his/her welfare and providing him/her with psychological, behavioural and psychiatric treatment.

---

[43]   [2006] EWHC 2584 (Fam), [2007] 1 FLR 1600 (para 37).

3.19.2 Procedural guide for applications to Court of Protection

When can an application be made	Before standard authorisation is given	
	After standard authorisation is given	
	After urgent authorisation is given	
Steps to be taken		
Before the application is issued	The applicant must contact the DoL team or at the same time as lodging the application and give the team the following information:	
	(1) that an application is to be made	
	(2) how urgent it is	
	(3) by when the decision should be given	
If an urgent application is to be made	(4) details of the parties and their addresses	
	(5) issue to be decided	
	(6) date of standard/urgent authorisation	
	(7) details of parties' legal representatives	
	(8) details of family members	
	(9) details of previous court proceedings	
Permission is not needed Where the application is made by	The patient his appointed representative, attorney or deputy; where an application is made under s 21A of the Act	MCA 2005, s 51 COP Rules 2007, Parts 8 and 10A
In an emergency	Application can be made out of hours by calling security officer at the RCJ on 020 7947 6000	PD10A, para 7
	In the Family Division judge can be contacted through the FD duty officer. The security officer will contact the duty officer	
How to apply		
The applicant must file	Form DLA Form DLB (plus draft) If possible an electronic version of order sought on disc	PD10A, para 15
	In an emergency an undertaking will be required that Forms will be filed and fee paid	
Court Fee	£400	PD10A, para 15(c)

Possible directions which may be sought on issue	(1) Upon whom, by whom and how service should be effected	PD10A, para 17
	(2) Dispensing with acknowledgement of service or seeking abridgement of time	
	(3) Whether lay or expert evidence required whether P or OS or other persons should be made parties	
	(4) Whether family member should be notified and joined as a party	
	(5) Fixing trial window or date for hearing allocation	
	(6) Whether it is appropriate to transfer to the High Court	
	(7) Directions for the preparation of bundles	
Court Office	Take steps to place application before a Nominated judge to hear DoL cases will notify the judge to put him/her on stand by and the judge will consider the application and give directions if appropriate	PD10A, paras 19 and 20
Steps after judge's order	DoL team will notify parties of order Action every point on judge's note Refer queries to the judge Make arrangements for transfer	
Steps to be taken by applicant	Comply with the order made File DLD if appropriate Serve Form DLE with other documents Prepare indexed and paginated Court bundle to include skeleton arguments and draft order Provide a copy of index to all parties and a copy of bundle to unrepresented party	PD10A, para 22
First Hearing	Court will attempt to hear case within 5 days. The hearing will be in private unless r 93 applies and court so directs	PD10A, paras 23-25 COP Rules, r 90
Orders that may be made	s 21A of MCA 2005	
Costs	No order	COP Rules 2007, r 157 PD10A para 50
Appeal	Permission to appeal required	PD10A, para 51 COP Rules 2007, r 171B and 172

Permission will only be granted if court considers it has a real prospect of success or there are some other compelling reasons	COP Rules 2007, r 173 PD10A, para 51

For DoLS applications which do not relate to urgent or standard authorisations, see Chapters 4 and 5.

CHAPTER 4

JUDICIAL AUTHORISATION OF DEPRIVATION OF LIBERTY

4.1 INTRODUCTION

In amending the MCA 2005 it was not contemplated that DoLS would be required for provision other than residential care. The Sch A1 regime therefore applied to care, nursing homes and hospitals only where it was considered sufficient to bridge the *Bournewood* gap. It was, after all, HL's confinement in institutional care which had given rise to the litigation. Further the Court of Protection had been given power to authorise deprivation of liberty by virtue of s 4A.

The Supreme Court in *P v Cheshire West and Chester County Council and P&Q v Surrey County Council*[1] extended the need to protect P's Art 5 rights of liberty and security to a wider range of state provisions provided for the care and support of P. This includes high level secure care at the upper end to some domiciliary care packages at the other even when commissioned from private contractors but paid for from health or social services budgets. Furthermore the Supreme Court defined the interpretation of deprivation of liberty more broadly, so some placements in hospitals and care homes which did not previously attract the protection of the Sch A1 regime now do so. Providers, particularly local authorities, who would have used the Sch A1 administrative procedure previously, find themselves unable to resource the increased number of applications immediately and instead seek authorisation from the court. The effect has been to increase enormously the numbers of people lacking capacity who require their arrangements to be authorised by the court where they amount to a deprivation of liberty. Consequently, concerns were raised about the impact of an increase in applications to the overloaded Court of Protection already tasked with reviewing its own orders authorising a deprivation of liberty.

The DoLS set out in Sch A1 to the Act relate only to those cases where P is accommodated in a hospital or local authority care homes. All other situations require authorisation of the court under s 16(2) for an order authorising deprivation of liberty. The law relating to whether actions taken in respect of P in domiciliary care amounts to deprivation of liberty is the same as that when P is cared for by a public body (see Chapter 2) but P in such cases does not have

---

[1]   [2014] UKSC 19.

the safeguards set out in Sch A1. It is thus necessary in every case where the action taken concerning P's care may amount to deprivation of P's liberty to apply to the court for authorisation.

4.2   THE STREAMLINED PROCESS PROPOSAL

In order to address the increase in workload the President arranged for a number of deprivation of liberty case to be listed before him for an initial direction hearing on 8 May 2014 which resulted in 25 questions being formulated which are set out in the Annex to the judgment. Interested parties were invited to contribute at a hearing on 5 June 2014 in addition to the advocates in the referred cases. So advocates for the Secretary of State for Health, the Lord Chancellor and the Secretary of State for Justice, the Law Society for England and Wales, the Association of Directors of Adult Social Services, eight local authorities, two NHS clinical commissioning groups, Mind, an NHS trust and others put forward their respective arguments and proposals.

On 7 August the President, in a preliminary judgment in *Re X and Others*,[2] set out a 'streamlined process' which he considered would be Art 5 compliant and which would speed up certain types of applications which involve or could potentially involve a deprivation of liberty. The President made it clear however that his judgment was not concerned with either analysing the Supreme Court's decision or exploring the implications as a matter of substantive law. The objective as he put it was:[3]

> 'to devise, if this is feasible, a standardised, and so far as possible "streamlined" process, compatible with all the requirements of Article 5, which will enable the Court of Protection to deal with all DOL cases in a timely but just and fair way. The process needs, if this is feasible, to distinguish between those DOL cases that can properly be dealt with on the papers and without an oral hearing, and those that require an oral hearing.'

Subsequently, the President handed down a further judgment in which he elaborated on his reasons for proposing the 'streamline process' and that this judgment will also deal with issues relating to possible issues relating to the extension of an urgent authorisation by a court order pending completion of assessments under Part 5 of Sch A1 to the MCA. In *Re X and Others (No 2)*[4] the President dealt with the issue of whether the detained resident should be joined as a party to any application under s 21A and in particular dealt with the following outstanding questions relating to P's involvement in the proceedings:

- 'Does P need to be joined to any application to the court seeking authorisation of a deprivation of liberty in order to meet the requirements of Article 5(1) ECHR or Article 6 or both;

---

[2]   [2014] EWCOP 25.
[3]   See para 5.
[4]   [2014] EWCOP 37.

- If so, should there be a requirement that P ... must have a litigation friend (whether by reference to the requirements of Article 5 ECHR and/or by reference to the requirements of Article 6 ECHR)?
- If P or the detained resident requires a litigation friend, then: (a) Can a litigation friend who does not otherwise have the right to conduct litigation or provide advocacy services provide those services, in other words without instructing legal representatives, by virtue of their acting as litigation friend and without being authorised by the court under the Legal Services Act 2007 to do either or both ...?'

He concluded that there was no requirement in domestic law or under the ECHR for P to be joined as a party to welfare proceedings and in particular deprivation of liberty proceedings; that P should be given an opportunity to express his wishes and to participate in proceedings and that although he will need assistance in so doing it was not necessary for this to be legal assistance; that there is no fundamental principle in domestic law which dictates that P if joined as a party should have a litigation friend, and, finally, that the litigation friend does not have to act through a legal representative – he can act and conduct the litigation on behalf of P, but will require the court's permission to act as an advocate. The President's conclusion were driven by expediency and resource because he stated in concluding his judgment:

'It is essential that where the issue concerns P's deprivation of liberty the Court of Protection's processes are rigorous, so that the circumstances of the individual case are subjected, as they must be, to the strict scrutiny demanded by the Convention. Both our domestic law and the Convention impose demanding standards. But the need to meet this challenge must not be allowed to lead to a system of technical requirements which may, in the real world, operate to deny P the speedy access to a judicial determination which is the very essence of what is required. To speak plainly, the Committee will have to consider how best to craft a process which, while it meets the demanding requirement of the law, also has regard to the realities consequent upon (a) the legal aid regime and (b) the exposure of a litigation friend to a costs risk. There is no point in a system which requires there to be a litigation friend, let alone which requires the litigation friend to instruct lawyers, if the reality is that there is, because of an absence of legal aid and possible exposure to an adverse costs order, no-one willing and able to accept appointment as litigation friend. Indeed, such a system would be self-defeating. And in this connection it needs to be remembered that the Official Solicitor can never be compelled to accept appointment. Moreover, as I understand it, he is not funded to act as a litigation friend in deprivation of liberty cases, so he is dependent on external funding which in many cases will not be available in the absence of legal aid.'

4.3 THE CURRENT POSITION

This decision was the subject of an appeal to the Court of Appeal. The Court of Appeal has disagreed with the President's analysis. The Court of Appeal was critical of the basis on which the streamline process was advocated and held that the President had not had the jurisdiction to engage in the procedure that he had adopted. It also disapproved the President's decision that a person who might be deprived of his liberty did not always have to be joined as a party to proceedings which concern the deprivation of his liberty (see further Chapter 6 as to P's status and participation in proceedings). The streamline procedure in its original form as proposed by the President has been abandoned as it relates to P's participation. However, the forms etc have been retained because they provide a vehicle for valuable and pertinent information about P to come before the court. The Law Commission on 7 July 2015 published its consultation paper CP222 on deprivation of liberty, in which it is recommending a new process. The consultation process ends in November 2015. It is anticipated that the final report and recommendation with a draft bill will be published in 2016-2017. However the consultation makes no reference to the Court of Appeal decision in *Re X* and this will have to be taken into account when new procedures are proposed.

4.4 AUTHORISATION OF A DEPRIVATION OF LIBERTY ANCILLARY TO OTHER APPLICATIONS

Where the court makes orders under s 16 MCA 2005 in respect of P's welfare, particularly residence, the effect of the order may be to deprive P of his or her liberty which will require authorisation. Where the deprivation of liberty is authorised by the court periodic review will be necessary by the court, at least annually (see *Salford City Council v GJ NJ & BJ (by their litigation friends)*[5]).

However, where the order requires P to live in accommodation covered by Sch A1, ie hospitals, nursing or care homes, authorisation of the deprivation of liberty[6] should be authorised using the statutory regime. In *Re HA*[6] Charles J noted the Sch A1 regime had 'checks and balances that generally should be preferred to review by the court'. In cases where the statutory regime does not apply there is currently no alternative but for the court to authorise and review the deprivation itself.

4.5 PRACTICE AND PROCEDURE IN RELATION TO COURT-AUTHORISED DEPRIVATION OF LIBERTY

On 17 November 2014 Practice Direction 10AA (Deprivation of Liberty Applications), supplementing the Court of Protection Rules 2007, came into force. This Practice Direction has been amended alongside the amendments made to the Court of Protection Rules 2007 with effect from 1 July 2015. In addition to addressing in Part 1, the procedure to be followed in applications to the court for orders under s 21A of the Mental Capacity Act 2005 relating to a standard or urgent authorisation under Sch A1 of MCA 2005 to deprive a person of his or her liberty (see Chapter 3), this Practice Direction also sets out in Part 2 the procedure to be followed in applications under s 16(2)(a) of the Act to authorise deprivation of liberty under s 4A(3) and (4) pursuant to a

---

[5]   [2008] EWHC 1097 (Fam).
[6]   [2012] EWHC 1068 (COP).

streamline procedure and makes provision common to applications under both Parts 1 and 2. Part 2 of the amended PD10A applies to health and welfare applications under s 16(2)(a) where authorisation for deprivation of liberty is sought under s 4A(3) and (4). The procedure to be followed in relation to applications for court authorisation of deprivation of liberty which fall outside the Sch A1 regime are set out within paras 27–48.

4.5.1 Steps to be taken before issuing the application

(1) It is mandatory for the applicant to consult with and inform P:
  (a) that the applicant is making an application to the court;
  (b) that it is to consider whether P lacks capacity to make decision in relation to his or her residence and care arrangements and whether to authorise the deprivation of liberty in connection with the care arrangements set out in the care plan;
  (c) what the proposed arrangements for which authorisation is sought;
  (d) his or her right to express his or her views wishes and feelings in relation to the proposed care arrangements and that these will be conveyed to the court by the person undertaking the consultation. In this regard P must be supported and assisted to express his views wishes and feelings;
  (e) that the person is entitled to apply to take part in the proceedings by being joined as a party or otherwise, what that means, and that the person undertaking the consultation will ensure that any such request is communicated to the court. P must be supported assisted and encouraged to take part in the proceedings to the extent that s/he wishes; and
  (f) that the person undertaking the consultation can help to obtain advice and assistance if s/he does not agree with the proposed arrangements (PD10A, para 35).

(2) The person undertaking the consultation must complete Annex C to form COPDOL 10.

(3) The applicant must also confirm that the person the application is about has been supported and assisted to express his or her views, wishes and feelings in relation to the application and the arrangements proposed in it, and encouraged to take part in the proceedings to the extent that he or she wishes in accordance with s 4(4) of the Act.

(4) It is also mandatory for the applicant to ensure that the following persons are consulted about the intention to make the application:
  (a) A donee of a LPA granted by P;
  (b) A deputy appointed for P by the court and if possible;
  (c) Anyone named by P who should be consulted in relation to the issues raised in the application;
  (d) Any one engaged in caring for P or interested in his or her welfare (PD10A, para 39).

(5) The persons consulted must be informed of the following matters:
  (a) that the applicant is making an application to the court;

(b) that the application is to consider whether P lacks capacity to make decisions in relation to his or her residence and care and whether he or she should be deprived of liberty in connection with the arrangements set out in the care plan;
(c) what the proposed arrangements under the order are; and
(d) that the applicant is under an obligation to inform P about the matters listed under (1) above unless in the circumstances it is inappropriate for the applicant to give P such information (PD10A, para 40).

4.5.2   Dispensing with notification or service of the application form

The court may dispense with the requirements of informing P of the application and other matters outlined above under (1) provided it is satisfied as to the adequacy of the consultation that has taken place with P and with other persons with whom consultations should have taken place (see under (4) above).

4.5.3   Permission to apply

Prior to 1 July 2015, save for those cases identified in COP Rules, r 51, permission to apply to make the application was mandatory. Rule 51 has been amended by the Court of Protection (Amendment) Rules 2015. Permission is no longer necessary where an application is made for an order under s 16(2)(a) of the MCA 2005 which is to be relied on to authorise the deprivation of P's liberty pursuant to s 4A(3) of the Act.

4.5.4   Form of application

A new application form COPDOL 10 with annexes and attachments has been issued to ensure that all the essential information and evidence is provided to the court to enable an initial assessment as to whether authorisation of deprivation of liberty is: (a) appropriate; and (b) suitable to be dealt with on the papers without an oral hearing. The form must be fully completed and verified by a statement of truth. Where a number of individuals are the subject of proceedings a separate application form for each individual must be filed but where the arrangements are common to the individuals who are the subject of the proceedings a generic statement of evidence may be filed dealing with the common arrangements.[7]

The President was quite clear that separate applications must be made for each individual, even if there are a number of people in the same placement. The reason is obvious and identified namely: P's circumstances must be considered

---

[7]   PD10A, para 31.

separately and on its own merits and with the passage of time, people's circumstances may change (for example P1 and P2 may no longer be in the same placement).[8]

The application form must be accompanied by:

- **Annex A.** The applicant is under a duty to make full and frank disclosure to disclose all facts and matters which may have an impact on the court's decision. Paragraph 33 of the PD10A sets out the factors which must be clearly identified in the evidence in support in Annex A to form COPDOL 10.

- **Annex B.** The applicant must identify the person who were not consulted as required in para 39 with an explanation why they were not consulted.

- **Annex C.** Must be completed by the person who undertook the consultation process with P as required under para 35. Confirmation that P was supported and assisted to express his /her views wishes and feelings and encouraged to take part in the proceedings to the extent that s/he wishes must also be provided.

- **Court fee.** For each application. If on considering the papers it is determined that a hearing is necessary before a decision can be made a separate hearing fee will be payable.

- **Draft order.** The order must set out the order sought, the duration of deprivation of liberty, provision for review and permission to apply for reconsideration. Draft orders have been issued which should be used as guide when drafting the proposed draft order.

Note that there is no need to for the same individual to complete and verify the statement of truth, the form and each of the annex.[9]

However, it should be noted that the Court of Appeal in *Re X* considered that PD10A was not Convention compliant and said:

> 'First, it is heavily dependent upon P conveying a wish to be joined in the proceedings or opposition to the arrangements proposed for him, or someone else who has his interests at heart taking these points on his behalf. Secondly, it depends entirely on the reliability and completeness of the information transmitted to the court by those charged with the task. In many cases, this will be the very person/organisation seeking authorisation for P to be deprived of his liberty and the possibility of a conflict of interest is clear.'

4.5.5 The evidence in support of the application

The evidence must be succinct and focused. Statements and reports need not be lengthy and the total material including the evidence and other supporting material should not exceed 50 pages at most. The evidence should include:

---

[8]   PD10A, para 38.
[9]   PD10A, para 32.

(1) A draft of the precise order sought, including in particular the duration of the authorisation sought and appropriate directions for automatic review and liberty to apply and/or seek a redetermination in accordance with r 89.

(2) Proof that P is 16 years old or more and is not ineligible to be deprived of liberty under the 2005 Act. This will usually take the form of exhibiting P's birth certificate or where this is not available providing an age assessment of P's likely age.

(3) The basis upon which it is said that P suffers from unsoundness of mind (together with the relevant medical evidence). Professional medical evidence is necessary to establish unsoundness of mind, but where the facts are clear this need not involve expert psychiatric opinion (there will be cases where the general practitioner's evidence will suffice). This requirement may be considered slightly ambiguous and open to several interpretations. However, it is submitted that until the matter is made clear either in any further judgment or when the Rules are amended it would be essential to obtain professional medical evidence of P's mental state (cf with the requirement under the standard qualifying requirements and the DoLS Code of Practice, paras 4.35–4.39).

(4) The nature of P's care arrangements (together with a copy of P's treatment plan) and why it is said that they do or may amount to a deprivation of liberty. This will require the applicant to consider issues raised by the acid test and provide evidence to explain/provide reasons for any restraint considered to be necessary.

(5) The basis upon which it is said that P lacks the capacity to consent to the care arrangements (together with the relevant medical evidence). Clearly the key principles set out in s 1 of the Act and the provisions of ss 2 and 3 must be applied in assessing whether the person lacks capacity.

(6) The basis upon which it is said that the arrangements are or may be imputable to the state.

(7) The basis upon which it is said that the arrangements are necessary in P's best interests and why there is no less restrictive option (including details of any investigation into less restrictive options and confirmation that a best interests assessment, which should be attached, has been carried out). Although the judgment is silent on the nature of the assessment required and the qualification of the assessor, presumably it is intended that this assessment will be undertaken by a person who is qualified as a 'best interests assessor' and someone who is not involved in the care or making decision about the care of P. Similarly, the assessor should not be a person who is employed by the public body making the application; ie the person should be totally independent.

(8) The steps that have been taken to notify P and all other relevant people in P's life (who should be identified) of the application and to canvass their wishes, feelings and views.

(9) Any relevant wishes and feelings expressed by P and any views expressed by any relevant person.

(10) Details of any relevant advance decision by P and any relevant decisions under a lasting power of attorney or by P's deputy (who should be identified). This requirement is similar to the no refusal requirement under Sch A1, paras 18 and 19.

(11) P's eligibility for public funding.

(12) The identification of anyone who might act as P's litigation friend.

(13) Any reasons for particular urgency in determining the application (the recently introduced Family Court children application forms provide a useful precedent).

(14) Any factors that ought to be brought specifically to the court's attention (the applicant being under a specific duty to make full and frank disclosure to the court of all facts and matters that might impact upon the court's decision), being factors:

- needing particular judicial scrutiny; or
- suggesting that the arrangements may not in fact be in P's best interests or be the least restrictive option; or
- otherwise indicating that the order sought should not be made (PD10A, para 33).

(15) The applicant must also identify those person not consulted by the applicant and those persons must be listed in Annex B to Form COPDOL 10 together with an explanation in that Annex of why they have not been consulted.

(16) The applicant must also consider who should complete the form and each annex with regard to the nature of the evidence required by each. There is no requirement that the same individual should complete and verify by statement of truth the form and each annex. It might be inappropriate where different people are best placed to provide evidence in different matters.

(17) The application form and witness statement must be verified by the statement of truth. If a document is not verified by a statement of truth the applicant or the respondent, as the case may be, may not rely upon the document as evidence of any of the matters set out in it unless the court permits.[10] Similarly, if a witness statement is not verified by a statement of truth it will not be admissible in evidence unless the court permits.[11] If a person makes or causes to be made a false statement in a document verified by a statement of truth without an honest belief in its truth proceedings for contempt of court may be brought against that person by the Attorney General or with the permission of the Court.[12]

4.5.6 What fee is payable?

The current fee for an application is £400. Since separate applications must be made for each individual it follows that a separate fee is payable for each

---

[10] COP Rules 2007, r 12.
[11] COP Rules 2007, r 13.
[12] COP Rules 2007, r 14(2).

individual. This will undoubtedly place an enormous financial burden on cash strapped public bodies. Since the President has made reference to the Family Court and children proceedings being a model for COP cases it may well be the case that the practice in CA cases of taking only one fee where the application concerns more than one child will be adopted as a reasonable compromise.

4.5.7   Does P need to be joined as a party to the application?

See above under **4.1**; **4.2**; **4.5.4** and Chapter 6.

4.5.8   After issue

After issue the application will be considered by a court officer from the dedicated team set up to deal with the streamlined process, to determine whether it is suitable for allocation as a paper determination or to be considered for an oral hearing (see below – Hearing). Those applications considered suitable to be dealt with on the papers will be allocated to a judge as soon as practicable.

4.5.9   Service of application

The court may dispense with service under COP Rules rr 42, 69 and 70 if it is satisfied that adequate and appropriate consultation has taken place as required (see also PD10A, para 41). However, following the Court of Appeal judgment in *Re X* it is unlikely that an order will be appropriate which dispenses with service upon P.

4.5.10   Which tribunal should hear this type of DoL case?

The question was posed as to whether an official of the Court of Protection could authorise a deprivation of liberty of an individual or must such authorisation be judicial in order to comply with Art 5(1) of the ECHR. The President made it clear that any authorisation of deprivation of liberty must be made by a judge and not a court officer.

The reason for this was spelt out by the President in his judgment that although:[13]

> 'Article 5(1) does not require a judicial determination, but anyone lawfully deprived of their liberty in accordance with article 5(1) is entitled to a "speedy" decision by a "court" of the lawfulness of the detention. The decision must be judicial, so the "court" for this purpose must be a judge and not an official. There is therefore no purpose in creating a procedure (which in any event would require amendment of PD3A) involving initial decision in a DOL case by a court officer. Even if otherwise appropriate (which it is not) it would simply create additional duplicated and unnecessary work for the Court of Protection.'

---

[13]   See para 11.

4.5.11 A paper exercise or an oral hearing?

Neither Art 5(1) nor the COP Rules require that the initial determination should be made at an oral hearing. Therefore the initial determination can properly be made on the papers but with 'an unimpeded right to request a speedy review (re-consideration in accordance with r 89(1)) at an oral hearing' (para 12). However, the President identified certain triggers which would indicate to the court the need for an oral hearing and the inappropriateness of dealing with the application on paper. These 'triggers' are identified as follows:[14]

(1)   any contest whether by P or anyone else to any of the matters set out in paras 35(ii)-(vii) of the judgment (see below under application form);

(2)   any failure to comply with any of the requirement set out in para 35(viii) ie steps taken to notify P and all other relevant people in P's life (who should be identified) of the application and to canvass their wishes feelings and views;

(3)   any concerns arising out of information supplied in relation to the wishes and feeling expressed by P and those of any relevant person; any reason given on the application for any particular urgency in determining the application and any factor which suggest that judicial scrutiny is needed or that the arrangements proposed may not be in P's best interests or be the least restrictive option or information which indicates that the order sought should not be made;

(4)   any objections by P;

(5)   any potential conflict with any advance decision by P and any relevant decisions under a lasting power of attorney or by P's deputy; or

(6)   If for any other reason the court thinks that an oral hearing is necessary or appropriate.

In view of the Court of Appeal decision in *Re X*, it is now unlikely in practice that authorisations will be made on the papers unless P participates (see Chapter 6 on P's participation).

If an oral hearing is required in accordance with the general rule the hearing will takes place in private. Usually the issue of whether the hearing should be held in public and whether any document relating to the proceedings should be a public document; if so, to what extent it should be redacted will be dealt with at a case management hearing (see r 5(2)(l) and (m)). Where the hearing is held in public the court may make an order excluding any person or class of persons from attending a public hearing or a part of it. It may also impose restrictions on the publication of the identity of P, any party or witnesses; prohibit publication of information that may lead to any such person being identified; prohibit the further publication of information relating to the proceedings; or impose such other restrictions on the publication of information relating to the proceedings as the court may specify (r 92).

---

[14]   See para 13.

4.5.12   Costs

In accordance with the general rule in relation to health and welfare there will be no order for costs (see COP Rules, r 157).

4.5.13   Form of order

A model *Re X* order is available to download from the freely available Family Law website: www.familylaw.co.uk. This form of order should be used as a guide/check list to draft the order required and submitted with the application form for the judge hearing the application to complete.

4.5.14   Service of the order

P and all persons who were consulted must be served with a copy of the order made pursuant to the streamline procedure by the applicant.

4.5.15   Review

The order must provide for a review. An application for review of the authorisation must be made in accordance with the terms provided for in the order.

After considering authorities the President's decision in *Re X* was that annual review by a judge would be the norm unless circumstances required a shorter period. Upholding earlier decisions in *Re GJ, NJ and BJ (Incapacitated Adults)*[15] and *Re BJ (Incapacitated Adult)*[16] the President held that an oral hearing is not required in every case. The review can take place on the papers. The President did not give any guidance on the form and nature of such reviews.

In the *Cheshire West* case Lady Hale said that periodic independent checks on whether the arrangements made for P were in his/her best interests were necessary but that such checks need not be as elaborate as those currently provided for in the Court of Protection or the DoL regime.

Similarly, in view of the Court of Appeal's decision in *Re X*, it is now unlikely that reviews will be carried out on the papers without P's participation.

4.5.16   Appeals

Permission to appeal is required (r 172). It will be granted where the court considers that there is a real prospect of success or there is some compelling reason why the appeal should be heard (r 173).

---

[15]   [2008] EWHC 1097 (Fam), [2008] 2 FLR 1295.
[16]   [2009] EWHC 3310 (Fam), [2010] 1 FLR 1373.

Part III deals with provisions common to both applications under the Sch A1 regime and the streamline process. These relate to form of hearing, costs and appeals. These provisions have been included above.

A dedicated team for dealing with *Re X* applications has been set up. The contact details for the DoL team are:

Court of Protection
PO Box 70185
First Avenue House
42–49 High Holborn
London WC1A 9J
DX: 160013 Kingsway
Enquiries: 0300 456 4600.

The Practice Direction and Form COPDOL 10 Form and draft Orders may be downloaded from:

https://www.judiciary.gov.uk/publications/court-of-protection-practice-directions/ and

https://www.gov.uk/guidance/deprivation-of-liberty-orders.

4.6   The future

The practice and procedure set out above emanated from the President's point of view as set out in the *Re X* case. The manner in which the procedure was formulated has received strong criticism from the Court of Appeal in the appeal from the President's decision:

> 'the particular course he [the President] adopted was not one that was open to him ...'[17]

> He engaged in an illegitimate approach to the determination of what he and all legal representatives regarded as generic academic issues without any, or any proper, identification of the particular issues which arose in the specific cases before him, he had no jurisdiction to make the determinations which he did.

> In consequence and, with respect, what are merely his opinions in relation to those matters ...'[18]

and that:

---

[17]   Black LJ at [58].
[18]   Gloster LJ at [127].

'... involved an inappropriate use of the court's process ... It was in substance a consultative exercise intended to promote the development of new rules of procedure and for that reason it was not ... one which the court was entitled to undertake.'[19]

The Law Commission in its consultation did not refer to the Court of Appeal decision in *Re X* and the issue of how P participates in the authorisation of deprivation of liberty. This will need to be addressed in its final report and recommended legislation. Meantime, further rules may be introduced to cover the interim.

---

[19]   Moore-Bick LJ at [146].

CHAPTER 5

URGENT AUTHORISATION OF RESTRAINT/DETENTION

5.1 INTRODUCTION

As a general rule any act taken to restrain a person lacking capacity (P) is likely to result in liability under the civil law. It becomes more so when the restraining action or the use of force relates to someone who is entrusted with the care and treatment of P. It has to be recognised, however, that some situations require some degree of restraint to be exercised for the safety and protection of P. In some situations restraint may be necessary over a long period of time in other circumstances it may be necessary only for a short period. On occasions events occur suddenly or as an emergency, requiring restraint to be used to protect P and or third parties from P's actions. Provision is therefore made in the MCA 2005 for restraint to be used in limited circumstances subject to conditions or restraint and physical force to be used in order to protect P from harm. The common law also recognises the need for restraint to be used under the doctrine of necessity. It is however advisable to err on the side of caution and seek authorisation from the court where possible.

The statutory definition of 'restraint', the provisions which provide the limited protection from liability when restraint is used in connection with care and treatment and the court's powers to authorise it are considered below.

5.2 RESTRAINT

5.2.1 Statutory meaning of restraint

Section 6(4) of the Act provides that a person restrains an incapacitated person if:
(1) he uses, or threatens to use, force to secure the doing of an act which the person lacking capacity resists; or
(2) restricts that person's liberty of movement, whether or not there is resistance.

There is no clear defining line when it can be said that an act of restraint becomes one of deprivation of liberty. Much depends on the circumstances of the individual case, degree of force used, the manner in which it is exercised, its duration and its effect on the person lacking capacity. The question that needs to be considered is whether in the circumstances of the individual the manner and degree of restraint is such as to amount to deprivation of liberty and, if it does, does the court have power to authorise such restraint or detention. Case-law set out at **2.3** gives some indication of the factors which influence the court in determining the distinction between restraint and deprivation of liberty. More recent examples are the following:

In *W City Council v Mrs L*,[1] a 93-year-old woman with Alzheimer's dementia was cared for in her home, an upper-floor flat, with safety arrangements set up by agreement between her daughters and the local authority. Bodey J held that her circumstances did not amount to deprivation of liberty or if it did it was not imputable to the State. Bodey J distinguished this case from *Cheshire West* on factual considerations. He considered that it was a finely balanced case; but on the totality of the evidence he came to the conclusion that 'whilst the arrangements (clearly) constitute restrictions on Mrs L's liberty, they do not cross the line to being deprivation of it' (para [27]). He regarded the arrangements:[2]

> '[a] shared arrangement set up by agreement with a caring and pro-active family; and the responsibility of the State is, it seems to me, diluted by the strong role which the family has played and continues to play. I do not consider in such circumstances that the mischief of State interference at which Article 5 was and is directed, sufficiently exists.'

It is not known whether this decision will be appealed. It should however be noted that Bodey J clearly indicated that this was a borderline case, and that his decision was very much dependant on the particular factual situation of the individual. It does not in any way seek to challenge the UKSC's decision in *Cheshire West*.

Re AJ (Deprivation of Liberty Safeguards)[3] is a textbook example of the pitfalls when the DoL Safeguards are not strictly followed. It also sets out useful guidance on the procedure to be adopted where restraint is or is likely to be used. Baker J has suggested that:[4]

> '... in any case in which physical restraint is used in the care of an incapacitated adult, any physical intervention, whether considered to amount to "restraint" or not, should be recorded in the care plan maintained by the service provider and monitored by the statutory body responsible for commissioning the person's care. Furthermore, precise details of all physical interventions should be ascertained and documented as part of the Deprivation of Liberty Safeguards process or indeed any best interest assessment from direct discussion with care staff implementing the interventions.'

---

[1] [2015] EWCOP 20.
[2] At para 27.
[3] [2015] EWCOP 5.
[4] At para 25.

Commissioner of the Police for the Metropolis v ZH,[5] although not a case under the MCA, nevertheless is one which is relevant because it concerned a severely autistic 19-year-old who also suffered from epilepsy and had learning difficulties and speech defect. When he was taken by the specialist school for a visit to a swimming pool with a view to initiating him to the environment and to him becoming accustomed to it, difficulties arose with his behaviour which resulted in the manager calling the police. The attendance of the police escalated and aggravated the situation with the result that, in order to control his behaviour he was handcuffed, his legs were restrained, and eventually he was removed and transported in a cage in the back of a police van for 40 minutes. In civil proceedings it was alleged inter alia that his Art 3.5 and Art 8 rights had been breached. Both the trial judge and the Court of Appeal ruled that, despite the circumstances in which the restraint was used and the purpose being to protect ZH and others, the action taken amounted to deprivation of liberty notwithstanding that it was only for a short period.

5.2.2 Guidance set out in Code of Practice

The *Deprivation of Liberty Safeguards Code of Practice*, para 2.8–2.11 and the *Mental Capacity Act 2005 Code of Practice* (the main Code of Practice), paras 6.40–6.48 contains guidance on what amounts to restraint and when it might be appropriate and considered to be proportionate to use restraint to prevent harm to P, but clearly warns that where the restriction or restraint is frequent, cumulative and ongoing, or if there are other factors present, then care providers should consider whether this has gone beyond permissible restraint, as defined in the Act. If so, then they must either apply for authorisation or change their care provision to reduce the level of restraint (para 2.12).

5.2.3 When is restraint permitted?

5.2.3.1 A statutory provisions – ss 4A and 4B powers

Section 4A permits a person (D) to deprive P of his liberty, if by doing so, D is giving effect to a decision made by a order under s 16(2)(a) in relation to P's personal welfare.

It provides:

4A Restriction on deprivation of liberty

(1) This Act does not authorise any person ("D") to deprive any other person ("P") of his liberty.

(2) But that is subject to –

    (a)   the following provisions of this section, and
    (b)   section 4B.

---

[5]   [2013] EWCA Civ 69.

(3) D may deprive P of his liberty if, by doing so, D is giving effect to a relevant decision of the court.

(4) A relevant decision of the court is a decision made by an order under section 16(2)(a) in relation to a matter concerning P's personal welfare.

(5) D may deprive P of his liberty if the deprivation is authorised by Schedule A1 (hospital and care home residents: deprivation of liberty).

Section 4B of the Act sets out the condition which must apply before a person may lawfully deprive P of his/her liberty while a decision is sought from the court as follows:

4B Deprivation of liberty necessary for life-sustaining treatment etc

(1) If the following conditions are met, D is authorised to deprive P of his liberty while a decision as respects any relevant issue is sought from the court.

(2) The first condition is that there is a question about whether D is authorised to deprive P of his liberty under section 4A.

(3) The second condition is that the deprivation of liberty –

    (a)   is wholly or partly for the purpose of –
        (i)   giving P life-sustaining treatment, or
        (ii)   doing any vital act, or

    (b)   consists wholly or partly of –
        (i)   giving P life-sustaining treatment, or
        (ii)   doing any vital act.

(4) The third condition is that the deprivation of liberty is necessary in order to –

    (a)   give the life-sustaining treatment, or
    (b)   do the vital act.

(5) A vital act is any act which the person doing it reasonably believes to be necessary to prevent a serious deterioration in P's condition.

The conditions that must be satisfied are therefore:

(1)   there is a question about whether that person is authorised to deprive P of his liberty under s 4A;

(2)   the deprivation of liberty is wholly or partly for the purpose of giving life sustaining treatment or doing any act which the person doing it reasonably believes to be necessary to prevent a serious deterioration in P's condition; and

(3)   the deprivation of liberty is necessary in order to give the life sustaining treatment or doing any act which the person undertaking it reasonably believes to be necessary to prevent a serious deterioration in the P's condition.

5.2.3.2 B Section 5 – use of restraint in connection with care and treatment

MCA 2005, s 5 permits the use of some form of restraint by carers and health and social care professionals in connection with the care or treatment of P if the person has taken reasonable steps to establish that P lacks capacity in relation the matter in question, and when doing the act the person reasonably believes that it will be in P's best interests for the act to be done. The use of restraint in these limited circumstances may exempt the doer from liability provided two conditions are satisfied. First, that the person using restraint must reasonably believe that it is necessary to do the act in order to prevent harm to P and secondly, that the act done must be a proportionate response to:

(a)   the likelihood of P suffering harm; and

(b)   the seriousness of that harm.[6]

The circumstances of P and the situation which necessitates the use of restraint must be assessed and, if restraint is used, the degree of force used must only be just enough to prevent harm to P.

This allows the carers to do whatever is considered necessary and in the best interests of P in order to safeguard his/her welfare and health. When carrying out such acts the carer must also apply the key principles set out in s 1. These are:

- the person must be assumed to have capacity unless it is established that he lacks capacity;

- a person is not be treated as unable to make a decision unless all practicable steps to help him to do so have been taken without success;

- a person is not to be treated as unable to make a decision merely because he makes an unwise decision;

- an act done, or decision made, under MCA 2005 for or on behalf of a person who lacks capacity must be done, or made in his best interests;

- before the act is done, or decision is made, regard must be had to whether the purpose for which it is needed can be as effectively achieved in a way that is less restrictive of the person's rights and freedom of action.

The best interests check list set out in s 4 of the Act must also be considered. These are that the person making the determination:

(1)   must not make it merely on the basis of the person's age or appearance or a condition of his, or an aspect of his behaviour which might lead others to make unjustified assumptions about what might be in his best interests;

(2)   must consider whether it is likely that P will at some time have capacity in relation to the matter in question and if it appears likely that he will when that is likely to be;

---

[6]   MCA 2005, s 6(2) and (3).

(3) he must so far as reasonably practicable, permit and encourage P to participate, or to improve his ability to participate, as fully as possible in any act done for him and any decision affecting him;

(4) where the decision relates to life-sustaining treatment he must not, in considering whether the treatment is in the best interests of P, be motivated by a desire to bring about his death;

(5) he must consider at far as reasonably ascertainable P's past and present wishes and feeling, his beliefs and values that would be likely to influence his decision if he had capacity and other factors that he would be likely to consider if he were able to do so;

(6) he must take into account if it is practicable and appropriate to consult them, the views of anyone named by P as someone to be consulted on the matter in question; anyone engaged in caring for P or interested in his welfare; any donee of a lasting power of attorney and any deputy appointed for P by the court.

Provided these conditions are met, the carer is afforded protection from liability for their actions and such acts can be carried out as if P had capacity and had given his/her consent. However, the protection from liability does not cover any act which is intended to restrain P.[7]

These provisions are most relevant in cases where those treating P have to undertake a balancing exercise between continuing treatment forcibly and deciding not continue with it. Where the treating professional is doubtful about the use of force or the extent of force to be used, an application should be made to the court for authorisation. In such cases it is desirable that authorisation is sought before it becomes an urgent or emergency situation as these cases are bound to raise ethical and legal issues and infringement of P's human rights. Cases where this is more likely to arise are those where P is suffering from severe anorexia nervosa and forcible feeding or medical treatment has to be considered where P does not qualify for treatment under the Mental Health Act. If the matter is dealt with under the MCA the issue of whether the action proposed would also amount to deprivation of liberty would need to be considered. Two recent COP cases have resulted in two different outcomes. *A Local Authority v E & Others*[8] concerned a 32-year-old intelligent woman who suffered from emotionally unstable borderline personality disorder, alcohol and opiate dependency. She had been compulsorily detained under the Mental Health Act 1983 on numerous occasions and had expressed a wish to end her life. The medical team had concluded that it was in E's interest to die in comfort. Proceedings were commenced. One of the issues before the court was whether, if her advance decision was not valid, it was in her best interests to force feed her. The court had to decide on two options; on the one hand to respect her autonomy and freedom and for palliative care to be given and allow her to die or, on the other hand to allow her to be transferred to be stabilised and fed through a nasogastric tube or PEG tube inserted through her stomach

---

[7]   MCA 2005, s 6(1).
[8]   [2012] EWHC 1639 (COP).

wall, with any resistance on her part being dealt with by physical restraint or sedation – a process which would continue on a regular basis for a year or more. In concluding that it was in her best interests to be force-fed Jackson J undertook the 'balance sheet approach' and took into account the risks involved; E's wishes and feelings, beliefs and values; the wishes of her parents, evidence of the consultant gastroenterologist and psychiatrist; and considerations of her rights under the ECHR.

However, in *NHS Trust v L and the Psychiatric NHS Trust & Others*[9] the application was for a declaration that it was not in the best interests of L to be the subject of forcible feeding or medical treatment notwithstanding the fact that this would result in her death. She was critically ill and there had already been a decision made that she should not be resuscitated (DNR-CPR) Her condition further deteriorated. The medical opinion was that in order to force-feed her it would be necessary to sedate her and her medical condition was such that the likelihood of death, if force-feeding were to be attempted on a chemically sedated basis, would run at close to 100%. In the unlikely event of her surviving she would suffer severe physical and psychological consequences. Sedation or restraint for the purposes of forced feeding would be disproportionate and would worsen her long term physical and psychological condition. Having determined that L lacked capacity the court applied the s 4 criteria and her rights under the ECHR particularly the right to life in assessing her best interests, and concluded that it was not in L's best interest to provide her with nutrition and hydration with which she was non-compliant and which could not be delivered without her co-operation and/or without the use of physical force. L's case was an extreme case of anorexia nervosa which justified the decision taken to withdraw life-sustaining treatment. Having considered all the evidence King J stated:[10]

> 'In my judgment this is one of those few cases where the only possible treatment, namely force feeding under sedation, is not to be countenanced in Ms L's best interests: to do so would be futile, carrying with it a near certainty that it would cause her death in any event. Such a course would be overly burdensome in that every calorie that enters her body is an enemy to Ms L.
>
> Ms L would I am satisfied be appallingly distressed and resistant to any suggestion that she was to be force fed and to what purpose? Her poor body is closing down, organ failure has begun, she can no longer resist infection and she is, at all times in imminent danger of cardiac arrest. Even if she could, by some miracle, agree to some miniscule increase in her nutrient intake her organ failure is nevertheless reversible and her anorexia so sever and deep rooted that there could be no real possibility of her maintaining her co-operation. Ms L on some occasion shows some small spark of insight – she said on the 1st August that she was frightened as she cannot help herself from "messing with the tube".'

Where a patient is non-compliant with a medical or surgical procedure the issue sometimes arises whether sedation should be used to make the patient more

---

[9] [2012] EWHC 2741 (COP).
[10] At paras 68 and 69.

compliant and whether physical restraint should be used so that the patient can be sedated in order to facilitate the treatment or the operation. These situations obviously raise ethical issues and the legality of administering the sedation in cases which involve those who lack capacity. In *DH NHS Foundation Trust v PS*[11] where the patient although agreeable to the surgical procedure suffered from needle phobia which prevented the operation proceeding, the court approved a plan which included provision of covert sedation mixed with a soft drink to enable her to be anaesthetised. In *An NHS Trust v K & Others*,[12] where the Official Solicitor acting on behalf of K was against the proposal that K should undergo an operation for treatment of cancer because of the considerable risk that she could die during the operation or in the post-operative recovery period and K had been resistant to the operation prior to anaesthesia, the court on balance ruled that the operation should go ahead but that as it could be very risky to apply physical restraint she should be sedated before being told of the operation in the hope that she might thereby be compliant to it. Holman J declared that it was in K's overall best interests to have the operation and it can be lawful and in her best interests to sedate her to enable it to take place and lawful to do so before she is told, after sedation but before anaesthesia, what is planned under the supervision of a qualified anesthetist. In both cases the court first determined the issue whether it was in the best interests of P to undergo the medical procedure and then went about deciding how best to achieve it without having to use physical restraint.

Other instances which occur as a matter of course are eg when transporting or conveying a person who lacks capacity to a hospital or care home. The DoLS Code of Practice at paras 2.13 and 2.14 gives the following guidance:

Within a hospital

2.13 If a person in hospital for mental health treatment, or being considered for admission to a hospital for mental health treatment, needs to be restrained, this is likely to indicate that they are objecting to treatment or to being in hospital. The care providers should consider whether the need for restraint means the person is objecting (see 4.6 of the Code for guidance on how to decide whether a person is objecting for this purpose). A person who objects to mental health treatment, and who meets the criteria for detention under the Mental Health Act 1983 is normally ineligible for an authorisation under the deprivation of liberty safeguards. If the care providers believe that it is necessary to detain the person, they may wish to consider use of the Mental Health Act 1983.

Taking someone to hospital

2.14 Transporting a person who lacks capacity from their home or another location, to a hospital or care home will not usually amount to deprivation of liberty (for example, to take them to hospital by ambulance in an emergency). Even when there is an expectation that the person will be deprived of liberty within the care home or hospital, it is unlikely that the journey itself will constitute deprivation of liberty so that an authorisation is needed before the journey

---

[11]   [2010] EWHC 1217 (Fam).
[12]   [2012] EWHC 2922 (COP).

commences. In most cases, it is likely that a person can be lawfully taken to a hospital or a care home under the wider provisions of the Act, as long as it is considered that being in the hospital or care home will be in their interests.

5.2.4 Permitted use of restraint under common law

Under common law healthcare and social work staff have a duty of care towards those for whom they provide services. It follows therefore that if P by his actions may cause harm to himself or others they have a duty to take appropriate necessary action to prevent harm both to P and to others. In this respect health and social welfare providers should follow the guidance on restraint given in any guidance issued by Government departments, such as the Department of Health and the Department of Education and Skills. The guidance given in the main Code of Practice and the DoLS Code of Practice should also be followed.

5.2.5 Limitations on acts of restrain

Under s 6 the two crucial factors which must be present when exercising restraint on P are that the restraint must be 'necessary' and 'proportionate'. In this regard the person exercising the restrain must be able to show that if restraint is not applied P is likely to suffer harm. Thus a carer may not use restraint simply because to do so would make the task undertaken more easy to perform. Additionally, the restraint used must be proportionate ie it must be the minimum amount of force necessary to secure the doing of the act which is resisted by P and for the shortest time possible and must not cross the line between restraint and deprivation of liberty. It will be necessary to show that other less restrictive options were considered and or tried to no avail or that the circumstances were such that there was a real need to take immediate action to prevent P suffering serious harm. Care should also be taken in ensuring that the resistance offered by P does not in fact amount to or indicate that P objects to the actions proposed.

Regimes where restriction or restraint is exercised frequently or regularly may be considered to amount to deprivation of liberty. In those cases it is desirable and advisable to seek the court's authorisation for the use of the particular form, degree and frequency of restraint. This can be an application for either an authorisation under the DoLS regime or for a declaration under s 15(1)(c) as to the lawfulness or otherwise of any act done or yet to be done in relation to P or under s 16 (see below). Careful assessment and preparation of a care plan will be crucial in such cases.

5.2.6 Meaning of 'serious harm'

The Act does not define what is meant by 'serious harm'. This is because each individual's circumstances will vary. Some examples to illustrate this point are set out in the main Code of Practice, para 6.45:

- A person with learning disabilities might run into a busy road without warning, if they do not understand the dangers of cars.

- A person with dementia may wander away from home and get lost, if they cannot remember where they live.

- A person with manic depression might engage in excessive spending during a manic phase, causing them to get into debt.

- A person may also be at risk of harm if they behave in a way that encourages others to assault or exploit them (for example, by behaving in a dangerously provocative way).

5.3   COURT'S POWERS TO MAKE DECLARATIONS AND INTERIM ORDERS

In its original form the MCA 2005 did not include a specific power to authorise an act of detention. Whether this could be implied was considered in a number of cases where the inherent jurisdiction of the High Court was invoked. In *Re PS Incapacitated or Vulnerable Adult*[13] it was held that the court has the power to make an order authorising the minimum of force or restraint necessary for detention of an adult who lacks capacity. This issue was further advanced in *Re GJ (Incapacitated Adults)*[14] where restraint was permitted to provide medical treatment to P, but this case too was decided under the inherent jurisdiction of the High Court. It was eventually in *Re P (Adult) Medical Treatment)*[15] that it was established that the Court did have powers to authorise detention under the provisions of s 15(1)(c) and s 48.

These powers are found under various sections of the MCA 2005:
- Sections 15(1)(c) of the Act confers on the court the general power to make declarations as to 'the lawfulness or otherwise of any act done, or yet to be done, in relation to' a person who lacks capacity to make a decision.

- Section 16 empowers the court by making an order to make decisions on P's behalf in relation to a matter or matters concerning inter alia P's personal welfare.

- Section 48 of the Act gives the court discretionary powers to make interim orders and directions, pending the determination of an application to it in relation to P if there is reason to believe that P lacks capacity in relation to the matter and the matter is one to which its powers extend and it is in P's best interests to make the order or to give direction without delay. These provision were intended to and do empower, the Court of Protection to make orders under the Act similar to those made by the High Court under its inherent jurisdiction before the amendments to the Act by the Mental Health Act 2007 came into effect on 1 April 2009.

---

[13]   [2007] 2 FLR 1083.
[14]   [2008] 2 FLR 1295.
[15]   [2009] 1 FCR 567.

The court therefore has power, if the circumstances and the welfare of the person concerned requires, to make a declaration under s 6(1)-(4), to render lawful an act of restraint that would otherwise amount to deprivation of liberty and to a breach of s 6(5) of the Act. Section 17 of the Act also provides that, in relation to the personal welfare of P, the powers of the Court under s 16 to grant an order making a decision or decisions on behalf of P in respect of issues concerning his welfare extend to 'giving or refusing' consent to the carrying out or continuation of a treatment by a person providing health care' for P.

The main Code of Practice at para 6.51 also provides that 'in some cases the Court of Protection might grant an order that permits the deprivation of a person's liberty, if it is satisfied that this is in the person's interests'.

> 'Thus where the facts justify, and the immediate welfare of an incapacitated adult so dictate, the Court may, by prior declaration in appropriate terms, render lawful an act of restraint under section 6(1)–(4) of the Act, which might otherwise amount to a deprivation of liberty under s 6(5), thus bridging the *Bournewood* Gap.'[16]

5.3.1   Interim orders

The court has powers to make interim orders pursuant to s 48 which provides:

48 Interim orders and directions

The court may, pending the determination of an application to it in relation to a person P, make an order or give directions in respect of any matter if –

(a)   there is reason to believe that P lacks capacity in relation to the matter;

(b)   the matter is one to which its powers under this Act extend, and

(c)   it is in the best interests to make the order, or give directions, without delay.

Where a decision needs to be made and an act done as a matter of urgency before it is possible to assess P's capacity, the court is empowered, following an application, to exercise its powers on an interim basis by applying a lower threshold if the conditions in s 48 are met. These powers extend to issues concerning the welfare of P. When determining such an application the court in the first instance will consider whether there is good cause for concern that the person might lack capacity in some relevant regard. Once that is raised as a serious possibility the court will decide what action, if any, it is in the best interests of P to take before the final determination of his or her capacity can be made. Where necessary, the court will make such orders as may be appropriate to authorise steps to be taken to safeguard P's health and well-being and as a matter of urgency, depending on the facts of the case and the urgency of the decision in question, balanced against P's right to autonomy and his best interests.

---

[16]   Per Sir Mark Potter P, *A Primary Care Trust & Anor v AH & Anor* [2008] EWHC 1403 (Fam).

5.4 AUTHORISATION UNDER THE COURT'S INHERENT JURISDICTION

In cases where P's capacity is in question or where the issues relate to a vulnerable adult proceedings may be issued in the Court of Protection for determination under the High Court's inherent jurisdiction to make the relevant orders as in pre-1 April 2009 cases such as *PS (Incapacitated or Vulnerable Adult)* and *Re GJ (Incapacitated Adults)* (above).

In *Sunderland v PS & Children Act 1989*[17] a case decided under the inherent jurisdiction of the High Court, the dispute was between the local authority and the daughter of the person concerned, over the care provided for her and her wish to leave the home. The issue was whether the local authority could detain the woman and whether the court under its inherent jurisdiction could make an order preventing the discharge of the woman from the care of the treatment unit preferred by the local authority and whether it could appoint a receiver to prevent the daughter dissipating her mother's savings and pensions in preference to the local authority applying for orders under the Mental Health Act 1983. Although not a case directly concerned with deprivation of liberty, the court set out some guidelines which may be relevant if the High Court's powers under its inherent jurisdiction is likely to be relied on. Munby J (as he then was) set the following minimum requirements which must be satisfied:

(1) The detention must be authorised on an application made before the detention commences.

(2) Except in an emergency, there must be evidence to establish that the person lacks capacity and that the restrictions or restraint proposed is appropriate.

(3) Any order authorising detention must contain provision for an adequate review procedure at reasonable intervals in particular to ascertain whether the lack of capacity persists or detention should continue.

(4) In *Salford County Council v GJ, MJ & BJ*[18] whilst accepting that safeguards would depend on the circumstances of the particular case, Munby J (as he then was) suggested an initial review hearing before the court within 4 weeks of the court order authorising deprivation of liberty or sooner if the Official Solicitor had not previously been involved in the proceedings.

(5) Regular review by the court at or about 12 months after the hearing or sooner if so directed by the court. The Official Solicitor should be involved at each review hearing and should be provided with up to date reports at least 4 weeks in advance of the hearing.

(6) Any party to the proceedings should be at liberty to apply for a review at any time, and where necessary at short notice.

(7) There must be regular internal reviews as required usually every 8-10 weeks, such reviews to include the Official Solicitor.

---

[17] [2007] EWHC 623 (Fam).
[18] [2008] EWHC 1097 (Fam).

5.5 PRACTICE AND PROCEDURE

The applicant for any welfare order under s 16(2)(a) of the Act which is to be relied on to authorise deprivation of liberty pursuant to s 4A(3) or which falls within Part 10 of the Court of Protection Rules no longer needs to apply for permission when making the application. Since these applications will usually arise in an emergency and as an interim measure the provisions of PD10B will apply to the procedure to be followed. These applications fall into two categories:

(1)   where an application form has already been issued; and

(2)   where an application has not yet been issued; and

in both cases the application is made without notice having been given to P.

Wherever possible the application should be made during court hours. Where there is extreme urgency the application may be made by telephone by calling 0300 456 4600 during business hours. When the application has to be made out of hours contact should be made with the security at the Royal Courts of Justice on 020 7947 6000. The security officer should be informed of the nature of the case. It should be noted however that if the judge hearing the urgent out of hours application has concerns that the application could have been made during court hours the judge may require the applicant or the applicant's representative to attend at a subsequent hearing to provide an explanation for the delay.

5.5.1   General requirements of without notice application

Where an application is anticipated, all possible steps should be taken to inform P and any other respondent(s). The notification may be made in writing, telephone, fax, text message or email unless it can be shown that if notice is given the relief sought would be defeated.

The applicant must also contact the DoL team to inform them with as much advance warning possible that the application is to be made, how urgent it is, and the order sought. Where the application is very urgent the court will require details of the names and addresses of the parties, the issue to be decide, and of any other court proceedings involving the parties.

Contact should be made to the Court of Protection at First Avenue House, 42-49 High Holborn; London WC1 9JA. Enquiries: 0300 456 4600.

The applicant will be required to give an undertaking to the court to serve the application notice, the evidence in support and any order made on P, and any respondent(s) and any other person the court may direct as soon as practicable or as ordered by the court any notice of the return date for a further hearing.[19]

---

[19]   PD10B, para 6(a) and (b).

5.5.2   Applications made before issue of an application form

Where the circumstances require an application to be made in an emergency an application may be made before filing the application form with the court's permission. The application for permission where time allows it should be made in writing. It can also be made orally but the court will require an undertaking to be given that the application form in Form DOL10 in the terms of the oral application will be filed on the next working day or as required by the court.[20] If the order is granted the order should state in the file after the names of the parties 'the Applicant and Respondent in an intended Application'.[21]

5.5.3   The application notice

It is advisable to indicate on the application notice that the application is:[22]

(1)   urgent;

(2)   should be dealt with by a particular judge or judge level within the court;

(3)   requires a hearing (not by way of a paper exercise);

(4)   any combination of the above.

5.5.4   Application made on issue of application form

To issue the application, the applicant will be required to file with the court in advance of the hearing where possible the following:[23]

(1)   application notice on Form COP9;

(2)   evidence in support;

(3)   draft order;

(4)   if the order is long and complex, a disk containing the draft order sought in a format compatible with word processing software used by the court;

(5)   the court fee.

Where it has not been possible to file these documents the applicant will be required to provide at the hearing a draft order with the evidence in support and to undertake to file the notice and the evidence in support with the court on the next working day or as ordered by the court.[24]

To assist the DoL team to deal with the matter with expediency and to ensure that the case is referred to the right level of judge, it is good practice for the application notice to set out the matters referred to under **5.6.3** above.

---

[20]   PD10B, para 9.

[21]   PD10B, para 10.

[22]   PD10B, para 13.

[23]   PD10B, para 7.

[24]   PD10B, para 8.

5.5.5   Other evidence and documents that the court will require

All supporting documents should be filed with the application. In addition the court will require evidence of capacity which should be in Form COP 3. Where a deputy has been appointed, Form COP4 (the declaration form) and, if appropriate, a copy of any lasting power of attorney should be filed. Where the applicant seeks to rely upon matters set out in the document as evidence it must be verified with a statement of truth. If the evidence is set out in a witness statement it should be verified by a statement of truth.

The court fee of £400 will have to be paid when the application is issued.

5.5.6   Application made by telephone

Where it is not possible to file an application form or notice, applications can be made by telephone. Contact should be made with the court during business hours on 0300 456 4600.

When it is not possible to apply within court hours contact should be made with the security office at the Royal Courts of Justice on 020 7947 6000. The security officer should be informed of the nature of the case.

5.5.7   Hearings conducted by telephone

Whenever practical hearings that take place by telephone, should be conducted by tape-recorded conference call, arranged and paid for in the first instance by the applicant. All parties and the judge should be informed that the call is being recorded by the service provider. It is also the applicant's duty and responsibility to order a transcript of the hearing from the service provider.

5.5.8   Steps the court will take

As soon as practicable after the application is issued the court should consider how to deal with it. Where permission is required the court will first consider whether to grant or refuse permission without a hearing or to direct a hearing to consider whether permission should be granted. If a hearing is directed the court will give notice of the hearing date to the parties and to any other person it directs and also give directions of what is to be dealt with at the hearing including whether the matter is to be disposed of at that hearing. It must also consider in each case whether it should make one or more of the direction set out in r 3A(2) concerning P's involvement in the proceedings. In deciding whether it should make any such direction the court will have regard to:

(1)   the nature and extent of the information before the court;

(2)   the issues raised in the case;

(3)   whether the matter is contentious; and

(4) whether P has been notified and what if anything P has said or done in response to such notification.

If P is joined as a party to the proceedings and a litigation friend is appointed or where a accredited legal representative or representative on behalf of P is appointed under r 3A, P must be notified of the appointment (r 41A). Notification must be effected by the applicant or such other person as the court may direct (r 41(1)(a)). The person effecting notification must, within 7 days of notification being given, file a certificate of notification which certifies the date on which and how P was notified and that P was notified in accordance with Part 7 of the COP Rules.

Where the court decides that it can deal with the matter without a hearing it will do so and serve a copy of its order on the parties and on any other person. Where an order is made without a hearing or without notice to any person who is affected by it P, any party to the proceedings or any other person affected by the order may apply to the court within 21 days of the order being served or such other period as the court may direct for reconsideration of the order made. The court in this event will reconsider the order without a hearing or fix a date for the hearing and notify all the parties to the proceedings and such other persons as the court may direct.

In considering whether it is necessary to hold a hearing the court must have regard to:

(1) the nature of the proceedings and the orders sought;

(2) whether the application is opposed by a person who appears to the court to have an interest in matters relating to P's best interests;

(3) whether the application involves a substantial dispute of fact;

(4) the complexity of the facts and the law;

(5) any wider public interest in the proceedings;

(6) the circumstances of P and of any party as to whether their rights would be adequately protected if a hearing were not held;

(7) whether the parties agree that the court should dispose of the application without a hearing; and

(8) any other matter specified in the relevant practice direction.

Every respondent and any person who wishes to take part in the proceedings must file the acknowledgment of service within 21 days.

5.6 PRACTICE AND PROCEDURE IN RELATION TO SERIOUS/URGENT MEDICAL TREATMENT

In cases concerning urgent and or serious medical treatment the above provisions will apply and should be followed subject to the procedure set out in PD9E. These provisions are as follows:

5.6.1 The application form

The application form in Form COP 1 should be headed 'serious medical treatment' to draw the court's attention to this fact. It should state the issues which the court is asked to determine and the order sought. Where practicable a draft order should also be filed with the application. If the application is for a declaration the order sought should be in the following or similar terms:

- That P lacks capacity to make a decision in relation to the (proposed medical treatment or procedure), eg 'That P lacks capacity to make a decision in relation to sterilisation by vasectomy'; and

- That, having regard to the best interests of P, it is lawful for the (proposed medical treatment or procedure) to be carried out by (proposed healthcare provider).

Where the application is for the withdrawal of life-sustaining treatment, the order sought should be in the following or similar terms:

- That P lacks capacity to consent to continued life-sustaining treatment measures (and specify what these are); and

- That, having regard to the best interests of P, it is lawful for (name of healthcare provider) to withdraw the life-sustaining treatment from P.

The application form should also state:

(1) the name of the applicant and his/her address;

(2) the name and address of P;

(3) name and address of each respondent and details of his or her connection with P;

(4) the name and addresses of each person whom the applicant intends to notify of the application and details of his or her connection with P.

The application form must be verified by a statement of truth if it contains evidence on which the applicant seeks to rely.

The application form must:

- be supported by evidence relied on.[25] If that is contained in a witness statement, the statement must be verified by a statement of truth;

- an assessment of capacity form where this is required. If an assessment of capacity has not been completed and filed, a witness statement must be filed explaining why the assessment has not been obtained; what attempts have been made to obtain it and the basis on which it is believed that the person lacks capacity to make the specific decision;

- any other document referred to in the application form; and

- any other information and material which may be relevant and set out eg in PD10B.

---

[25] COP Rules 2007, r 64(a).

5.6.2   Should P be made a party to the proceedings?

Where the treatment involves the use of restraint or force being used, having regard to the Court of Appeal's decision in *Re X*, application should be made for P to be made a party to the proceedings.

CHAPTER 6

P'S STATUS, INVOLVEMENT IN PROCEEDINGS AND DECISIONS

6.1 INTRODUCTION

Unlike civil proceedings where parties resort to the court to determine a dispute between them, proceedings in the Court of Protection about P's finances and welfare may involve whole families, public bodies or institutions. The court's role is to make decisions in P's best interests.

However, the Court of Protection Rules do not provide for P automatically to be made a party to proceedings. COP Rules 2007, Part 9, r 63 provides that the application form must name the person who lacks capacity (P). Section 1 of the Act requires the applicant to give details of the person to whom the application relates, ie P. The rule also requires the applicant to provide details of any person who the applicant reasonably believes has an interest in the proceedings and ought to be heard. The applicant must notify P that the application form has been issued unless the court has dispensed with this requirement under r 49. Any person who is named in the form as a respondent and is served with or notified of an application and who wishes to take part in the proceedings must file an acknowledgement of service or notification within 21 days of being served or notified (r 72(1)).

6.2 CURRENT POSITION IN DEPRIVATION OF LIBERTY CASES

Reliance is often placed on Art 5(4) of the European Convention on Human Rights (ECHR) which entitles P who is deprived of his liberty to challenge the lawfulness of his detention, but there is no specific requirement for P to be made a party to the proceedings irrespective of whether the Sch A1 regime applies or if the court is to authorise detention. Article 5 however does not stand alone. Its provisions must be considered with the obligations imposed under Art 6 of the ECHR – the right to a fair trial.

The issue of whether the MCA 2005 sufficiently protects P's rights under these Articles has troubled many, especially in relation to those individuals who fall outside the Sch A1 regime and who, since *Cheshire West*, have had their deprivation of liberty authorised by the Court of Protection.

In *Re X & others*[1] the President proposed a streamline procedure to deal expeditiously with an anticipated flood of authorisation applications to the Court of Protection post-*Cheshire West*. In particular he looked at whether it was necessary to join P as a party to every application. Not to do so would speed up the process (see under Chapter 4). He concluded that there was no requirement in domestic law or under the ECHR for P to be joined as a party to welfare proceedings and in particular deprivation of liberty proceedings; that there is no fundamental principle in domestic law which dictates that P if is joined as a party he should have a litigation friend and finally, that the litigation friend does not have to act through a legal representative – he can conduct the litigation on behalf of P, but will require the court's permission to act as an advocate. The President's conclusions were driven by expediency and resource.

The President's decision in *Re X & others*[2] was the subject of an appeal to the Court of Appeal: *Re X (Court of Protection)*.[3] The Court of Appeal disagreed with the President. All three members of the Court of Appeal expressed the view that the fundamental principles of both domestic and Convention requirements demand that P should be a party to proceedings in which authorisation to deprive P of his liberty is applied for. Of particular significance are the following reasons given for their conclusions:[4]

> 'What this might indicate, it seems to me, is that it is generally considered indispensable in this country for the person whose liberty is at stake automatically to be a party to the proceedings in which the issue is to be decided. The President's conclusion that it was unnecessary for this to be so in relation to an adult without capacity appears therefore to run counter to normal domestic practice. It might, therefore, be thought to require very firm foundations if it is to be regarded as acceptable.
>
> Article 5 is not, of course, drafted in terms which reflect our domestic procedure and practice and nor does the jurisprudence of the ECtHR speak in those terms. It is not surprising therefore that it is not said explicitly that a person whose liberty is the subject of proceedings must be a party to those proceedings. It is necessary to consider the substance of what is said in the Article and the decisions concerning it and to determine how the required guarantees can be delivered in the procedural framework of the domestic legal system.
>
> What is essential is that the person concerned "should have access to a court and the opportunity to be heard either in person or, where necessary, through some form of representation". In so far as special procedural safeguards are required because the person is not fully capable of acting for himself, they are there to secure the right and must not impair the "very essence" of it. *MS v Croatia* is a practical demonstration of what is expected.'

Applying European jurisprudence Black LJ accepted that:[5]

---

[1]   [2014] EWCOP 37.
[2]   [2014] EWCOP 37.
[3]   [2015] EWCA Civ 599.
[4]   At paras 86, 93 and 94.
[5]   At para 96.

'in theory, P need not always be a party to the proceedings if his participation in them can reliably be secured by other means. The question is, however, whether this can be done and, more importantly, whether the streamlined procedure contemplated by the President could be sufficiently relied upon to achieve it. In considering this, it has to be borne in mind that the President was establishing a process which was to be universal. It would be translated into action by many who were expert and efficient but, inevitably, also by some who were lacking in time or expertise or judgment. In what follows, I am not suggesting bad faith on the part of those involved in the process, merely acknowledging the pressures and realities of everyday practice.'

But in her view the President's scheme presented two problems namely:[6]

'First, it is heavily dependent upon P conveying a wish to be joined in the proceedings or opposition to the arrangements proposed for him, or someone else who has his interests at heart taking these points on his behalf. Secondly, it depends entirely on the reliability and completeness of the information transmitted to the court by those charged with the task. In many cases, this will be the very person/organisation seeking authorisation for P to be deprived of his liberty and the possibility of a conflict of interest is clear.'

Having further explored the President's scheme against the provisions under the DoLS regime and the limitation with the consultation process in Annex C to the *Re X* forms, Black LJ concluded that:[7]

'A critical feature of the relevant person's representative is that he or she is independent of those who commission and provide the service that P is receiving and is charged, amongst other things, with making such application to the Court of Protection as is appropriate. This degree of independence and duty is lacking in the procedure followed in respect of an application to the Court of Protection under section 16(2)(a) for the court to authorise a deprivation of liberty. In a section 16 case, as I have already observed, the application is likely to be made by the body commissioning or providing care to P which has already formed the view that the deprivation of liberty is necessary in the best interests of P. As applicant, that body bears the primary responsibility for obtaining and providing to the court the information to enable the court to decide whether the case is appropriate for the streamlined procedure and ultimately, of course, if the streamlined procedure continues to apply, whether to grant the order sought. It is the applicant who sets out on the relevant court form why the proposed course is said to be required. Consultation with people with an interest in the application is also the responsibility of the applicant and the views of those consulted are reported to the court in Annex B to the application form filed by the applicant.

It is only in relation to the obligatory consultation with P that any significant degree of detachment is introduced. Annex C deals with this process and the notes to it advise that the consultation should be by someone who knows P and is best placed to express their wishes and views. The suggestion is made on the form that this could be a relative or close friend or someone the person has previously chosen to act on their behalf or, if no suitable person is available, then an IMCA or similar

---

[6] At para 100.
[7] At paras 102 and 103.

should be appointed. The results of the consultation are to be noted on the Annex C form and filed by the applicant with the application form. This consultation process has its limitations, however, as a safeguard for P. There is no equivalent to the relevant person's representative and no one whose role includes challenging the proposed deprivation of liberty. P may not have any family members or friends to advocate for him, or none with the detachment (or drive or competence or knowledge) required to safeguard his interests in respect of his liberty. It may be, for example, that P's family is simply happy to go along with the management of the case by those caring for P or is unaware of the existence of alternatives. Even if he does have family members or friends, or if an IMCA is appointed for him as Annex C suggests, it is vital to keep in mind the characteristics of someone in the position of P. The court will only be involved in making the decision to approve the proposed deprivation of liberty under section 16(2) if P has a difficulty of the type set out in section 3(1), which I set out above. Consulting him about his views, canvassing his wishes, explaining what it means to be a party to the proceedings (or not to be a party), and finding out whether he wishes to be joined can be anticipated to present significantly greater challenges than it would with a person of full capacity. Inevitably, even when consulted very skilfully, he is not likely to be in a position to make an informed decision himself about his participation in the proceedings or indeed about his living circumstances, particularly as he may have no conception of the alternatives that might be available for his care. In the light of all of this, it is not appropriate, in my view, for P's participation in proceedings to turn in any way upon whether he wishes to participate or indeed upon whether he expresses an objection to the form of care that is being provided or proposed. There is too high a risk of slip ups in such a scheme. Article 5 requires a greater guarantee against arbitrariness.'

She suggested that it might be possible to take the best of the Sch A1 procedure, which has been accepted as providing appropriate safeguards, to devise a less complex process which will still protect those whose liberty is in the balance. She could not agree that the streamlined process provides the elements required for compliance with Art 5 and that she could see no alternative to P being made a party to the deprivation of liberty proceedings because:[8]

'... In my view, however, it is not possible to place sufficient reliance on the process devised for it to be said to constitute such an opportunity. It is not only that there is too significant a risk that cases would slip through the net, going unrecognised by the applicant and by the court despite the best efforts of all involved. In addition, I agree with the submission that the process set up by the President amounts to placing an additional hurdle in the way of P participating in the proceedings – instead of being a party automatically, there is an additional process to be gone through before he is joined, namely the collection/provision of material to persuade the court that he wishes/needs to be joined. I remind myself that no other example could be found of an adult whose liberty was in question in proceedings before a court or tribunal not being automatically a party to those proceedings. P is therefore in a position which is the opposite of what the Strasbourg jurisprudence requires, namely that the essence of the Article 5 right must not be impaired and there might, in fact, need to be additional assistance provided to P to ensure that it is effective.'

---

[8]   At para 106.

Black LJ took into consideration the concern about the increased workload and the delay that may result but concluded:[9]

> '... There is no reason to suppose that the automatic joinder of P as a party would be likely to generate dispute where there would not otherwise have been dispute and, where P and his litigation friend are content that what is proposed is necessary in his best interests, the proceedings need not be protracted or elaborate. In any event, pressure on resources and even considerations of increased delay are not material to a determination of whether there are adequate safeguards to satisfy Article 5. For the reasons I have explained, had I been in a position to determine the issue in these proceedings, I would have held that in order that deprivations of liberty are reliably subjected to thorough scrutiny, and effective procedural safeguards are provided against arbitrary detention in practice, it is presently necessary for P to be a party in the relevant proceedings.'

In agreeing with Black LJ's judgment, LJs Gloster and Moore-Bick said that the President's approach to P's party status:

> 'is not consistent with fundamental principles of domestic law and does not provide the degree of protection required by the Convention and the Strasbourg jurisprudence [127] ...

> These are essentially practical considerations, but they invite consideration of what is actually meant by being a party to proceedings. In my view a party can best be described for these purposes as a natural or juridical person who has come before the court in order to obtain vindication of his rights and relief of some kind (usually described in the proceedings as a claimant) or who has been brought before the court by another under compulsion in order that the court's powers may be invoked against him (usually described as a defendant). Such persons are directly affected by the court's decision and are therefore entitled to play a full part in the proceedings in accordance with the rules of procedure. Other persons whose interests are directly affected may sometimes be joined as parties to ensure that they are bound by the outcome (usually as defendants), in which case they are also entitled to play a full part in the proceedings. The decision of the court on matters in issue binds all parties to the proceedings, but not others. In order to obtain a decision which binds a person of full age and sound mind it is necessary to make him a party to the proceedings and in the light of the approach adopted in *Cheshire West*, it is difficult to see why the same should not be true of a person who lacks capacity, despite the fact that he must act by a litigation friend, when his liberty is at stake.

> The decision in *Winterwerp v The Netherlands* (1979) 2 EHRR 387 makes it clear that a person who lacks capacity must have access to a court and an effective opportunity to be heard, either in person or by means of representation. The fullest right to participation in proceedings is that which is enjoyed by the parties, but the streamlined procedure envisaged by the President contemplates that there will be cases in which a person lacking capacity will not be made a party because someone considers that it is unnecessary for that step to be taken. I agree with Black LJ for the reasons she gives that a procedure under which such a person need not be made a party in order to ensure that the proceedings are properly to constituted

---

[9]   At para 108.

(even though he may be joined as a party at his request) is not consistent with fundamental principles of domestic law and does not provide the degree of protection required by the Convention and the Strasbourg jurisprudence.' [170-171]

Clearly the Court of Appeal were aware of the obiter nature of their observations on the party status of P. However, they would hardly have given such detailed consideration to the issues if it were expected they would be ignored. Having regard to the fact that the issue before the court was fully argued on all fronts by experienced counsel and considered by the court in a very detailed judgment, it is also unlikely that, however inconvenient the ruling may be, it will be ignored. P therefore must be made a party to all deprivation of liberty proceedings with a litigation friend appointed to look after P's interests in relation to the litigation. In so doing, stated Black LJ, 'the court will have done what is reasonably practicable to permit and encourage him to participate as fully as possible in any decision affecting him, fulfilling section 4 of the MCA 2005'. The court did not give any indication on whether the litigation friend should act through a solicitor. Having regard to what all three Lord Justices said and the decision of ECtHR in *MS v Croatia (No 2)*[10] it is submitted that any suggestion that a litigation friend should act for P without legal representation would not be Convention compliant because it would not provide effective independent legal representation in deprivation of liberty cases.

It may be suggested that the provisions set out in the new r 3A (see below) adequately deal with the concerns raised by the court. Although these provisions are a step forward, do they go far enough to meet the degree of protection required by the ECHR and referred to by the Court of Appeal; do they meet the universal test advocated by the UKSC in *Cheshire*? When the options available to P under the new rules to be involved in proceedings are scrutinised it is unlikely that they provide the protection envisaged by either domestic or European jurisprudence. The available options are considered below under **6.5–6.11**.

6.2.1　Recent developments: Charles J's conclusions in *Re NRA & Others* [2015] EWCOP 59

On 25 September Charles J handed down his judgment in a number of welfare cases referred to him by the district bench of the Court of Protection at First Avenue House (*Re NRA & Others* [2015] EWCOP 59). These cases all involved deprivation of liberty issues but the circumstances of each individual varied. His task was to decide whether or not P needed to be made a party to proceedings to ensure Art 5 compliant safeguards when the care package involved a deprivation of liberty, and how P could be best represented generally. Charles J was mindful of the burden not only upon the Court of Protection in processing these cases but also upon the public purse by placing additional financial demands upon local authorities and diverting resources from frontline

---

[10]　[2015] ECHR 196.

personal social services [6–33]. In determining these issues he felt bound by the Supreme Court's decision in *Cheshire West* but not by the conclusions of the Court of Appeal in *Re X*. Although he acknowledged that the Court of Appeal's decision was persuasive and cogently argued [22] it was clear from the judgment that his focus was on containing financial resources. His view was that P's interests may be represented by family and friends. In so doing he formulated a qualitative test to guide the court in its approach in determining the ability of lay people to represent P's interests. Can they:

(i)   elicit P's wishes and feelings and make them and the matters mentioned in s 4(6) of the MCA known to the court without causing P any or any unnecessary distress,

(ii) critically examine P's best interests, and with a detailed knowledge of P, the pros and cons of a care package, and whether it is the least restrictive available option; and

(iii) keep the implementation of the care package under review and raise points relating to it and changes in P's behaviour or health [164].

He concluded that:

- Family members and friends, who had supported and cared for P and effectively promoted P's interests and 'fought P's corner over a long time would be the best and appropriate litigation friend or Rule 3A representative and would be best placed to ensure the promotion of P's interests, P's participation in the decisions relating the care package, the determinative test (above) and the proceedings ([164–175], [230–238], [239–240]). Where there is no family member or friend who could act as a litigation friend or a Rule 3A representative the solution he said is (a) for the court to make an order for s 49 reports and issue witness summonses; and (b) for the court to appoint a Rule 3A representative if and when the Secretary of State takes steps to make sure that one is available in practice [241–244].

- There was no requirement under European law or common law that there must be an oral hearing of a non-controversial case because it involves deprivation of liberty, or a person who lacks capacity to litigate, or otherwise.

- It was not necessary for P to be made a party to an application for a welfare order which requires authorisation of deprivation of liberty [176–196].

- The President streamlined the process, subject to certain improvements (see below) to the information provided under the procedure (see paras 226(i)–(xi) – a web link is provided in **Appendix 8**), provided the necessary safeguards and should be reinstated.

He agreed that the present forms and process, direct the minds of applicants to the key issues so that they can provide all the required information but considered that it would be an improvement if these provisions 'were summarised and the questions raised in the forms were answered by reference to that summary (or provisions in the care package not mentioned therein.)'. The summary should in particular include the level of supervision (1:1, 2:1, etc) the periods of the day when supervision is provided; the use or possible use of sedation or restraint; the use of technology; and what would happen if P tried to leave [224–225].

The improvements he suggested are:

(i)   if the proposed placement is planned and has not yet taken place, there should be an explanation of whether or not a transition plan has been produced, a provision to append the transition plan and an explanation as to how the placement will be reviewed, particularly in the context of responding to P's reaction to his or her new placement. This would inform the timing of a review by the court,

(i)   if P is already living at the placement in respect of which a welfare order is sought the following information should be provided, namely the date P moved there, where he or she lived before, why the move took place, and how the move was working,

(iii) any recent change or planned change in the care package and the reasons for it should be provided,

(iv)   there should be a specific requirement to explain why the identified sedation or restraint are or may be used, and why they are the least restrictive measures to deal with the relevant issues,

(v)   there should be a question about the tenancy agreement (if there is one) and who has the authority or needs to apply for the authority to sign it on P's behalf,

(vi)   there should be a specific question as to why it is thought the case is not controversial and can be dealt with on the papers,

(vii) there should be a question directed to participation of family and friends over the years and the nature of the care and support they have provided and their approach to issues relating to its provision in the past and so whether and the reasons why it is thought that family or friends have provided and will provide balanced support for P in his or her best interests,

(viii) there should be a question that requires the reasons why family and friends support the care package to be set out,

(ix)   there should be a question directed to the willingness of a family member or friend to be a litigation friend or a Rule 3A representative and their ability to keep the care package under review,

(x)   there should be questions directed to the suitability of family members or friends for such appointment that direct the author of the answers to particularise the answers by reference to the history of P's care, and

(xi)   there should be a question on what options have been considered and why the care package advanced has been chosen as the appropriate one. [226]

6.2.2 Analysis

Whilst many commentators agree that the CA's decision is obiter and not binding, Charles J's decision flies in the face of underlying jurisprudence that, to comply with the provisions of domestic and European law, P should be made a party where the issue to determined involves a deprivation of liberty. It is therefore more than likely that an appeal will be mounted so as to give the CA a framework upon which to properly give judgment upon the proposals. Given that all these cases involve live issues rather than a hypothetical situation, it is intended to avoid the CA finding themselves without jurisdiction to hear the appeal, which was the problem in *Re X*.

The Law Commission in its consultation paper CP122 has not made any reference to the implications of the Court of Appeal's decision in *Re X* when making its provisional recommendations. In this respect the report is deficient but no doubt this shortcoming will be addressed when it makes it final recommendation.

6.3 THE GENERAL RULE ON P'S PARTICIPATION BEFORE 1 JULY 2015

Although P must be notified of the proceedings P is not named as a respondent unless the court directs that he/she be made a respondent.[11] The issue of whether P should be made a party should be considered by the court early on in the proceedings as there is a duty on the court when managing the case to identify who should be made a party to the proceedings.[12] In every case therefore the court has a duty to consider P's party status, and, if P is not made a party, to consider how P is to be involved in the proceedings and his voice heard. The issue of P's status in the proceedings becomes even more crucial when it is proposed that P should be deprived of his/her liberty. In any event however, irrespective of whether P is joined as a party to the proceedings, the court may hear P on the question of whether or not an order should be made[13] but the court may proceed with a hearing in the absence of P if it considers that it would be appropriate to do so.[14]

If P is joined as a party, a litigation friend must be appointed. If P is not joined as a party, he must still be notified of the application and the date of the hearing.[15] The person notifying P must also explain to P who the applicant is; the issue which is the subject of the proceedings and that the application raises the question of whether P lacks capacity in relation to those matters and what that means. P must also be given an explanation of what will happen to him if the court makes the order or gives the direction which is being sought. The person notifying P must also inform him that he may seek legal advice and

---

[11] Rule 73(4).
[12] Rule 5(2)(b).
[13] Rule 88.
[14] Rule 88(2).
[15] Rule 42(2)-(4).

assistance. When an order is made P must be informed personally and in a manner which is appropriate to P's circumstances.[16] We submit that if a person lacks capacity, notifying him and advising him of his right to seek legal advice and assistance without more and without actively promoting and securing access to a lawyer is tantamount to merely paying lip service to the requirement of 'effective representation'.

6.4 GENERAL RULE POST-1 JULY 2015

As from 1 July 2015, pursuant to the Court of Protection (Amendment) Rules 2015, new r 3A of the COP Rules (set out in **Appendix 2**) makes it mandatory for the court in each case, on its own initiative or on the application of any person to consider whether it should make one or more of the directions set out in r 3A(2). These are:

(a) P should be joined as a party;

(b) P's participation should be secured by the appointment of an accredited legal representative to represent P in the proceedings and to discharge such other functions as the court may direct;

(c) P's participation should be secured by the appointment of a representative whose function shall be to provide the court with information as to the matters set out in s 4(6) of the Act and to discharge such other functions as the court may direct;

(d) P should have the opportunity to address (directly or indirectly) the judge determining the application and, if so directed, the circumstances in which that should occur;

(e) P's interests and position can properly be secured without any direction under sub-paragraphs (a) to (d) being made or by the making of an alternative direction meeting the overriding objective.

6.4.1 The criteria to be applied

COP Rules 2007, r 3(1) requires the court to have regard to the overriding objective ie to deal with a case justly having regard to the principles set out in the Act, when it exercises any power under the Rules or interprets any rule or practice direction. Rule 3A also requires the court to ensure that the overriding objective is met.

The criteria and the issues the court should consider are set out in r 3(3). Of these the ones that are relevant to P's involvement in the proceedings are:

(a) ensuring that P's interests and position are properly considered;

(b) dealing with the case in ways which are proportionate to the nature and importance and complexity of the issues; and

(c) ensuring that the parties are on an equal footing.

---

[16] Rule 46.

In addition, when determining whether to make or more of the directions relating to P's participation in proceedings the court should have regard to:

(a)   the nature and extent of the information before the court;

(b)   the issues raised in the case;

(c)   whether a matter is contentious; and

(d)   whether P has been notified in accordance with the provisions of Part 7 and what, if anything, P has said or done in response to such notification.

If P is joined as a party, unless P has capacity to conduct the proceedings, the order joining him/her will only take effect on the appointment of a litigation friend or the appointment of an accredited legal representative (ALR).

6.5   THE VARIOUS OPTIONS FOR P'S VOICE TO BE HEARD UNDER THE CURRENT RULES

6.5.1   Accredited legal representative (ALR)

6.5.1.1   *What is an ALR?*

Rule 6 of the Court of Protection Rules 2007 as amended defines an ALR to mean 'a legal representative authorised pursuant to a scheme of accreditation approved by the President to represent person meeting the definition of "P" on proceedings before the court'.

The only qualification apparently required to act as an ALR for P is that the person can fairly and competently discharge his or her functions on behalf of P.[17]

6.5.1.2   *How and by whom is an ALR appointed?*

The court may make an order appointing a person to act as an ALR for P either on its own initiative or on the application of any person but only with the consent of the person appointed.[18] The court must however be satisfied that the person to be appointed can fairly and competently discharge his or her functions on behalf of P.[19]

6.5.1.3   *Duration of the appointment*

The appointment may be made for a specific period but otherwise the appointment continues until it is brought to an end by a court order.[20] The court must bring an end the appointment if P has capacity to appoint a

---

[17]   Rule 148(3).
[18]   Rule 148(2).
[19]   Rule 148(3).
[20]   Rule 148B(4).

representative and does not wish the appointment by the court to continue.[21] The court also has the power either of its own initiative or on the application of any person to direct that a person may not act as an ALR and terminate the appointment.[22] The P must be notified where a direction is made of the appointment of an ALR.[23]

6.5.1.4   Qualification

The only qualification apparently required to act as an ALR for P is that the person can fairly and competently discharge his or her functions on behalf of P, but since the appointment is made for the purpose of giving P a voice in any proceedings and the person appointed must be accredited, it is assumed that he/she must have some legal qualification and experience in dealing with persons lacking capacity and court proceedings.

6.5.1.5   Functions of an ALR

The function of the ALR is to represent P in the proceedings and to discharge such other functions as the court may direct.[24] The court may also at any stage of the proceedings give directions as to the terms of appointment of an ALR.[25] Similarly, an ALR may at any time and without giving notice to the other parties apply to the court for directions relating to the performance, terms of appointment or continuation of his or her appointment. The court may also vary the terms of an ALR's appointment.[26]

To date the 'scheme of accreditation' has not been established. It is not known what qualification experience, training or other conditions that will be required for a person to be approved as an ALR. No regulations have as yet been issued providing for the functions of an ALR besides that which is set out in the definition clause to the rules. It is also not known what powers an ALR will have nor how he/she will be remunerated and funded to undertake work on behalf of P and exactly what role he/she will play in proceedings.

6.5.2   A r 3A representative

A representative is a person appointed under r 3A(2)(c).[27]

The only qualification apparently required to act as an r 3A representative for P is that the person can fairly and competently discharge his or her functions on behalf of P.[28]

---

[21]   Rule 148B(5).
[22]   Rule 148(1)(a), (b).
[23]   Rule 41A.
[24]   Rule 3A.
[25]   Rule 148(4).
[26]   Rule 148B(1)(c).
[27]   Rule 3.
[28]   Rules 147 and 148(3).

6.5.2.1   How and by whom is a r 3A representative appointed?

The court may make an order appointing a person to act as representative for P either on its own initiative or on the application of any person but only with the consent of the person appointed.[29] The court must however be satisfied that the person to be appointed can fairly and competently discharge his or her functions on behalf of P.[30]

6.5.2.2   Duration of the appointment

The appointment may be made for a specific period but otherwise the appointment continues until it is brought to an end by a court order.[31] The court must bring an end the appointment if P has capacity to appoint a representative and does not wish the appointment by the court to continue.[32] The court also has the power either of its own initiative or on the application of any person to direct that a person may not act as a representative and terminate the appointment.[33] P must be notified where a direction is made of the appointment of an ALR.[34]

6.5.2.3   Function of a r 3A representative

His function is to provide the court with information as to the matters set out in s 4(6) of MCA 2005 and to discharge such other functions as the court may direct.

Section 4(6) matters are:

(a)   P's past and present wishes and feeling (and in particular any relevant written statement made by him when he had capacity);

(b)   the beliefs and values that would be likely to influence P decision if he had capacity; and

(c)   the other factors that P would be likely to consider if he were able to do so.

The court may also at any stage of the proceedings give directions as to the terms of appointment of a representative.[35] Similarly, a representative may at any time and without giving notice to the other parties apply to the court for directions relating to the performance, terms of appointment or continuation of his or her appointment. The court may also vary the terms of a representative's appointment.

---

[29]   Rule 148(2).
[30]   Rule 148 (3).
[31]   Rule 148B(4).
[32]   Rule 148B(5).
[33]   Rule 148 (1)(a), (b).
[34]   Rule 41A.
[35]   Rule 148(4).

6.5.3   Opportunity to address (directly or indirectly) the judge

Under the new r 3A the court is required to consider whether it should give
directions on whether P should have an opportunity to address the judge
determining the application and if so the circumstances in which that should
occur. There are no supplementary or supporting provisions on how, by whom
any directions given by the court should be implemented and how the
directions given will be resourced.

6.5.4   P's interests and position to be secured without any directions for P either to be made a party or to facilitate P's participation (r 3A(1)(e)) or making alternative directions

This provision is meaningless because it is left to chance. Those who drafted
this rule could only have inserted this provision in the hope that the voluntary
sector could be relied on to step in to assist and support P and his case.

6.5.5   Litigation friend

6.5.5.1   *How and by whom appointed*

The court may by order appoint the Official Solicitor or some other person to
act as a litigation friend for P if P is joined as a party, either on its own initiative
or on the application of any person provided it is satisfied that the person to be
appointed can fairly and competently conduct the proceedings on behalf of P
and that he has no interests adverse to those of P and the person appointed
consents to the appointment.[36] If a litigation friend cannot be appointed P
cannot be joined as party. In this event an alternative is not suggested. The
court's duty in this event is to record the act that no such appointment was
made and the reasons given for it.[37]

The rule provides for a practice direction to be made to add to or supplement
these provisions.

For more details on the criteria for appointment and duties of a litigation friend
in DoL case, see *Court of Protection Practice 2015*.

6.5.5.2   *Duration*

The appointment of a litigation friend continues until brought to an end by a
court order.[38]

---

[36]   Rules 140(1) and 143.
[37]   Rule 3A(5).
[38]   Rule 144.

6.5.6   Relevant person's representative (RPR)

The appointment of RPR is made when a case falls within the Sch A1 regime and a standard authorisations has been issued.[39] **It is thus not available to those who do not come within the Sch A1 regime.** The process for appointing an RPR must begin as soon as the best interests assessor is selected by the supervisory body for the purposes of a request for standard authorisation. The Mental Capacity (Deprivation of Liberty: Appointment of Relevant Person's Representative) Regulation 2008 as amended (set out in **Appendix 5**) provides for the selection and termination of appointment of a RPR; the formalities of the appointment and its termination.

6.5.6.1   Appointment and function of RPR

The supervisory body has a duty to appoint an RPR and that person must if appointed maintain, represent and support P in matters relating to or connected with his/her deprivation of liberty. The selection of the person to act a RPR however may be made by P if the best assessor determines that he has capacity to do so in which case a family member, friend or carer may be selected by P.

The selection of an RPR may also be recommended by a donee, deputy or best assessor as follows:

(1)   Where the best interest assessor determines that P lacks capacity to select a representative and P has a donee or deputy and the donee's or deputy's scope of authority permits the selection of a family member, friend or carer of the relevant person, the donee or deputy may select an RPR.

(2)   A donee or deputy may select himself or herself to the RPR.

(3)   The best assessor may select a family member, friend or carer as a RPR where:
    (a)   the relevant person has the capacity to make a selection under reg 5(1) but does not wish to do so;
    (b)   the relevant person's donee or deputy does not wish to make a selection under reg 6(1) or (2); or
    (c)   the relevant person lacks the capacity to make a selection and —
        (i)   does not have a donee or deputy, or
        (ii)   has a donee or deputy but the donee's or deputy's scope of authority does not permit the selection of a representative (para 8).

(4)   Where a supervisory body is given notice by the best interests assessor that they do not intend to select a person who is eligible to be a representative it may select a person to be the RPR who:
    (a)   would be performing the role in a professional capacity;
    (b)   has satisfactory skills and experience to perform the role;
    (c)   is not a family member, friend or carer of the relevant person;

---

[39]   See Sch A1, Pt 10, paras 139–140.

(d) is not employed by, or providing services to, the relevant person's managing authority, where the relevant person's managing authority is a care home;

(e) is not employed to work in the relevant person's managing authority in a role that is, or could be, related to the relevant person's case, where the relevant person's managing authority is a hospital; and

(f) is not employed to work in the supervisory body that is appointing the representative in a role that is, or could be, related to the relevant person's case.

6.5.6.2 Qualification

A person can only be selected to be a RPR if they are:

(1) 18 years of age or over;

(2) able to keep in contact with the relevant person;

(3) willing to be the relevant person's representative;

(4) not financially interested in the relevant person's managing authority;

(5) not a relative of a person who is financially interested in the managing authority;

(6) not employed by, or providing services to, the relevant person's managing authority, where the relevant person's managing authority is a care home;

(7) not employed to work in the relevant person's managing authority in a role that is, or could be, related to the relevant person's case, where the relevant person's managing authority is a hospital; and

(8) not employed to work in the supervisory body that is appointing the representative in a role that is, or could be, related to the relevant person's case.

The pitfalls of selecting the wrong person to be appointed RPR are discussed by Baker J in *In the matter of the Mental Capacity Act 2005 Re AJ (Deprivation of Liberty Safeguards)*[40] (see Chapter 3). For ease of reference a web link for the case is set out in **Appendix 8**.

6.5.6.3 Formalities for appointing an RPR

The offer of an appointment must be made in writing. It must state the duties of a RPR and the duration of the appointment (para 12(1)). The appointment must be made for the period of the authorisation (para 12(3)). Acceptance of the appointment must also be in writing with confirmation that the person understands his or her duties. Notice of the appointment when made must be sent to the following persons:

(a) the appointed person;

(b) the relevant person;

(c) the relevant person's managing authority;

---

[40] [2015] EWCOP 6.

(d) any donee or deputy of the relevant person;

(e) any independent mental capacity advocate appointed in accordance with ss 37–39D of the Act, involved in the relevant person's case; and

(f) every interested person named by the best interests assessor in their report as somebody the assessor has consulted in carrying out the assessment.

6.5.6.4 Termination of appointment

An RPR ceases to act if:

(1) the person dies;

(2) the person informs the supervisory body that they are no longer willing to continue as representative;

(3) the period of the appointment ends;

(4) a relevant person who has selected a family member, friend or carer under reg 5(1) who has been appointed as their representative informs the supervisory body that they object to the person continuing to be a representative;

(5) a donee or deputy who has selected a family member, friend or carer of the relevant person under reg 6(1) who has been appointed as a representative informs the supervisory body that they object to the person continuing to be a representative;

(6) the supervisory body terminates the appointment because it is satisfied that the representative is not maintaining sufficient contact with the relevant person in order to support and represent them;

(7) the supervisory body terminates the appointment because it is satisfied that the representative is not acting in the best interests of the relevant person; or

(8) the supervisory body terminates the appointment because it is satisfied that the person is no longer eligible or was not eligible at the time of appointment, to be a representative.

Notice of termination of the appointment must be sent to all persons referred to in under formalities (2) to (6) (above).

6.5.6.5 Payment

The supervisory body is permitted to make payments to a RPR where it has selected the RPR on receipt of a notice from the best interests assessor they do not intend to select a person who is eligible to be a RPR (para 15).

6.5.7 Independent mental capacity advocate (IMCA)

In any case where an NHS body or local authority proposes to make arrangements for the provision of accommodation for P in a hospital or care home (in the case of the NHS) or the provision of residential accommodation (in the case of a local authority) or a change in P's accommodation and it is satisfied that there is no family member or friend of P whom it would be appropriate for the NHS body or the local authority, as the case may be, to consult in determining what would be in P's best interests, it must instruct an IMCA to represent P. There are exceptions to this requirement. In the case of an NHS body the provision does not apply if it is satisfied that:

(1) the accommodation is likely to be provided for a continuous period which is less than 28 days, if the accommodation is to be provided in a hospital, or 8 weeks if it is in a care home; or

(2) the arrangements need to be made as a matter of urgency.

In the case of a local authority the provision to instruct an IMCA does not apply if it is satisfied that:

(1) the accommodation is likely to be provided for a continuous period of less than 8 weeks, or

(2) the arrangements need to be made as a matter of urgency.

In either case, if subsequently the NHS body or the local authority (as the case may be) have reason to believe that the accommodation is likely to be provided for a continuous period which is longer than that specified above it must instruct an IMCA to represent P.

In deciding what arrangements to make for P, the NHS body and the local authority (as the case may be) should take into account any information given or submission made, by the IMCA.

6.5.7.1 Functions of the IMCA

The IMCA is required to take such steps as he may be required for the purpose of:

(1) providing support to the person whom he has instructed to represent (P) so that P may participate as fully as possible in any relevant decision;

(2) obtaining and evaluating relevant information;

(3) ascertaining what P's wishes and feelings would be likely to be, and the beliefs and values that would be likely to influence P if he had capacity;

(4) ascertaining what alternative courses of action are available in relation to P;

(5) obtaining a further medical opinion where treatment is proposed and the advocate thinks that one should be obtained;

(6) the advocate may challenge or provide assistance for the purpose of challenging any relevant decision.

The Mental Capacity Act 2005 (Independent Mental Capacity Advocates) (General) Regulations 2006, SI 2006/1832 (see **Appendix 6**) provide that the

IMCA must determine in all the circumstances how best to represent and support P and in particular the IMCA must:

(1) verify that the instructions were issued by an authorised person;

(2) to the extent that it is practicable and appropriate to do so, interview P and examine the records relevant to P to which the IMCA has access under s 35(6) of the Act;

(3) to the extent that it is practicable and appropriate to do so, consult persons engaged in providing care or treatment for P in a professional capacity or for remuneration, and other persons who may be in a position to comment on P's wishes, feelings, beliefs or values;

(4) take all practicable steps to obtain such other information about P or the act or decision that is proposed in relation to P, as the IMCA considers necessary;

(5) evaluate all the information he has obtained for the purpose of ascertaining the extent of the support provided to P to enable him to participate in making any decision about the matter in relation to which the IMCA has been instructed and what the patient's wishes and feeling are likely to be and the beliefs and values that would be likely to influence him/her if he/she had capacity in relation to the proposed act or decision and to consider what alternative courses of action are available and whether P is likely to benefit from a further medical opinion.

In accordance with the provisions of s 37(3) the IMCA is given the right to challenge the decision taken or proposed as if he were a person engaged in caring for P or interested in his welfare. In most cases this can be achieved by using the complaints procedure to resolve disputes but there may be circumstances where the IMCA may be obliged to apply to the Court of Protection for relief.

Regulation 5 of the General Regulations provides certain minimum requirements that a person must meet in order to be appointed as an IMCA. In order to act as an IMCA, a person must be approved by a local authority as meeting the appointment requirements, or he must be a member of a class which has been so approved. The appointment requirements are that:

• he/she must have appropriate experience/training;

• he/she be a person of integrity and good character;

• he/she must be able to act independently of anyone who instructs him to act as an IMCA.

APPENDIX 1

EXTRACTS FROM THE MENTAL CAPACITY ACT 2005

4 Best interests

(1) In determining for the purposes of this Act what is in a person's best interests, the person making the determination must not make it merely on the basis of –

(a) the person's age or appearance, or

(b) a condition of his, or an aspect of his behaviour, which might lead others to make unjustified assumptions about what might be in his best interests.

(2) The person making the determination must consider all the relevant circumstances and, in particular, take the following steps.

(3) He must consider –

(a) whether it is likely that the person will at some time have capacity in relation to the matter in question, and

(b) if it appears likely that he will, when that is likely to be.

(4) He must, so far as reasonably practicable, permit and encourage the person to participate, or to improve his ability to participate, as fully as possible in any act done for him and any decision affecting him.

(5) Where the determination relates to life-sustaining treatment he must not, in considering whether the treatment is in the best interests of the person concerned, be motivated by a desire to bring about his death.

(6) He must consider, so far as is reasonably ascertainable –

(a) the person's past and present wishes and feelings (and, in particular, any relevant written statement made by him when he had capacity),

(b) the beliefs and values that would be likely to influence his decision if he had capacity, and

(c) the other factors that he would be likely to consider if he were able to do so.

(7) He must take into account, if it is practicable and appropriate to consult them, the views of –

(a) anyone named by the person as someone to be consulted on the matter in question or on matters of that kind,

(b) anyone engaged in caring for the person or interested in his welfare,

(c) any donee of a lasting power of attorney granted by the person, and

(d)   any deputy appointed for the person by the court,

as to what would be in the person's best interests and, in particular, as to the matters mentioned in subsection (6).

(8) The duties imposed by subsections (1) to (7) also apply in relation to the exercise of any powers which –

(a)   are exercisable under a lasting power of attorney, or
(b)   are exercisable by a person under this Act where he reasonably believes that another person lacks capacity.

(9) In the case of an act done, or a decision made, by a person other than the court, there is sufficient compliance with this section if (having complied with the requirements of subsections (1) to (7)) he reasonably believes that what he does or decides is in the best interests of the person concerned.

(10) "Life-sustaining treatment" means treatment which in the view of a person providing health care for the person concerned is necessary to sustain life.

(11) "Relevant circumstances" are those –

(a)   of which the person making the determination is aware, and
(b)   which it would be reasonable to regard as relevant.

4A Restriction on deprivation of liberty

(1) This Act does not authorise any person ("D") to deprive any other person ("P") of his liberty.

(2) But that is subject to –

(a)   the following provisions of this section, and
(b)   section 4B.

(3) D may deprive P of his liberty if, by doing so, D is giving effect to a relevant decision of the court.

(4) A relevant decision of the court is a decision made by an order under section 16(2)(a) in relation to a matter concerning P's personal welfare.

(5) D may deprive P of his liberty if the deprivation is authorised by Schedule A1 (hospital and care home residents: deprivation of liberty).

4B Deprivation of liberty necessary for life-sustaining treatment etc

(1) If the following conditions are met, D is authorised to deprive P of his liberty while a decision as respects any relevant issue is sought from the court.

(2) The first condition is that there is a question about whether D is authorised to deprive P of his liberty under section 4A.

(3) The second condition is that the deprivation of liberty –

(a)   is wholly or partly for the purpose of –
  (i)   giving P life-sustaining treatment, or
  (ii)   doing any vital act, or

(b) consists wholly or partly of –

    (i) giving P life-sustaining treatment, or

    (ii) doing any vital act.

(4) The third condition is that the deprivation of liberty is necessary in order to –

(a) give the life-sustaining treatment, or

(b) do the vital act.

(5) A vital act is any act which the person doing it reasonably believes to be necessary to prevent a serious deterioration in P's condition.

5 Acts in connection with care or treatment

(1) If a person ("D") does an act in connection with the care or treatment of another person ("P"), the act is one to which this section applies if –

(a) before doing the act, D takes reasonable steps to establish whether P lacks capacity in relation to the matter in question, and

(b) when doing the act, D reasonably believes –

    (i) that P lacks capacity in relation to the matter, and

    (ii) that it will be in P's best interests for the act to be done.

(2) D does not incur any liability in relation to the act that he would not have incurred if P –

(a) had had capacity to consent in relation to the matter, and

(b) had consented to D's doing the act.

(3) Nothing in this section excludes a person's civil liability for loss or damage, or his criminal liability, resulting from his negligence in doing the act.

(4) Nothing in this section affects the operation of sections 24 to 26 (advance decisions to refuse treatment).

6 Section 5 acts: limitations

(1) If D does an act that is intended to restrain P, it is not an act to which section 5 applies unless two further conditions are satisfied.

(2) The first condition is that D reasonably believes that it is necessary to do the act in order to prevent harm to P.

(3) The second is that the act is a proportionate response to –

(a) the likelihood of P's suffering harm, and

(b) the seriousness of that harm.

(4) For the purposes of this section D restrains P if he –

(a) uses, or threatens to use, force to secure the doing of an act which P resists, or

(b) restricts P's liberty of movement, whether or not P resists.

(5) . . .

(6) Section 5 does not authorise a person to do an act which conflicts with a decision made, within the scope of his authority and in accordance with this Part, by –

(a)   a donee of a lasting power of attorney granted by P, or
(b)   a deputy appointed for P by the court.

(7) But nothing in subsection (6) stops a person –

(a)   providing life-sustaining treatment, or
(b)   doing any act which he reasonably believes to be necessary to prevent a serious deterioration in P's condition,

while a decision as respects any relevant issue is sought from the court.

16A Section 16 powers: Mental Health Act patients etc

(1) If a person is ineligible to be deprived of liberty by this Act, the court may not include in a welfare order provision which authorises the person to be deprived of his liberty.

(2) If –

(a)   a welfare order includes provision which authorises a person to be deprived of his liberty, and
(b)   that person becomes ineligible to be deprived of liberty by this Act,

the provision ceases to have effect for as long as the person remains ineligible.

(3) Nothing in subsection (2) affects the power of the court under section 16(7) to vary or discharge the welfare order.

(4) For the purposes of this section –

(a)   Schedule 1A applies for determining whether or not P is ineligible to be deprived of liberty by this Act;
(b)   "welfare order" means an order under section 16(2)(a).

21A Powers of court in relation to Schedule A1

(1) This section applies if either of the following has been given under Schedule A1 –

(a)   a standard authorisation;
(b)   an urgent authorisation.

(2) Where a standard authorisation has been given, the court may determine any question relating to any of the following matters –

(a)   whether the relevant person meets one or more of the qualifying requirements;
(b)   the period during which the standard authorisation is to be in force;
(c)   the purpose for which the standard authorisation is given;
(d)   the conditions subject to which the standard authorisation is given.

(3) If the court determines any question under subsection (2), the court may make an order –

(a) varying or terminating the standard authorisation, or
(b) directing the supervisory body to vary or terminate the standard authorisation.

(4) Where an urgent authorisation has been given, the court may determine any question relating to any of the following matters –

(a) whether the urgent authorisation should have been given;
(b) the period during which the urgent authorisation is to be in force;
(c) the purpose for which the urgent authorisation is given.

(5) Where the court determines any question under subsection (4), the court may make an order –

(a) varying or terminating the urgent authorisation, or
(b) directing the managing authority of the relevant hospital or care home to vary or terminate the urgent authorisation.

(6) Where the court makes an order under subsection (3) or (5), the court may make an order about a person's liability for any act done in connection with the standard or urgent authorisation before its variation or termination.

(7) An order under subsection (6) may, in particular, exclude a person from liability.

SCHEDULE A1
Hospital and Care Home Residents: Deprivation of Liberty

PART 1
AUTHORISATION TO DEPRIVE RESIDENTS OF LIBERTY ETC

Application of Part

1 (1) This Part applies if the following conditions are met.

(2) The first condition is that a person ("P") is detained in a hospital or care home – for the purpose of being given care or treatment – in circumstances which amount to deprivation of the person's liberty.

(3) The second condition is that a standard or urgent authorisation is in force.

(4) The third condition is that the standard or urgent authorisation relates –

(a) to P, and
(b) to the hospital or care home in which P is detained.

Authorisation to deprive P of liberty

2 The managing authority of the hospital or care home may deprive P of his liberty by detaining him as mentioned in paragraph 1(2).

No liability for acts done for purpose of depriving P of liberty

3 (1) This paragraph applies to any act which a person ("D") does for the purpose of detaining P as mentioned in paragraph 1(2).

(2) D does not incur any liability in relation to the act that he would not have incurred if P –

    (a)   had had capacity to consent in relation to D's doing the act, and

    (b)   had consented to D's doing the act.

No protection for negligent acts etc

4 (1) Paragraphs 2 and 3 do not exclude a person's civil liability for loss or damage, or his criminal liability, resulting from his negligence in doing anything.

(2) Paragraphs 2 and 3 do not authorise a person to do anything otherwise than for the purpose of the standard or urgent authorisation that is in force.

(3) In a case where a standard authorisation is in force, paragraphs 2 and 3 do not authorise a person to do anything which does not comply with the conditions (if any) included in the authorisation.

PART 2
INTERPRETATION: MAIN TERMS

Introduction

5 This Part applies for the purposes of this Schedule.

Detained resident

6 "Detained resident" means a person detained in a hospital or care home – for the purpose of being given care or treatment – in circumstances which amount to deprivation of the person's liberty.

Relevant person etc

7 In relation to a person who is, or is to be, a detained resident –

"relevant person" means the person in question;
"relevant hospital or care home" means the hospital or care home in question;
"relevant care or treatment" means the care or treatment in question.

Authorisations

8 "Standard authorisation" means an authorisation given under Part 4.

9 "Urgent authorisation" means an authorisation given under Part 5.

10 "Authorisation under this Schedule" means either of the following –

    (a)   a standard authorisation;

    (b)   an urgent authorisation.

11 (1) The purpose of a standard authorisation is the purpose which is stated in the authorisation in accordance with paragraph 55(1)(d).

(2) The purpose of an urgent authorisation is the purpose which is stated in the authorisation in accordance with paragraph 80(d).

PART 3
THE QUALIFYING REQUIREMENTS

The qualifying requirements

12 (1) These are the qualifying requirements referred to in this Schedule –

(a)   the age requirement;
(b)   the mental health requirement;
(c)   the mental capacity requirement;
(d)   the best interests requirement;
(e)   the eligibility requirement;
(f)   the no refusals requirement.

(2) Any question of whether a person who is, or is to be, a detained resident meets the qualifying requirements is to be determined in accordance with this Part.

(3) In a case where –

(a)   the question of whether a person meets a particular qualifying requirement arises in relation to the giving of a standard authorisation, and
(b)   any circumstances relevant to determining that question are expected to change between the time when the determination is made and the time when the authorisation is expected to come into force,

those circumstances are to be taken into account as they are expected to be at the later time.

The age requirement

13 The relevant person meets the age requirement if he has reached 18.

The mental health requirement

14 (1) The relevant person meets the mental health requirement if he is suffering from mental disorder (within the meaning of the Mental Health Act, but disregarding any exclusion for persons with learning disability).

(2) An exclusion for persons with learning disability is any provision of the Mental Health Act which provides for a person with learning disability not to be regarded as suffering from mental disorder for one or more purposes of that Act.

The mental capacity requirement

15 The relevant person meets the mental capacity requirement if he lacks capacity in relation to the question whether or not he should be accommodated in the relevant hospital or care home for the purpose of being given the relevant care or treatment.

The best interests requirement

16 (1) The relevant person meets the best interests requirement if all of the following conditions are met.

(2) The first condition is that the relevant person is, or is to be, a detained resident.

(3) The second condition is that it is in the best interests of the relevant person for him to be a detained resident.

(4) The third condition is that, in order to prevent harm to the relevant person, it is necessary for him to be a detained resident.

(5) The fourth condition is that it is a proportionate response to –

   (a)   the likelihood of the relevant person suffering harm, and
   (b)   the seriousness of that harm,

for him to be a detained resident.

The eligibility requirement

17 (1) The relevant person meets the eligibility requirement unless he is ineligible to be deprived of liberty by this Act.

(2) Schedule 1A applies for the purpose of determining whether or not P is ineligible to be deprived of liberty by this Act.

The no refusals requirement

18 The relevant person meets the no refusals requirement unless there is a refusal within the meaning of paragraph 19 or 20.

19 (1) There is a refusal if these conditions are met –

   (a)   the relevant person has made an advance decision;
   (b)   the advance decision is valid;
   (c)   the advance decision is applicable to some or all of the relevant treatment.

(2) Expressions used in this paragraph and any of sections 24, 25 or 26 have the same meaning in this paragraph as in that section.

20 (1) There is a refusal if it would be in conflict with a valid decision of a donee or deputy for the relevant person to be accommodated in the relevant hospital or care home for the purpose of receiving some or all of the relevant care or treatment –

(a)   in circumstances which amount to deprivation of the person's liberty, or

(b)   at all.

(2) A donee is a donee of a lasting power of attorney granted by the relevant person.

(3) A decision of a donee or deputy is valid if it is made –

(a)   within the scope of his authority as donee or deputy, and

(b)   in accordance with Part 1 of this Act.

PART 4
STANDARD AUTHORISATIONS

Supervisory body to give authorisation

21 Only the supervisory body may give a standard authorisation.

22 The supervisory body may not give a standard authorisation unless –

(a)   the managing authority of the relevant hospital or care home have requested it, or

(b)   paragraph 71 applies (right of third party to require consideration of whether authorisation needed).

23 The managing authority may not make a request for a standard authorisation unless –

(a)   they are required to do so by paragraph 24 (as read with paragraphs 27 to 29),

(b)   they are required to do so by paragraph 25 (as read with paragraph 28), or

(c)   they are permitted to do so by paragraph 30.

Duty to request authorisation: basic cases

24 (1) The managing authority must request a standard authorisation in any of the following cases.

(2) The first case is where it appears to the managing authority that the relevant person –

(a)   is not yet accommodated in the relevant hospital or care home,

(b)   is likely – at some time within the next 28 days – to be a detained resident in the relevant hospital or care home, and

(c)   is likely –
   (i)   at that time, or
   (ii)   at some later time within the next 28 days,

to meet all of the qualifying requirements.

(3) The second case is where it appears to the managing authority that the relevant person –

(a)   is already accommodated in the relevant hospital or care home,

(b)   is likely –at some time within the next 28 days –to be a detained resident in the relevant hospital or care home, and

(c)   is likely –
       (i)   at that time, or
       (ii)   at some later time within the next 28 days,

to meet all of the qualifying requirements.

(4) The third case is where it appears to the managing authority that the relevant person –

(a)   is a detained resident in the relevant hospital or care home, and

(b)   meets all of the qualifying requirements, or is likely to do so at some time within the next 28 days.

(5) This paragraph is subject to paragraphs 27 to 29.

Duty to request authorisation: change in place of detention

25 (1) The relevant managing authority must request a standard authorisation if it appears to them that these conditions are met.

(2) The first condition is that a standard authorisation –

(a)   has been given, and

(b)   has not ceased to be in force.

(3) The second condition is that there is, or is to be, a change in the place of detention.

(4) This paragraph is subject to paragraph 28.

26 (1) This paragraph applies for the purposes of paragraph 25.

(2) There is a change in the place of detention if the relevant person –

(a)   ceases to be a detained resident in the stated hospital or care home, and

(b)   becomes a detained resident in a different hospital or care home ("the new hospital or care home").

(3) The stated hospital or care home is the hospital or care home to which the standard authorisation relates.

(4) The relevant managing authority are the managing authority of the new hospital or care home.

Other authority for detention: request for authorisation

27 (1) This paragraph applies if, by virtue of section 4A(3), a decision of the court authorises the relevant person to be a detained resident.

(2) Paragraph 24 does not require a request for a standard authorisation to be made in relation to that detention unless these conditions are met.

(3) The first condition is that the standard authorisation would be in force at a time immediately after the expiry of the other authority.

(4) The second condition is that the standard authorisation would not be in force at any time on or before the expiry of the other authority.

(5) The third condition is that it would, in the managing authority's view, be unreasonable to delay making the request until a time nearer the expiry of the other authority.

(6) In this paragraph –

(a)   the other authority is –
   (i)   the decision mentioned in sub-paragraph (1), or
   (ii)   any further decision of the court which, by virtue of section 4A(3), authorises, or is expected to authorise, the relevant person to be a detained resident;

(b)   the expiry of the other authority is the time when the other authority is expected to cease to authorise the relevant person to be a detained resident.

Request refused: no further request unless change of circumstances

28 (1) This paragraph applies if –

(a)   a managing authority request a standard authorisation under paragraph 24 or 25, and
(b)   the supervisory body are prohibited by paragraph 50(2) from giving the authorisation.

(2) Paragraph 24 or 25 does not require that managing authority to make a new request for a standard authorisation unless it appears to the managing authority that –

(a)   there has been a change in the relevant person's case, and
(b)   because of that change, the supervisory body are likely to give a standard authorisation if requested.

Authorisation given: request for further authorisation

29 (1) This paragraph applies if a standard authorisation –

(a)   has been given in relation to the detention of the relevant person, and
(b)   that authorisation ("the existing authorisation") has not ceased to be in force.

(2) Paragraph 24 does not require a new request for a standard authorisation ("the new authorisation") to be made unless these conditions are met.

(3) The first condition is that the new authorisation would be in force at a time immediately after the expiry of the existing authorisation.

(4) The second condition is that the new authorisation would not be in force at any time on or before the expiry of the existing authorisation.

(5) The third condition is that it would, in the managing authority's view, be unreasonable to delay making the request until a time nearer the expiry of the existing authorisation.

(6) The expiry of the existing authorisation is the time when it is expected to cease to be in force.

Power to request authorisation

30 (1) This paragraph applies if –

(a) a standard authorisation has been given in relation to the detention of the relevant person,

(b) that authorisation ("the existing authorisation") has not ceased to be in force,

(c) the requirement under paragraph 24 to make a request for a new standard authorisation does not apply, because of paragraph 29, and

(d) a review of the existing authorisation has been requested, or is being carried out, in accordance with Part 8.

(2) The managing authority may request a new standard authorisation which would be in force on or before the expiry of the existing authorisation; but only if it would also be in force immediately after that expiry.

(3) The expiry of the existing authorisation is the time when it is expected to cease to be in force.

(4) Further provision relating to cases where a request is made under this paragraph can be found in –

(a) paragraph 62 (effect of decision about request), and

(b) paragraph 124 (effect of request on Part 8 review).

Information included in request

31 A request for a standard authorisation must include the information (if any) required by regulations.

Records of requests

32 (1) The managing authority of a hospital or care home must keep a written record of –

(a) each request that they make for a standard authorisation, and

(b) the reasons for making each request.

(2) A supervisory body must keep a written record of each request for a standard authorisation that is made to them.

Relevant person must be assessed

33 (1) This paragraph applies if the supervisory body are requested to give a standard authorisation.

(2) The supervisory body must secure that all of these assessments are carried out in relation to the relevant person –

   (a)   an age assessment;
   (b)   a mental health assessment;
   (c)   a mental capacity assessment;
   (d)   a best interests assessment;
   (e)   an eligibility assessment;
   (f)   a no refusals assessment.

(3) The person who carries out any such assessment is referred to as the assessor.

(4) Regulations may be made about the period (or periods) within which assessors must carry out assessments.

(5) This paragraph is subject to paragraphs 49 and 133.

Age assessment

34 An age assessment is an assessment of whether the relevant person meets the age requirement.

Mental health assessment

35 A mental health assessment is an assessment of whether the relevant person meets the mental health requirement.

36 When carrying out a mental health assessment, the assessor must also –

   (a)   consider how (if at all) the relevant person's mental health is likely to be affected by his being a detained resident, and
   (b)   notify the best interests assessor of his conclusions.

Mental capacity assessment

37 A mental capacity assessment is an assessment of whether the relevant person meets the mental capacity requirement.

Best interests assessment

38 A best interests assessment is an assessment of whether the relevant person meets the best interests requirement.

39 (1) In carrying out a best interests assessment, the assessor must comply with the duties in sub-paragraphs (2) and (3).

(2) The assessor must consult the managing authority of the relevant hospital or care home.

(3) The assessor must have regard to all of the following –

   (a)   the conclusions which the mental health assessor has notified to the best interests assessor in accordance with paragraph 36(b);
   (b)   any relevant needs assessment;

(c)   any relevant care plan.

(4) A relevant needs assessment is an assessment of the relevant person's needs which –

    (a)   was carried out in connection with the relevant person being accommodated in the relevant hospital or care home, and

    (b)   was carried out by or on behalf of –
        (i)   the managing authority of the relevant hospital or care home, or
        (ii)   the supervisory body.

(5) A relevant care plan is a care plan which –

    (a)   sets out how the relevant person's needs are to be met whilst he is accommodated in the relevant hospital or care home, and

    (b)   was drawn up by or on behalf of –
        (i)   the managing authority of the relevant hospital or care home, or
        (ii)   the supervisory body.

(6) The managing authority must give the assessor a copy of –

    (a)   any relevant needs assessment carried out by them or on their behalf, or

    (b)   any relevant care plan drawn up by them or on their behalf.

(7) The supervisory body must give the assessor a copy of –

    (a)   any relevant needs assessment carried out by them or on their behalf, or

    (b)   any relevant care plan drawn up by them or on their behalf.

(8) The duties in sub-paragraphs (2) and (3) do not affect any other duty to consult or to take the views of others into account.

40 (1) This paragraph applies whatever conclusion the best interests assessment comes to.

(2) The assessor must state in the best interests assessment the name and address of every interested person whom he has consulted in carrying out the assessment.

41 Paragraphs 42 and 43 apply if the best interests assessment comes to the conclusion that the relevant person meets the best interests requirement.

42 (1) The assessor must state in the assessment the maximum authorisation period.

(2) The maximum authorisation period is the shorter of these periods –

    (a)   the period which, in the assessor's opinion, would be the appropriate maximum period for the relevant person to be a detained resident under the standard authorisation that has been requested;

    (b)   1 year, or such shorter period as may be prescribed in regulations.

(3) Regulations under sub-paragraph (2)(b) –

   (a)   need not provide for a shorter period to apply in relation to all standard authorisations;

   (b)   may provide for different periods to apply in relation to different kinds of standard authorisations.

(4) Before making regulations under sub-paragraph (2)(b) the Secretary of State must consult all of the following –

   (a)   each body required by regulations under paragraph 162 to monitor and report on the operation of this Schedule in relation to England;

   (b)   such other persons as the Secretary of State considers it appropriate to consult.

(5) Before making regulations under sub-paragraph (2)(b) the National Assembly for Wales must consult all of the following –

   (a)   each person or body directed under paragraph 163(2) to carry out any function of the Assembly of monitoring and reporting on the operation of this Schedule in relation to Wales;

   (b)   such other persons as the Assembly considers it appropriate to consult.

43 The assessor may include in the assessment recommendations about conditions to which the standard authorisation is, or is not, to be subject in accordance with paragraph 53.

44 (1) This paragraph applies if the best interests assessment comes to the conclusion that the relevant person does not meet the best interests requirement.

(2) If, on the basis of the information taken into account in carrying out the assessment, it appears to the assessor that there is an unauthorised deprivation of liberty, he must include a statement to that effect in the assessment.

(3) There is an unauthorised deprivation of liberty if the managing authority of the relevant hospital or care home are already depriving the relevant person of his liberty without authority of the kind mentioned in section 4A.

45 The duties with which the best interests assessor must comply are subject to the provision included in appointment regulations under Part 10 (in particular, provision made under paragraph 146).

Eligibility assessment

46 An eligibility assessment is an assessment of whether the relevant person meets the eligibility requirement.

47 (1) Regulations may –

   (a)   require an eligibility assessor to request a best interests assessor to provide relevant eligibility information, and

   (b)   require the best interests assessor, if such a request is made, to provide such relevant eligibility information as he may have.

(2) In this paragraph –

"best interests assessor" means any person who is carrying out, or has carried out, a best interests assessment in relation to the relevant person;

"eligibility assessor" means a person carrying out an eligibility assessment in relation to the relevant person;

"relevant eligibility information" is information relevant to assessing whether or not the relevant person is ineligible by virtue of paragraph 5 of Schedule 1A.

No refusals assessment

48 A no refusals assessment is an assessment of whether the relevant person meets the no refusals requirement.

Equivalent assessment already carried out

49 (1) The supervisory body are not required by paragraph 33 to secure that a particular kind of assessment ("the required assessment") is carried out in relation to the relevant person if the following conditions are met.

(2) The first condition is that the supervisory body have a written copy of an assessment of the relevant person ("the existing assessment") that has already been carried out.

(3) The second condition is that the existing assessment complies with all requirements under this Schedule with which the required assessment would have to comply (if it were carried out).

(4) The third condition is that the existing assessment was carried out within the previous 12 months; but this condition need not be met if the required assessment is an age assessment.

(5) The fourth condition is that the supervisory body are satisfied that there is no reason why the existing assessment may no longer be accurate.

(6) If the required assessment is a best interests assessment, in satisfying themselves as mentioned in sub-paragraph (5), the supervisory body must take into account any information given, or submissions made, by –

(a)   the relevant person's representative,
(b)   any section 39C IMCA, or
(c)   any section 39D IMCA.

(7) It does not matter whether the existing assessment was carried out in connection with a request for a standard authorisation or for some other purpose.

(8) If, because of this paragraph, the supervisory body are not required by paragraph 33 to secure that the required assessment is carried out, the existing assessment is to be treated for the purposes of this Schedule –

(a)   as an assessment of the same kind as the required assessment, and

(b) as having been carried out under paragraph 33 in connection with the request for the standard authorisation.

Duty to give authorisation

50 (1) The supervisory body must give a standard authorisation if –

(a) all assessments are positive, and
(b) the supervisory body have written copies of all those assessments.

(2) The supervisory body must not give a standard authorisation except in accordance with sub-paragraph (1).

(3) All assessments are positive if each assessment carried out under paragraph 33 has come to the conclusion that the relevant person meets the qualifying requirement to which the assessment relates.

Terms of authorisation

51 (1) If the supervisory body are required to give a standard authorisation, they must decide the period during which the authorisation is to be in force.

(2) That period must not exceed the maximum authorisation period stated in the best interests assessment.

52 A standard authorisation may provide for the authorisation to come into force at a time after it is given.

53 (1) A standard authorisation may be given subject to conditions.

(2) Before deciding whether to give the authorisation subject to conditions, the supervisory body must have regard to any recommendations in the best interests assessment about such conditions.

(3) The managing authority of the relevant hospital or care home must ensure that any conditions are complied with.

Form of authorisation

54 A standard authorisation must be in writing.

55 (1) A standard authorisation must state the following things –

(a) the name of the relevant person;
(b) the name of the relevant hospital or care home;
(c) the period during which the authorisation is to be in force;
(d) the purpose for which the authorisation is given;
(e) any conditions subject to which the authorisation is given;
(f) the reason why each qualifying requirement is met.

(2) The statement of the reason why the eligibility requirement is met must be framed by reference to the cases in the table in paragraph 2 of Schedule 1A.

56 (1) If the name of the relevant hospital or care home changes, the standard authorisation is to be read as if it stated the current name of the hospital or care home.

(2) But sub-paragraph (1) is subject to any provision relating to the change of name which is made in any enactment or in any instrument made under an enactment.

Duty to give information about decision

57 (1) This paragraph applies if –

(a)   a request is made for a standard authorisation, and
(b)   the supervisory body are required by paragraph 50(1) to give the standard authorisation.

(2) The supervisory body must give a copy of the authorisation to each of the following –

(a)   the relevant person's representative;
(b)   the managing authority of the relevant hospital or care home;
(c)   the relevant person;
(d)   any section 39A IMCA;
(e)   every interested person consulted by the best interests assessor.

(3) The supervisory body must comply with this paragraph as soon as practicable after they give the standard authorisation.

58 (1) This paragraph applies if –

(a)   a request is made for a standard authorisation, and
(b)   the supervisory body are prohibited by paragraph 50(2) from giving the standard authorisation.

(2) The supervisory body must give notice, stating that they are prohibited from giving the authorisation, to each of the following –

(a)   the managing authority of the relevant hospital or care home;
(b)   the relevant person;
(c)   any section 39A IMCA;
(d)   every interested person consulted by the best interests assessor.

(3) The supervisory body must comply with this paragraph as soon as practicable after it becomes apparent to them that they are prohibited from giving the authorisation.

Duty to give information about effect of authorisation

59 (1) This paragraph applies if a standard authorisation is given.

(2) The managing authority of the relevant hospital or care home must take such steps as are practicable to ensure that the relevant person understands all of the following –

(a)   the effect of the authorisation;
(b)   the right to make an application to the court to exercise its jurisdiction under section 21A;
(c)   the right under Part 8 to request a review;
(d)   the right to have a section 39D IMCA appointed;

(e) how to have a section 39D IMCA appointed.

(3) Those steps must be taken as soon as is practicable after the authorisation is given.

(4) Those steps must include the giving of appropriate information both orally and in writing.

(5) Any written information given to the relevant person must also be given by the managing authority to the relevant person's representative.

(6) They must give the information to the representative as soon as is practicable after it is given to the relevant person.

(7) Sub-paragraph (8) applies if the managing authority is notified that a section 39D IMCA has been appointed.

(8) As soon as is practicable after being notified, the managing authority must give the section 39D IMCA a copy of the written information given in accordance with sub-paragraph (4).

Records of authorisations

60 A supervisory body must keep a written record of all of the following information −

(a) the standard authorisations that they have given;
(b) the requests for standard authorisations in response to which they have not given an authorisation;
(c) in relation to each standard authorisation given: the matters stated in the authorisation in accordance with paragraph 55.

Variation of an authorisation

61 (1) A standard authorisation may not be varied except in accordance with Part 7 or 8.

(2) This paragraph does not affect the powers of the Court of Protection or of any other court.

Effect of decision about request made under paragraph 25 or 30

62 (1) This paragraph applies where the managing authority request a new standard authorisation under either of the following −

(a) paragraph 25 (change in place of detention);
(b) paragraph 30 (existing authorisation subject to review).

(2) If the supervisory body are required by paragraph 50(1) to give the new authorisation, the existing authorisation terminates at the time when the new authorisation comes into force.

(3) If the supervisory body are prohibited by paragraph 50(2) from giving the new authorisation, there is no effect on the existing authorisation's continuation in force.

When an authorisation is in force

63 (1) A standard authorisation comes into force when it is given.

(2) But if the authorisation provides for it to come into force at a later time, it comes into force at that time.

64 (1) A standard authorisation ceases to be in force at the end of the period stated in the authorisation in accordance with paragraph 55(1)(c).

(2) But if the authorisation terminates before then in accordance with paragraph 62(2) or any other provision of this Schedule, it ceases to be in force when the termination takes effect.

(3) This paragraph does not affect the powers of the Court of Protection or of any other court.

65 (1) This paragraph applies if a standard authorisation ceases to be in force.

(2) The supervisory body must give notice that the authorisation has ceased to be in force.

(3) The supervisory body must give that notice to all of the following –

    (a)   the managing authority of the relevant hospital or care home;
    (b)   the relevant person;
    (c)   the relevant person's representative;
    (d)   every interested person consulted by the best interests assessor.

(4) The supervisory body must give that notice as soon as practicable after the authorisation ceases to be in force.

When a request for a standard authorisation is "disposed of"

66 A request for a standard authorisation is to be regarded for the purposes of this Schedule as disposed of if the supervisory body have given –

    (a)   a copy of the authorisation in accordance with paragraph 57, or
    (b)   notice in accordance with paragraph 58.

Right of third party to require consideration of whether authorisation needed

67 For the purposes of paragraphs 68 to 73 there is an unauthorised deprivation of liberty if –

    (a)   a person is already a detained resident in a hospital or care home, and
    (b)   the detention of the person is not authorised as mentioned in section 4A.

68 (1) If the following conditions are met, an eligible person may request the supervisory body to decide whether or not there is an unauthorised deprivation of liberty.

(2) The first condition is that the eligible person has notified the managing authority of the relevant hospital or care home that it appears to the eligible person that there is an unauthorised deprivation of liberty.

(3) The second condition is that the eligible person has asked the managing authority to request a standard authorisation in relation to the detention of the relevant person.

(4) The third condition is that the managing authority has not requested a standard authorisation within a reasonable period after the eligible person asks it to do so.

(5) In this paragraph "eligible person" means any person other than the managing authority of the relevant hospital or care home.

69 (1) This paragraph applies if an eligible person requests the supervisory body to decide whether or not there is an unauthorised deprivation of liberty.

(2) The supervisory body must select and appoint a person to carry out an assessment of whether or not the relevant person is a detained resident.

(3) But the supervisory body need not select and appoint a person to carry out such an assessment in either of these cases.

(4) The first case is where it appears to the supervisory body that the request by the eligible person is frivolous or vexatious.

(5) The second case is where it appears to the supervisory body that –

(a) the question of whether or not there is an unauthorised deprivation of liberty has already been decided, and
(b) since that decision, there has been no change of circumstances which would merit the question being decided again.

(6) The supervisory body must not select and appoint a person to carry out an assessment under this paragraph unless it appears to the supervisory body that the person would be –

(a) suitable to carry out a best interests assessment (if one were obtained in connection with a request for a standard authorisation relating to the relevant person), and
(b) eligible to carry out such a best interests assessment.

(7) The supervisory body must notify the persons specified in sub-paragraph (8) –

(a) that the supervisory body have been requested to decide whether or not there is an unauthorised deprivation of liberty;
(b) of their decision whether or not to select and appoint a person to carry out an assessment under this paragraph;
(c) if their decision is to select and appoint a person, of the person appointed.

(8) The persons referred to in sub-paragraph (7) are –

(a) the eligible person who made the request under paragraph 68;
(b) the person to whom the request relates;
(c) the managing authority of the relevant hospital or care home;
(d) any section 39A IMCA.

70 (1) Regulations may be made about the period within which an assessment under paragraph 69 must be carried out.

(2) Regulations made under paragraph 129(3) apply in relation to the selection and appointment of a person under paragraph 69 as they apply to the selection of a person under paragraph 129 to carry out a best interests assessment.

(3) The following provisions apply to an assessment under paragraph 69 as they apply to an assessment carried out in connection with a request for a standard authorisation –

    (a)   paragraph 131 (examination and copying of records);
    (b)   paragraph 132 (representations);
    (c)   paragraphs 134 and 135(1) and (2) (duty to keep records and give copies).

(4) The copies of the assessment which the supervisory body are required to give under paragraph 135(2) must be given as soon as practicable after the supervisory body are themselves given a copy of the assessment.

71 (1) This paragraph applies if –

    (a)   the supervisory body obtain an assessment under paragraph 69,
    (b)   the assessment comes to the conclusion that the relevant person is a detained resident, and
    (c)   it appears to the supervisory body that the detention of the person is not authorised as mentioned in section 4A.

(2) This Schedule (including Part 5) applies as if the managing authority of the relevant hospital or care home had, in accordance with Part 4, requested the supervisory body to give a standard authorisation in relation to the relevant person.

(3) The managing authority of the relevant hospital or care home must supply the supervisory body with the information (if any) which the managing authority would, by virtue of paragraph 31, have had to include in a request for a standard authorisation.

(4) The supervisory body must notify the persons specified in paragraph 69(8) –

    (a)   of the outcome of the assessment obtained under paragraph 69, and
    (b)   that this Schedule applies as mentioned in sub-paragraph (2).

72 (1) This paragraph applies if –

    (a)   the supervisory body obtain an assessment under paragraph 69, and
    (b)   the assessment comes to the conclusion that the relevant person is not a detained resident.

(2) The supervisory body must notify the persons specified in paragraph 69(8) of the outcome of the assessment.

73 (1) This paragraph applies if –

    (a)   the supervisory body obtain an assessment under paragraph 69,

(b)   the assessment comes to the conclusion that the relevant person is a detained resident, and

(c)   it appears to the supervisory body that the detention of the person is authorised as mentioned in section 4A.

(2) The supervisory body must notify the persons specified in paragraph 69(8) –

(a)   of the outcome of the assessment, and

(b)   that it appears to the supervisory body that the detention is authorised.

PART 5
URGENT AUTHORISATIONS

Managing authority to give authorisation

74 Only the managing authority of the relevant hospital or care home may give an urgent authorisation.

75 The managing authority may give an urgent authorisation only if they are required to do so by paragraph 76 (as read with paragraph 77).

Duty to give authorisation

76 (1) The managing authority must give an urgent authorisation in either of the following cases.

(2) The first case is where –

(a)   the managing authority are required to make a request under paragraph 24 or 25 for a standard authorisation, and

(b)   they believe that the need for the relevant person to be a detained resident is so urgent that it is appropriate for the detention to begin before they make the request.

(3) The second case is where –

(a)   the managing authority have made a request under paragraph 24 or 25 for a standard authorisation, and

(b)   they believe that the need for the relevant person to be a detained resident is so urgent that it is appropriate for the detention to begin before the request is disposed of.

(4) References in this paragraph to the detention of the relevant person are references to the detention to which paragraph 24 or 25 relates.

(5) This paragraph is subject to paragraph 77.

77 (1) This paragraph applies where the managing authority have given an urgent authorisation ("the original authorisation") in connection with a case where a person is, or is to be, a detained resident ("the existing detention").

(2) No new urgent authorisation is to be given under paragraph 76 in connection with the existing detention.

(3) But the managing authority may request the supervisory body to extend the duration of the original authorisation.

(4) Only one request under sub-paragraph (3) may be made in relation to the original authorisation.

(5) Paragraphs 84 to 86 apply to any request made under sub-paragraph (3).

Terms of authorisation

78 (1) If the managing authority decide to give an urgent authorisation, they must decide the period during which the authorisation is to be in force.

(2) That period must not exceed 7 days.

Form of authorisation

79 An urgent authorisation must be in writing.

80 An urgent authorisation must state the following things –

    (a)   the name of the relevant person;
    (b)   the name of the relevant hospital or care home;
    (c)   the period during which the authorisation is to be in force;
    (d)   the purpose for which the authorisation is given.

81 (1) If the name of the relevant hospital or care home changes, the urgent authorisation is to be read as if it stated the current name of the hospital or care home.

(2) But sub-paragraph (1) is subject to any provision relating to the change of name which is made in any enactment or in any instrument made under an enactment.

Duty to keep records and give copies

82 (1) This paragraph applies if an urgent authorisation is given.

(2) The managing authority must keep a written record of why they have given the urgent authorisation.

(3) As soon as practicable after giving the authorisation, the managing authority must give a copy of the authorisation to all of the following –

    (a)   the relevant person;
    (b)   any section 39A IMCA.

Duty to give information about authorisation

83 (1) This paragraph applies if an urgent authorisation is given.

(2) The managing authority of the relevant hospital or care home must take such steps as are practicable to ensure that the relevant person understands all of the following –

    (a)   the effect of the authorisation;

(b)   the right to make an application to the court to exercise its jurisdiction under section 21A.

(3) Those steps must be taken as soon as is practicable after the authorisation is given.

(4) Those steps must include the giving of appropriate information both orally and in writing.

Request for extension of duration

84 (1) This paragraph applies if the managing authority make a request under paragraph 77 for the supervisory body to extend the duration of the original authorisation.

(2) The managing authority must keep a written record of why they have made the request.

(3) The managing authority must give the relevant person notice that they have made the request.

(4) The supervisory body may extend the duration of the original authorisation if it appears to them that –

(a)   the managing authority have made the required request for a standard authorisation,

(b)   there are exceptional reasons why it has not yet been possible for that request to be disposed of, and

(c)   it is essential for the existing detention to continue until the request is disposed of.

(5) The supervisory body must keep a written record that the request has been made to them.

(6) In this paragraph and paragraphs 85 and 86 –

(a)   "original authorisation" and "existing detention" have the same meaning as in paragraph 77;

(b)   the required request for a standard authorisation is the request that is referred to in paragraph 76(2) or (3).

85 (1) This paragraph applies if, under paragraph 84, the supervisory body decide to extend the duration of the original authorisation.

(2) The supervisory body must decide the period of the extension.

(3) That period must not exceed 7 days.

(4) The supervisory body must give the managing authority notice stating the period of the extension.

(5) The managing authority must then vary the original authorisation so that it states the extended duration.

(6) Paragraphs 82(3) and 83 apply (with the necessary modifications) to the variation of the original authorisation as they apply to the giving of an urgent authorisation.

(7) The supervisory body must keep a written record of –

(a)   the outcome of the request, and
(b)   the period of the extension.

86 (1) This paragraph applies if, under paragraph 84, the supervisory body decide not to extend the duration of the original authorisation.

(2) The supervisory body must give the managing authority notice stating –

(a)   the decision, and
(b)   their reasons for making it.

(3) The managing authority must give a copy of that notice to all of the following –

(a)   the relevant person;
(b)   any section 39A IMCA.

(4) The supervisory body must keep a written record of the outcome of the request.

No variation

87 (1) An urgent authorisation may not be varied except in accordance with paragraph 85.

(2) This paragraph does not affect the powers of the Court of Protection or of any other court.

When an authorisation is in force

88 An urgent authorisation comes into force when it is given.

89 (1) An urgent authorisation ceases to be in force at the end of the period stated in the authorisation in accordance with paragraph 80(c) (subject to any variation in accordance with paragraph 85).

(2) But if the required request is disposed of before the end of that period, the urgent authorisation ceases to be in force as follows.

(3) If the supervisory body are required by paragraph 50(1) to give the requested authorisation, the urgent authorisation ceases to be in force when the requested authorisation comes into force.

(4) If the supervisory body are prohibited by paragraph 50(2) from giving the requested authorisation, the urgent authorisation ceases to be in force when the managing authority receive notice under paragraph 58.

(5) In this paragraph –

"required request" means the request referred to in paragraph 76(2) or (3);

"requested authorisation" means the standard authorisation to which the required request relates.

(6) This paragraph does not affect the powers of the Court of Protection or of any other court.

90 (1) This paragraph applies if an urgent authorisation ceases to be in force.

(2) The supervisory body must give notice that the authorisation has ceased to be in force.

(3) The supervisory body must give that notice to all of the following –

    (a)   the relevant person;
    (b)   any section 39A IMCA.

(4) The supervisory body must give that notice as soon as practicable after the authorisation ceases to be in force.

PART 6
ELIGIBILITY REQUIREMENT NOT MET: SUSPENSION OF STANDARD AUTHORISATION

91 (1) This Part applies if the following conditions are met.

(2) The first condition is that a standard authorisation –

    (a)   has been given, and
    (b)   has not ceased to be in force.

(3) The second condition is that the managing authority of the relevant hospital or care home are satisfied that the relevant person has ceased to meet the eligibility requirement.

(4) But this Part does not apply if the relevant person is ineligible by virtue of paragraph 5 of Schedule 1A (in which case see Part 8).

92 The managing authority of the relevant hospital or care home must give the supervisory body notice that the relevant person has ceased to meet the eligibility requirement.

93 (1) This paragraph applies if the managing authority give the supervisory body notice under paragraph 92.

(2) The standard authorisation is suspended from the time when the notice is given.

(3) The supervisory body must give notice that the standard authorisation has been suspended to the following persons –

    (a)   the relevant person;
    (b)   the relevant person's representative;
    (c)   the managing authority of the relevant hospital or care home.

94 (1) This paragraph applies if, whilst the standard authorisation is suspended, the managing authority are satisfied that the relevant person meets the eligibility requirement again.

(2) The managing authority must give the supervisory body notice that the relevant person meets the eligibility requirement again.

95 (1) This paragraph applies if the managing authority give the supervisory body notice under paragraph 94.

(2) The standard authorisation ceases to be suspended from the time when the notice is given.

(3) The supervisory body must give notice that the standard authorisation has ceased to be suspended to the following persons –

- (a)   the relevant person;
- (b)   the relevant person's representative;
- (c)   any section 39D IMCA;
- (d)   the managing authority of the relevant hospital or care home.

(4) The supervisory body must give notice under this paragraph as soon as practicable after they are given notice under paragraph 94.

96 (1) This paragraph applies if no notice is given under paragraph 94 before the end of the relevant 28 day period.

(2) The standard authorisation ceases to have effect at the end of the relevant 28 day period.

(3) The relevant 28 day period is the period of 28 days beginning with the day on which the standard authorisation is suspended under paragraph 93.

97 The effect of suspending the standard authorisation is that Part 1 ceases to apply for as long as the authorisation is suspended.

PART 7
STANDARD AUTHORISATIONS: CHANGE IN SUPERVISORY RESPONSIBILITY

Application of this Part

98 (1) This Part applies if these conditions are met.

(2) The first condition is that a standard authorisation –

- (a)   has been given, and
- (b)   has not ceased to be in force.

(3) The second condition is that there is a change in supervisory responsibility.

(4) The third condition is that there is not a change in the place of detention (within the meaning of paragraph 25).

99 For the purposes of this Part there is a change in supervisory responsibility if –

- (a)   one body ("the old supervisory body") have ceased to be supervisory body in relation to the standard authorisation, and
- (b)   a different body ("the new supervisory body") have become supervisory body in relation to the standard authorisation.

Effect of change in supervisory responsibility

100 (1) The new supervisory body becomes the supervisory body in relation to the authorisation.

(2) Anything done by or in relation to the old supervisory body in connection with the authorisation has effect, so far as is necessary for continuing its effect after the change, as if done by or in relation to the new supervisory body.

(3) Anything which relates to the authorisation and which is in the process of being done by or in relation to the old supervisory body at the time of the change may be continued by or in relation to the new supervisory body.

(4) But –

    (a)   the old supervisory body do not, by virtue of this paragraph, cease to be liable for anything done by them in connection with the authorisation before the change; and

    (b)   the new supervisory body do not, by virtue of this paragraph, become liable for any such thing.

PART 8
STANDARD AUTHORISATIONS: REVIEW

Application of this Part

101 (1) This Part applies if a standard authorisation –

    (a)   has been given, and
    (b)   has not ceased to be in force.

(2) Paragraphs 102 to 122 are subject to paragraphs 123 to 125.

Review by supervisory body

102 (1) The supervisory body may at any time carry out a review of the standard authorisation in accordance with this Part.

(2) The supervisory body must carry out such a review if they are requested to do so by an eligible person.

(3) Each of the following is an eligible person –

    (a)   the relevant person;
    (b)   the relevant person's representative;
    (c)   the managing authority of the relevant hospital or care home.

Request for review

103 (1) An eligible person may, at any time, request the supervisory body to carry out a review of the standard authorisation in accordance with this Part.

(2) The managing authority of the relevant hospital or care home must make such a request if one or more of the qualifying requirements appear to them to be reviewable.

Grounds for review

104 (1) Paragraphs 105 to 107 set out the grounds on which the qualifying requirements are reviewable.

(2) A qualifying requirement is not reviewable on any other ground.

Non-qualification ground

105 (1) Any of the following qualifying requirements is reviewable on the ground that the relevant person does not meet the requirement –

    (a)   the age requirement;
    (b)   the mental health requirement;
    (c)   the mental capacity requirement;
    (d)   the best interests requirement;
    (e)   the no refusals requirement.

(2) The eligibility requirement is reviewable on the ground that the relevant person is ineligible by virtue of paragraph 5 of Schedule 1A.

(3) The ground in sub-paragraph (1) and the ground in sub-paragraph (2) are referred to as the non-qualification ground.

Change of reason ground

106 (1) Any of the following qualifying requirements is reviewable on the ground set out in sub-paragraph (2) –

    (a)   the mental health requirement;
    (b)   the mental capacity requirement;
    (c)   the best interests requirement;
    (d)   the eligibility requirement;
    (e)   the no refusals requirement.

(2) The ground is that the reason why the relevant person meets the requirement is not the reason stated in the standard authorisation.

(3) This ground is referred to as the change of reason ground.

Variation of conditions ground

107 (1) The best interests requirement is reviewable on the ground that –

    (a)   there has been a change in the relevant person's case, and
    (b)   because of that change, it would be appropriate to vary the conditions to which the standard authorisation is subject.

(2) This ground is referred to as the variation of conditions ground.

(3) A reference to varying the conditions to which the standard authorisation is subject is a reference to –

    (a)   amendment of an existing condition,
    (b)   omission of an existing condition, or

(c) inclusion of a new condition (whether or not there are already any existing conditions).

Notice that review to be carried out

108 (1) If the supervisory body are to carry out a review of the standard authorisation, they must give notice of the review to the following persons –

(a) the relevant person;
(b) the relevant person's representative;
(c) the managing authority of the relevant hospital or care home.

(2) The supervisory body must give the notice –

(a) before they begin the review, or
(b) if that is not practicable, as soon as practicable after they have begun it.

(3) This paragraph does not require the supervisory body to give notice to any person who has requested the review.

Starting a review

109 To start a review of the standard authorisation, the supervisory body must decide which, if any, of the qualifying requirements appear to be reviewable.

No reviewable qualifying requirements

110 (1) This paragraph applies if no qualifying requirements appear to be reviewable.

(2) This Part does not require the supervisory body to take any action in respect of the standard authorisation.

One or more reviewable qualifying requirements

111 (1) This paragraph applies if one or more qualifying requirements appear to be reviewable.

(2) The supervisory body must secure that a separate review assessment is carried out in relation to each qualifying requirement which appears to be reviewable.

(3) But sub-paragraph (2) does not require the supervisory body to secure that a best interests review assessment is carried out in a case where the best interests requirement appears to the supervisory body to be non-assessable.

(4) The best interests requirement is non-assessable if –

(a) the requirement is reviewable only on the variation of conditions ground, and
(b) the change in the relevant person's case is not significant.

(5) In making any decision whether the change in the relevant person's case is significant, regard must be had to –

(a) the nature of the change, and

(b)   the period that the change is likely to last for.

Review assessments

112 (1) A review assessment is an assessment of whether the relevant person meets a qualifying requirement.

(2) In relation to a review assessment –

(a)   a negative conclusion is a conclusion that the relevant person does not meet the qualifying requirement to which the assessment relates;

(b)   a positive conclusion is a conclusion that the relevant person meets the qualifying requirement to which the assessment relates.

(3) An age review assessment is a review assessment carried out in relation to the age requirement.

(4) A mental health review assessment is a review assessment carried out in relation to the mental health requirement.

(5) A mental capacity review assessment is a review assessment carried out in relation to the mental capacity requirement.

(6) A best interests review assessment is a review assessment carried out in relation to the best interests requirement.

(7) An eligibility review assessment is a review assessment carried out in relation to the eligibility requirement.

(8) A no refusals review assessment is a review assessment carried out in relation to the no refusals requirement.

113 (1) In carrying out a review assessment, the assessor must comply with any duties which would be imposed upon him under Part 4 if the assessment were being carried out in connection with a request for a standard authorisation.

(2) But in the case of a best interests review assessment, paragraphs 43 and 44 do not apply.

(3) Instead of what is required by paragraph 43, the best interests review assessment must include recommendations about whether – and, if so, how – it would be appropriate to vary the conditions to which the standard authorisation is subject.

Best interests requirement reviewable but non-assessable

114 (1) This paragraph applies in a case where –

(a)   the best interests requirement appears to be reviewable, but

(b)   in accordance with paragraph 111(3), the supervisory body are not required to secure that a best interests review assessment is carried out.

(2) The supervisory body may vary the conditions to which the standard authorisation is subject in such ways (if any) as the supervisory body think are appropriate in the circumstances.

Best interests review assessment positive

115 (1) This paragraph applies in a case where –

(a)   a best interests review assessment is carried out, and
(b)   the assessment comes to a positive conclusion.

(2) The supervisory body must decide the following questions –

(a)   whether or not the best interests requirement is reviewable on the change of reason ground;
(b)   whether or not the best interests requirement is reviewable on the variation of conditions ground;
(c)   if so, whether or not the change in the person's case is significant.

(3) If the supervisory body decide that the best interests requirement is reviewable on the change of reason ground, they must vary the standard authorisation so that it states the reason why the relevant person now meets that requirement.

(4) If the supervisory body decide that –

(a)   the best interests requirement is reviewable on the variation of conditions ground, and
(b)   the change in the relevant person's case is not significant,

they may vary the conditions to which the standard authorisation is subject in such ways (if any) as they think are appropriate in the circumstances.

(5) If the supervisory body decide that –

(a)   the best interests requirement is reviewable on the variation of conditions ground, and
(b)   the change in the relevant person's case is significant,

they must vary the conditions to which the standard authorisation is subject in such ways as they think are appropriate in the circumstances.

(6) If the supervisory body decide that the best interests requirement is not reviewable on –

(a)   the change of reason ground, or
(b)   the variation of conditions ground,

this Part does not require the supervisory body to take any action in respect of the standard authorisation so far as the best interests requirement relates to it.

Mental health, mental capacity, eligibility or no refusals review assessment positive

116 (1) This paragraph applies if the following conditions are met.

(2) The first condition is that one or more of the following are carried out –

(a)   a mental health review assessment;
(b)   a mental capacity review assessment;
(c)   an eligibility review assessment;

(d) a no refusals review assessment.

(3) The second condition is that each assessment carried out comes to a positive conclusion.

(4) The supervisory body must decide whether or not each of the assessed qualifying requirements is reviewable on the change of reason ground.

(5) If the supervisory body decide that any of the assessed qualifying requirements is reviewable on the change of reason ground, they must vary the standard authorisation so that it states the reason why the relevant person now meets the requirement or requirements in question.

(6) If the supervisory body decide that none of the assessed qualifying requirements are reviewable on the change of reason ground, this Part does not require the supervisory body to take any action in respect of the standard authorisation so far as those requirements relate to it.

(7) An assessed qualifying requirement is a qualifying requirement in relation to which a review assessment is carried out.

One or more review assessments negative

117 (1) This paragraph applies if one or more of the review assessments carried out comes to a negative conclusion.

(2) The supervisory body must terminate the standard authorisation with immediate effect.

Completion of a review

118 (1) The review of the standard authorisation is complete in any of the following cases.

(2) The first case is where paragraph 110 applies.

(3) The second case is where –

    (a) paragraph 111 applies, and
    (b) paragraph 117 requires the supervisory body to terminate the standard authorisation.

(4) In such a case, the supervisory body need not comply with any of the other provisions of paragraphs 114 to 116 which would be applicable to the review (were it not for this sub-paragraph).

(5) The third case is where –

    (a) paragraph 111 applies,
    (b) paragraph 117 does not require the supervisory body to terminate the standard authorisation, and
    (c) the supervisory body comply with all of the provisions of paragraphs 114 to 116 (so far as they are applicable to the review).

Variations under this Part

119 Any variation of the standard authorisation made under this Part must be in writing.

Notice of outcome of review

120 (1) When the review of the standard authorisation is complete, the supervisory body must give notice to all of the following –

(a)   the managing authority of the relevant hospital or care home;
(b)   the relevant person;
(c)   the relevant person's representative;
(d)   any section 39D IMCA.

(2) That notice must state –

(a)   the outcome of the review, and
(b)   what variation (if any) has been made to the authorisation under this Part.

Records

121 A supervisory body must keep a written record of the following information –

(a)   each request for a review that is made to them;
(b)   the outcome of each request;
(c)   each review which they carry out;
(d)   the outcome of each review which they carry out;
(e)   any variation of an authorisation made in consequence of a review.

Relationship between review and suspension under Part 6

122 (1) This paragraph applies if a standard authorisation is suspended in accordance with Part 6.

(2) No review may be requested under this Part whilst the standard authorisation is suspended.

(3) If a review has already been requested, or is being carried out, when the standard authorisation is suspended, no steps are to be taken in connection with that review whilst the authorisation is suspended.

Relationship between review and request for new authorisation

123 (1) This paragraph applies if, in accordance with paragraph 24 (as read with paragraph 29), the managing authority of the relevant hospital or care home make a request for a new standard authorisation which would be in force after the expiry of the existing authorisation.

(2) No review may be requested under this Part until the request for the new standard authorisation has been disposed of.

(3) If a review has already been requested, or is being carried out, when the new standard authorisation is requested, no steps are to be taken in connection with that review until the request for the new standard authorisation has been disposed of.

124 (1) This paragraph applies if –

(a)   a review under this Part has been requested, or is being carried out, and
(b)   the managing authority of the relevant hospital or care home make a request under paragraph 30 for a new standard authorisation which would be in force on or before, and after, the expiry of the existing authorisation.

(2) No steps are to be taken in connection with the review under this Part until the request for the new standard authorisation has been disposed of.

125 In paragraphs 123 and 124 –

(a)   the existing authorisation is the authorisation referred to in paragraph 101;
(b)   the expiry of the existing authorisation is the time when it is expected to cease to be in force.

PART 9
ASSESSMENTS UNDER THIS SCHEDULE

Introduction

126 This Part contains provision about assessments under this Schedule.

127 An assessment under this Schedule is either of the following –

(a)   an assessment carried out in connection with a request for a standard authorisation under Part 4;
(b)   a review assessment carried out in connection with a review of a standard authorisation under Part 8.

128 In this Part, in relation to an assessment under this Schedule –

"assessor" means the person carrying out the assessment;
"relevant procedure" means –
(a)   the request for the standard authorisation, or
(b)   the review of the standard authorisation;

"supervisory body" means the supervisory body responsible for securing that the assessment is carried out.

Supervisory body to select assessor

129 (1) It is for the supervisory body to select a person to carry out an assessment under this Schedule.

(2) The supervisory body must not select a person to carry out an assessment unless the person –

(a) appears to the supervisory body to be suitable to carry out the assessment (having regard, in particular, to the type of assessment and the person to be assessed), and

(b) is eligible to carry out the assessment.

(3) Regulations may make provision about the selection, and eligibility, of persons to carry out assessments under this Schedule.

(4) Sub-paragraphs (5) and (6) apply if two or more assessments are to be obtained for the purposes of the relevant procedure.

(5) In a case where the assessments to be obtained include a mental health assessment and a best interests assessment, the supervisory body must not select the same person to carry out both assessments.

(6) Except as prohibited by sub-paragraph (5), the supervisory body may select the same person to carry out any number of the assessments which the person appears to be suitable, and is eligible, to carry out.

130 (1) This paragraph applies to regulations under paragraph 129(3).

(2) The regulations may make provision relating to a person's –

(a) qualifications,

(b) skills,

(c) training,

(d) experience,

(e) relationship to, or connection with, the relevant person or any other person,

(f) involvement in the care or treatment of the relevant person,

(g) connection with the supervisory body, or

(h) connection with the relevant hospital or care home, or with any other establishment or undertaking.

(3) The provision that the regulations may make in relation to a person's training may provide for particular training to be specified by the appropriate authority otherwise than in the regulations.

(4) In sub-paragraph (3) the "appropriate authority" means –

(a) in relation to England: the Secretary of State;

(b) in relation to Wales: the National Assembly for Wales.

(5) The regulations may make provision requiring a person to be insured in respect of liabilities that may arise in connection with the carrying out of an assessment.

(6) In relation to cases where two or more assessments are to be obtained for the purposes of the relevant procedure, the regulations may limit the number, kind or combination of assessments which a particular person is eligible to carry out.

(7) Sub-paragraphs (2) to (6) do not limit the generality of the provision that may be made in the regulations.

Examination and copying of records

131 An assessor may, at all reasonable times, examine and take copies of –

(a)   any health record,

(b)   any record of, or held by, a local authority and compiled in accordance with a social services function, and

(c)   any record held by a person registered under Part 2 of the Care Standards Act 2000 or Chapter 2 of Part 1 of the Health and Social Care Act 2008,

which the assessor considers may be relevant to the assessment which is being carried out.

Representations

132 In carrying out an assessment under this Schedule, the assessor must take into account any information given, or submissions made, by any of the following –

(a)   the relevant person's representative;

(b)   any section 39A IMCA;

(c)   any section 39C IMCA;

(d)   any section 39D IMCA.

Assessments to stop if any comes to negative conclusion

133 (1) This paragraph applies if an assessment under this Schedule comes to the conclusion that the relevant person does not meet one of the qualifying requirements.

(2) This Schedule does not require the supervisory body to secure that any other assessments under this Schedule are carried out in relation to the relevant procedure.

(3) The supervisory body must give notice to any assessor who is carrying out another assessment in connection with the relevant procedure that they are to cease carrying out that assessment.

(4) If an assessor receives such notice, this Schedule does not require the assessor to continue carrying out that assessment.

Duty to keep records and give copies

134 (1) This paragraph applies if an assessor has carried out an assessment under this Schedule (whatever conclusions the assessment has come to).

(2) The assessor must keep a written record of the assessment.

(3) As soon as practicable after carrying out the assessment, the assessor must give copies of the assessment to the supervisory body.

135 (1) This paragraph applies to the supervisory body if they are given a copy of an assessment under this Schedule.

(2) The supervisory body must give copies of the assessment to all of the following –

    (a)   the managing authority of the relevant hospital or care home;
    (b)   the relevant person;
    (c)   any section 39A IMCA;
    (d)   the relevant person's representative.

(3) If –

    (a)   the assessment is obtained in relation to a request for a standard authorisation, and
    (b)   the supervisory body are required by paragraph 50(1) to give the standard authorisation,

the supervisory body must give the copies of the assessment when they give copies of the authorisation in accordance with paragraph 57.

(4) If –

    (a)   the assessment is obtained in relation to a request for a standard authorisation, and
    (b)   the supervisory body are prohibited by paragraph 50(2) from giving the standard authorisation,

the supervisory body must give the copies of the assessment when they give notice in accordance with paragraph 58.

(5) If the assessment is obtained in connection with the review of a standard authorisation, the supervisory body must give the copies of the assessment when they give notice in accordance with paragraph 120.

136 (1) This paragraph applies to the supervisory body if –

    (a)   they are given a copy of a best interests assessment, and
    (b)   the assessment includes, in accordance with paragraph 44(2), a statement that it appears to the assessor that there is an unauthorised deprivation of liberty.

(2) The supervisory body must notify all of the persons listed in sub-paragraph (3) that the assessment includes such a statement.

(3) Those persons are –

    (a)   the managing authority of the relevant hospital or care home;
    (b)   the relevant person;
    (c)   any section 39A IMCA;
    (d)   any interested person consulted by the best interests assessor.

(4) The supervisory body must comply with this paragraph when (or at some time before) they comply with paragraph 135.

PART 10
RELEVANT PERSON'S REPRESENTATIVE

The representative

137 In this Schedule the relevant person's representative is the person appointed as such in accordance with this Part.

138 (1) Regulations may make provision about the selection and appointment of representatives.

(2) In this Part such regulations are referred to as "appointment regulations".

Supervisory body to appoint representative

139 (1) The supervisory body must appoint a person to be the relevant person's representative as soon as practicable after a standard authorisation is given.

(2) The supervisory body must appoint a person to be the relevant person's representative if a vacancy arises whilst a standard authorisation is in force.

(3) Where a vacancy arises, the appointment under sub-paragraph (2) is to be made as soon as practicable after the supervisory body becomes aware of the vacancy.

140 (1) The selection of a person for appointment under paragraph 139 must not be made unless it appears to the person making the selection that the prospective representative would, if appointed –

    (a)   maintain contact with the relevant person,
    (b)   represent the relevant person in matters relating to or connected with this Schedule, and
    (c)   support the relevant person in matters relating to or connected with this Schedule.

141 (1) Any appointment of a representative for a relevant person is in addition to, and does not affect, any appointment of a donee or deputy.

(2) The functions of any representative are in addition to, and do not affect –

    (a)   the authority of any donee,
    (b)   the powers of any deputy, or
    (c)   any powers of the court.

Appointment regulations

142 Appointment regulations may provide that the procedure for appointing a representative may begin at any time after a request for a standard authorisation is made (including a time before the request has been disposed of).

143 (1) Appointment regulations may make provision about who is to select a person for appointment as a representative.

(2) But regulations under this paragraph may only provide for the following to make a selection –

(a)   the relevant person, if he has capacity in relation to the question of which person should be his representative;

(b)   a donee of a lasting power of attorney granted by the relevant person, if it is within the scope of his authority to select a person;

(c)   a deputy, if it is within the scope of his authority to select a person;

(d)   a best interests assessor;

(e)   the supervisory body.

(3) Regulations under this paragraph may provide that a selection by the relevant person, a donee or a deputy is subject to approval by a best interests assessor or the supervisory body.

(4) Regulations under this paragraph may provide that, if more than one selection is necessary in connection with the appointment of a particular representative –

(a)   the same person may make more than one selection;

(b)   different persons may make different selections.

(5) For the purposes of this paragraph a best interests assessor is a person carrying out a best interests assessment in connection with the standard authorisation in question (including the giving of that authorisation).

144 (1) Appointment regulations may make provision about who may, or may not, be –

(a)   selected for appointment as a representative, or

(b)   appointed as a representative.

(2) Regulations under this paragraph may relate to any of the following matters –

(a)   a person's age;

(b)   a person's suitability;

(c)   a person's independence;

(d)   a person's willingness;

(e)   a person's qualifications.

145 Appointment regulations may make provision about the formalities of appointing a person as a representative.

146 In a case where a best interests assessor is to select a person to be appointed as a representative, appointment regulations may provide for the variation of the assessor's duties in relation to the assessment which he is carrying out.

Monitoring of representatives

147 Regulations may make provision requiring the managing authority of the relevant hospital or care home to –

(a)   monitor, and

(b)   report to the supervisory body on,

the extent to which a representative is maintaining contact with the relevant person.

Termination

148 Regulations may make provision about the circumstances in which the appointment of a person as the relevant person's representative ends or may be ended.

149 Regulations may make provision about the formalities of ending the appointment of a person as a representative.

Suspension of representative's functions

150 (1) Regulations may make provision about the circumstances in which functions exercisable by, or in relation to, the relevant person's representative (whether under this Schedule or not) may be –

(a)   suspended, and
(b)   if suspended, revived.

(2) The regulations may make provision about the formalities for giving effect to the suspension or revival of a function.

(3) The regulations may make provision about the effect of the suspension or revival of a function.

Payment of representative

151 Regulations may make provision for payments to be made to, or in relation to, persons exercising functions as the relevant person's representative.

Regulations under this Part

152 The provisions of this Part which specify provision that may be made in regulations under this Part do not affect the generality of the power to make such regulations.

Effect of appointment of section 39C IMCA

153 Paragraphs 159 and 160 make provision about the exercise of functions by, or towards, the relevant person's representative during periods when –

(a)   no person is appointed as the relevant person's representative, but
(b)   a person is appointed as a section 39C IMCA.

PART 11
IMCAS

Application of Part

154 This Part applies for the purposes of this Schedule.

The IMCAs

155 A section 39A IMCA is an independent mental capacity advocate appointed under section 39A.

156 A section 39C IMCA is an independent mental capacity advocate appointed under section 39C.

157 A section 39D IMCA is an independent mental capacity advocate appointed under section 39D.

158 An IMCA is a section 39A IMCA or a section 39C IMCA or a section 39D IMCA.

Section 39C IMCA: functions

159 (1) This paragraph applies if, and for as long as, there is a section 39C IMCA.

(2) In the application of the relevant provisions, references to the relevant person's representative are to be read as references to the section 39C IMCA.

(3) But sub-paragraph (2) does not apply to any function under the relevant provisions for as long as the function is suspended in accordance with provision made under Part 10.

(4) In this paragraph and paragraph 160 the relevant provisions are –

    (a)   paragraph 102(3)(b) (request for review under Part 8);
    (b)   paragraph 108(1)(b) (notice of review under Part 8);
    (c)   paragraph 120(1)(c) (notice of outcome of review under Part 8).

160 (1) This paragraph applies if –

    (a)   a person is appointed as the relevant person's representative, and
    (b)   a person accordingly ceases to hold an appointment as a section 39C IMCA.

(2) Where a function under a relevant provision has been exercised by, or towards, the section 39C IMCA, there is no requirement for that function to be exercised again by, or towards, the relevant person's representative.

Section 39A IMCA: restriction of functions

161 (1) This paragraph applies if –

    (a)   there is a section 39A IMCA, and
    (b)   a person is appointed under Part 10 to be the relevant person's representative (whether or not that person, or any person subsequently appointed, is currently the relevant person's representative).
    (2)   The duties imposed on, and the powers exercisable by, the section 39A IMCA do not apply.
    (3)   The duties imposed on, and the powers exercisable by, any other person do not apply, so far as they fall to be performed or exercised towards the section 39A IMCA.
    (4)   But sub-paragraph (2) does not apply to any power of challenge exercisable by the section 39A IMCA.

(5)   And sub-paragraph (3) does not apply to any duty or power of any other person so far as it relates to any power of challenge exercisable by the section 39A IMCA.

(6)   Before exercising any power of challenge, the section 39A IMCA must take the views of the relevant person's representative into account.

(7)   A power of challenge is a power to make an application to the court to exercise its jurisdiction under section 21A in connection with the giving of the standard authorisation.

PART 12
MISCELLANEOUS

Monitoring of operation of Schedule

162 (1) Regulations may make provision for, and in connection with, requiring one or more prescribed bodies to monitor, and report on, the operation of this Schedule in relation to England.

(2) The regulations may, in particular, give a prescribed body authority to do one or more of the following things –

(a)   to visit hospitals and care homes;

(b)   to visit and interview persons accommodated in hospitals and care homes;

(c)   to require the production of, and to inspect, records relating to the care or treatment of persons.

(3) "Prescribed" means prescribed in regulations under this paragraph.

163 (1) Regulations may make provision for, and in connection with, enabling the National Assembly for Wales to monitor, and report on, the operation of this Schedule in relation to Wales.

(2) The National Assembly may direct one or more persons or bodies to carry out the Assembly's functions under regulations under this paragraph.

Disclosure of information

164 (1) Regulations may require either or both of the following to disclose prescribed information to prescribed bodies –

(a)   supervisory bodies;

(b)   managing authorities of hospitals or care homes.

(2) "Prescribed" means prescribed in regulations under this paragraph.

(3) Regulations under this paragraph may only prescribe information relating to matters with which this Schedule is concerned.

Directions by National Assembly in relation to supervisory functions

165 (1) The National Assembly for Wales may direct a Local Health Board to exercise in relation to its area any supervisory functions which are specified in the direction.

(2) Directions under this paragraph must not preclude the National Assembly from exercising the functions specified in the directions.

(3) In this paragraph "supervisory functions" means functions which the National Assembly have as supervisory body, so far as they are exercisable in relation to hospitals (whether NHS or independent hospitals, and whether in Wales or England).

166 (1) This paragraph applies where, under paragraph 165, a Local Health Board ("the specified LHB") is directed to exercise supervisory functions ("delegated functions").

(2) The National Assembly for Wales may give directions to the specified LHB about the Board's exercise of delegated functions.

(3) The National Assembly may give directions for any delegated functions to be exercised, on behalf of the specified LHB, by a committee, sub-committee or officer of that Board.

(4) The National Assembly may give directions providing for any delegated functions to be exercised by the specified LHB jointly with one or more other Local Health Boards.

(5) Where, under sub-paragraph (4), delegated functions are exercisable jointly, the National Assembly may give directions providing for the functions to be exercised, on behalf of the Local Health Boards in question, by a joint committee or joint sub-committee.

167 (1) Directions under paragraph 165 must be given in regulations.

(2) Directions under paragraph 166 may be given –

    (a)   in regulations, or
    (b)   by instrument in writing.

168 The power under paragraph 165 or paragraph 166 to give directions includes power to vary or revoke directions given under that paragraph.

Notices

169 Any notice under this Schedule must be in writing.

Regulations

170 (1) This paragraph applies to all regulations under this Schedule, except regulations under paragraph 162, 163, 167 or 183.

(2) It is for the Secretary of State to make such regulations in relation to authorisations under this Schedule which relate to hospitals and care homes situated in England.

(3) It is for the National Assembly for Wales to make such regulations in relation to authorisations under this Schedule which relate to hospitals and care homes situated in Wales.

171 It is for the Secretary of State to make regulations under paragraph 162.

172 It is for the National Assembly for Wales to make regulations under paragraph 163 or 167.

173 (1) This paragraph applies to regulations under paragraph 183.

(2) It is for the Secretary of State to make such regulations in relation to cases where a question as to the ordinary residence of a person is to be determined by the Secretary of State.

(3) It is for the National Assembly for Wales to make such regulations in relation to cases where a question as to the ordinary residence of a person is to be determined by the National Assembly.

PART 13
INTERPRETATION

Introduction

174 This Part applies for the purposes of this Schedule.

Hospitals and their managing authorities

175 (1) "Hospital" means –

(a)   an NHS hospital, or
(b)   an independent hospital.

(2) "NHS hospital" means –

(a)   a health service hospital as defined by section 275 of the National Health Service Act 2006 or section 206 of the National Health Service (Wales) Act 2006, or
(b)   a hospital as defined by section 206 of the National Health Service (Wales) Act 2006 vested in a Local Health Board.

(3) "Independent hospital" –

(a)   in relation to England, means a hospital as defined by section 275 of the National Health Service Act 2006 that is not an NHS hospital; and
(b)   in relation to Wales, means a hospital as defined by section 2 of the Care Standards Act 2000 that is not an NHS hospital.

176 (1) "Managing authority", in relation to an NHS hospital, means –

(a)   if the hospital –
   (i)   is vested in the appropriate national authority for the purposes of its functions under the National Health Service Act 2006 or of the National Health Service (Wales) Act 2006, or
   (ii) consists of any accommodation provided by a local authority and used as a hospital by or on behalf of the appropriate national authority under either of those Acts,

the . . . Local Health Board or Special Health Authority responsible for the administration of the hospital;

(aa) in relation to England, if the hospital falls within paragraph (a)(i) or (ii) and no Special Health Authority has responsibility for its administration, the Secretary of State;

(b) if the hospital is vested in a . . . National Health Service trust or NHS foundation trust, that trust;

(c) if the hospital is vested in a Local Health Board, that Board.

(2) For this purpose the appropriate national authority is –

(a) in relation to England: the Secretary of State;

(b) in relation to Wales: the National Assembly for Wales;

(c) in relation to England and Wales: the Secretary of State and the National Assembly acting jointly.

177 "Managing authority", in relation to an independent hospital, means –

(a) in relation to England, the person registered, or required to be registered, under Chapter 2 of Part 1 of the Health and Social Care Act 2008 in respect of regulated activities (within the meaning of that Part) carried on in the hospital, and

(b) in relation to Wales, the person registered, or required to be registered, under Part 2 of the Care Standards Act 2000 in respect of the hospital.

Care homes and their managing authorities

178 "Care home" has the meaning given by section 3 of the Care Standards Act 2000.

179 "Managing authority", in relation to a care home, means –

(a) in relation to England, the person registered, or required to be registered, under Chapter 2 of Part 1 of the Health and Social Care Act 2008 in respect of the provision of residential accommodation, together with nursing or personal care, in the care home, and

(b) in relation to Wales, the person registered, or required to be registered, under Part 2 of the Care Standards Act 2000 in respect of the care home.

Supervisory bodies: hospitals

180 (1) The identity of the supervisory body is determined under this paragraph in cases where the relevant hospital is situated in England.

(2) If the relevant person is ordinarily resident in the area of a local authority in England, the supervisory body are that local authority.

(3) If the relevant person is not ordinarily resident in England and the National Assembly for Wales or a Local Health Board commission the relevant care or treatment, the National Assembly are the supervisory body.

(4) In any other case, the supervisory body are the local authority for the area in which the relevant hospital is situated.

(4A) "Local authority" means –

    (a)   the council of a county;
    (b)   the council of a district for which there is no county council;
    (c)   the council of a London borough;
    (d)   the Common Council of the City of London;
    (e)   the Council of the Isles of Scilly.

(5) If a hospital is situated in the areas of two (or more) local authorities, it is to be regarded for the purposes of sub-paragraph (4) as situated in whichever of the areas the greater (or greatest) part of the hospital is situated.

181 (1) The identity of the supervisory body is determined under this paragraph in cases where the relevant hospital is situated in Wales.

(2) The National Assembly for Wales are the supervisory body.

(3) But if the relevant person is ordinarily resident in the area of a local authority in England, the supervisory body are that local authority.

(4) "Local authority" means –

    (a)   the council of a county;
    (b)   the council of a district for which there is no county council;
    (c)   the council of a London borough;
    (d)   the Common Council of the City of London;
    (e)   the Council of the Isles of Scilly.

Supervisory bodies: care homes

182 (1) The identity of the supervisory body is determined under this paragraph in cases where the relevant care home is situated in England or in Wales.

(2) The supervisory body are the local authority for the area in which the relevant person is ordinarily resident.

(3) But if the relevant person is not ordinarily resident in the area of a local authority, the supervisory body are the local authority for the area in which the care home is situated.

(4) In relation to England "local authority" means –

    (a)   the council of a county;
    (b)   the council of a district for which there is no county council;
    (c)   the council of a London borough;
    (d)   the Common Council of the City of London;
    (e)   the Council of the Isles of Scilly.

(5) In relation to Wales "local authority" means the council of a county or county borough.

(6) If a care home is situated in the areas of two (or more) local authorities, it is to be regarded for the purposes of sub-paragraph (3) as situated in whichever of the areas the greater (or greatest) part of the care home is situated.

Supervisory bodies: determination of place of ordinary residence

183 (1) Subsections (5) and (6) of section 24 of the National Assistance Act 1948 (deemed place of ordinary residence) apply to any determination of where a person is ordinarily resident for the purposes of paragraphs 180, 181 and 182 as those subsections apply to such a determination for the purposes specified in those subsections.

(2) In the application of section 24(6) of the 1948 Act by virtue of subsection (1) to any determination of where a person is ordinarily resident for the purposes of paragraph 182, section 24(6) is to be read as if it referred to a hospital vested in a Local Health Board as well as to hospitals vested in the Secretary of State and the other bodies mentioned in section 24(6).

(2A) Section 39(1), (2) and (4) to (6) of the Care Act 2014 and paragraphs 1(1), 2(1) and 8 of Schedule 1 to that Act apply to any determination of where a person is ordinarily resident for the purposes of paragraphs 180, 181 and 182 as they apply for the purposes of Part 1 of that Act.

(3) Any question arising as to the ordinary residence of a person is to be determined by the Secretary of State or by the National Assembly for Wales.

(4) The Secretary of State and the National Assembly must make and publish arrangements for determining which cases are to be dealt with by the Secretary of State and which are to be dealt with by the National Assembly.

(5) Those arrangements may include provision for the Secretary of State and the National Assembly to agree, in relation to any question that has arisen, which of them is to deal with the case.

(6) Regulations may make provision about arrangements that are to have effect before, upon, or after the determination of any question as to the ordinary residence of a person.

(7) The regulations may, in particular, authorise or require a local authority to do any or all of the following things –

  (a) to act as supervisory body even though it may wish to dispute that it is the supervisory body;
  (b) to become the supervisory body in place of another local authority;
  (c) to recover from another local authority expenditure incurred in exercising functions as the supervisory body.

Same body managing authority and supervisory body

184 (1) This paragraph applies if, in connection with a particular person's detention as a resident in a hospital or care home, the same body are both –

  (a) the managing authority of the relevant hospital or care home, and
  (b) the supervisory body.

(2) The fact that a single body are acting in both capacities does not prevent the body from carrying out functions under this Schedule in each capacity.

(3) But, in such a case, this Schedule has effect subject to any modifications contained in regulations that may be made for this purpose.

Interested persons

185 Each of the following is an interested person –

(a)   the relevant person's spouse or civil partner;

(b)   where the relevant person and another person are not married to each other, nor in a civil partnership with each other, but are living together as if they were a married couple: that other person;

(d)   the relevant person's children and step-children;

(e)   the relevant person's parents and step-parents;

(f)   the relevant person's brothers and sisters, half-brothers and half-sisters, and stepbrothers and stepsisters;

(g)   the relevant person's grandparents;

(h)   a deputy appointed for the relevant person by the court;

(i)   a donee of a lasting power of attorney granted by the relevant person.

186 (1) An interested person consulted by the best interests assessor is any person whose name is stated in the relevant best interests assessment in accordance with paragraph 40 (interested persons whom the assessor consulted in carrying out the assessment).

(2) The relevant best interests assessment is the most recent best interests assessment carried out in connection with the standard authorisation in question (whether the assessment was carried out under Part 4 or Part 8).

187 Where this Schedule imposes on a person a duty towards an interested person, the duty does not apply if the person on whom the duty is imposed –

(a)   is not aware of the interested person's identity or of a way of contacting him, and

(b)   cannot reasonably ascertain it.

188 The following table contains an index of provisions defining or otherwise explaining expressions used in this Schedule –

age assessment	paragraph 34
age requirement	paragraph 13
age review assessment	paragraph 112(3)
appointment regulations	paragraph 138
assessment under this Schedule	paragraph 127
assessor (except in Part 8)	paragraph 33
assessor (in Part 8)	paragraphs 33 and 128
authorisation under this Schedule	paragraph 10
best interests (determination of)	section 4
best interests assessment	paragraph 38
best interests requirement	paragraph 16

APPENDIX 2

EXTRACTS FROM THE COURT OF PROTECTION RULES 2007, SI 2007/1744

3A Participation of P

(1) The court shall in each case, on its own initiative or on the application of any person, consider whether it should make one or more of the directions in paragraph (2), having regard to –

(a) the nature and extent of the information before the court;

(b) the issues raised in the case;

(c) whether a matter is contentious; and

(d) whether P has been notified in accordance with the provisions of Part 7 and what, if anything, P has said or done in response to such notification.

(2) The directions are that –

(a) P should be joined as a party;

(b) P's participation should be secured by the appointment of an accredited legal representative to represent P in the proceedings and to discharge such other functions as the court may direct;

(c) P's participation should be secured by the appointment of a representative whose function shall be to provide the court with information as to the matters set out in section 4(6) of the Act and to discharge such other functions as the court may direct;

(d) P should have the opportunity to address (directly or indirectly) the judge determining the application and, if so directed, the circumstances in which that should occur;

(e) P's interests and position can properly be secured without any direction under sub-paragraphs (a) to (d) being made or by the making of an alternative direction meeting the overriding objective.

(3) Any appointment or directions made pursuant to paragraph (2)(b) to (e) may be made for such period or periods as the court thinks fit.

(4) Unless P has capacity to conduct the proceedings, an order joining P as a party shall only take effect –

(a) on the appointment of a litigation friend on P's behalf; or

(b) if the court so directs, on or after the appointment of an accredited legal representative.

(5) If the court has directed that P should be joined as a party but such joinder does not occur because no litigation friend or accredited legal representative is appointed, the court shall record in a judgment or order –

  (a)   the fact that no such appointment was made; and
  (b)   the reasons given for that appointment not being made.

(6) A practice direction may make additional or supplementary provision in respect of any of the matters set out in this rule.

> (The appointment of litigation friends, accredited legal representatives and representatives under paragraph (2)(c) is dealt with under Part 17.)

> ("Accredited legal representative" is defined in rule 6.).

41A Notifying P of appointment of a litigation friend, etc

P must be notified –

  (a)   where a direction has been made under rule 3A; and
  (b)   of the appointment of a litigation friend, accredited legal representative or representative on P's behalf.

PART 10A
DEPRIVATION OF LIBERTY

82A

The practice direction to this Part sets out procedure governing –

  (a)   applications to the court for orders relating to the deprivation, or proposed deprivation, of liberty of P; and
  (b)   proceedings (for example, relating to costs or appeals) connected with or consequent upon such applications.

* * *

PART 17
LITIGATION FRIENDS AND RULE 3A REPRESENTATIVES
SECTION 1 – LITIGATION FRIENDS

Who may act as a litigation friend

140 (1) A person may act as a litigation friend on behalf of a person mentioned in paragraph (2) if that person –

  (a)   can fairly and competently conduct proceedings on behalf of that person; and
  (b)   has no interests adverse to those of that person.

(2) The persons for whom a litigation friend may act are –

  (a)   P;
  (b)   a child;
  (c)   a protected party.

Requirement for a litigation friend

141 (1) This rule does not apply to P (whether P is an adult or a child).

(2) A protected party (if a party to the proceedings) must have a litigation friend.

(3) A child (if a party to the proceedings) must have a litigation friend to conduct those proceedings on that child's behalf unless the court makes an order under paragraph (4).

(4) The court may make an order permitting a child to conduct proceedings without a litigation friend.

(5) An application for an order under paragraph (4) –

    (a)   may be made by the child;
    (b)   if the child already has a litigation friend, must be made on notice to the litigation friend; and
    (c)   if the child has no litigation friend, may be made without notice.

(6) Where –

    (a)   the court has made an order under paragraph (4); and
    (b)   it subsequently appears to the court that it is desirable for a litigation friend to conduct the proceedings on behalf of the child,

the court may appoint a person to the child's litigation friend.

Litigation friend without a court order

142 (1) This rule does not apply –

    (a)   in relation to P;
    (b)   where the court has appointed a person under rule 143 or 144; or
    (c)   where the Official Solicitor is to act as a litigation friend.

(2) A deputy with the power to conduct legal proceedings in the name of a protected party or on the protected party's behalf is entitled to be a litigation friend of the protected party in any proceedings to which the deputy's power relates.

(3) If no-one has been appointed by the court or, in the case of a protected party, there is no deputy with the power to conduct proceedings, a person who wishes to act as a litigation friend must –

    (a)   file a certificate of suitability stating that they satisfy the conditions in rule 140(1); and
    (b)   serve the certificate of suitability on –
        (i)   the person on whom an application form is to be served in accordance with rule 32 (service on children and protected parties); and
        (ii)   every other person who is a party to the proceedings.

(4) If the person referred to in paragraph (2) wishes to act as a litigation friend for the protected party, that person must file and serve on the persons mentioned in paragraph (3)(b) a copy of the court order which appointed that person.

Litigation friend by court order

143 (1) The court may make an order appointing –

    (a)   the Official Solicitor; or
    (b)   some other person,

to act as a litigation friend for a protected party, a child or P.

(2) The court may make an order under paragraph (1) –

    (a)   either on its own initiative or on the application of any person; but
    (b)   only with the consent of the person to be appointed.

(3) An application for an order under paragraph (1) must be supported by evidence.

(4) The court may not appoint a litigation friend under this rule unless it is satisfied that the person to be appointed satisfies the conditions in rule 140(1).

(5) The court may at any stage of the proceedings give directions as to the appointment of a litigation friend.

> (Rule 3A requires the court to consider how P should participate in the proceedings, which may be by way of being made a party and the appointment of a litigation friend under this Part.)

Court's power to prevent a person from acting as a litigation friend or to bring an end to an appointment of a person as a litigation friend or to appoint another one

144 (1) The court may either on its own initiative or on the application of any person –

    (a)   direct that a person may not act as a litigation friend;
    (b)   bring to an end a litigation friend's appointment; or
    (c)   appoint a new litigation friend in place of an existing one.

(2) If an application for an order under paragraph (1) is based on the conduct of the litigation friend, it must be supported by evidence.

(3) The court may not appoint a litigation friend under this rule unless it is satisfied that the person to be appointed satisfies the conditions in rule 140(1).

(4) The appointment of a litigation friend continues until brought to an end by court order.

> (Rule 87 applies if P has capacity in relation to the matter or matters to which the application relates.)

Appointment of litigation friend by court order – supplementary

145 The applicant must serve a copy of an application for an order under rule 143 or 144 on –

(a) the person on whom an application form is to be served in accordance with rule 32 (service on children and protected parties);
(b) every other person who is a party to the proceedings;
(c) any person who is the litigation friend, or who is purporting to act as the litigation friend, when the application is made; and
(d) unless that person is the applicant, the person who it is proposed should be the litigation friend,

as soon as practicable and in any event within 14 days of the date on which the application was issued.

Procedure where appointment of a litigation friend comes to an end for a child

145A When a child reaches 18, provided the child is neither –

(a) P; nor
(b) a protected party,

the litigation friend's appointment ends and the child must serve notice on every other party –

(i) stating that the child has reached full age;
(ii) stating that the appointment of the litigation friend has ended; and
(iii) providing an address for service.

Practice direction in relation to litigation friends

146 A practice direction may make additional or supplementary provision in relation to litigation friends.

SECTION 2 – RULE 3A REPRESENTATIVES

Interpretation

146A In this Section, references to "rule 3A representatives" are references to both accredited legal representatives and representatives.

("Accredited legal representative" and "representative" are defined in rule 6.)

Who may act as a rule 3A representative for P

147 A person may act as an accredited legal representative, or a representative, for P, if that person can fairly and competently discharge his or her functions on behalf of P.

Rule 3A representative by court order

148 (1) The court may make an order appointing a person to act as a representative, or an accredited legal representative, for P.

(2) The court may make an order under paragraph (1) −

(a)   either of its own initiative or on the application of any person; but

(b)   only with the consent of the person to be appointed.

(3) The court may not appoint a representative or an accredited legal representative under this rule unless it is satisfied that the person to be appointed satisfies the conditions in rule 147.

(4) The court may at any stage of the proceedings give directions as to the terms of appointment of a representative or an accredited legal representative.

> (Rule 3A requires the court to consider how P should participate in the proceedings, which may be by way of the appointment of a representative or accredited legal representative under this Part.)

Application by rule 3A representative or by P for directions

148A A representative, an accredited legal representative or P may, at any time and without giving notice to the other parties, apply to the court for directions relating to the performance, terms of appointment or continuation of the appointment of the representative or accredited legal representative.

Court's power to prevent a person from acting as a rule 3A representative or to bring an end to an appointment of a person as a rule 3A representative or appoint another one

148B (1) The court may, either of its own initiative or on the application of any person −

(a)   direct that a person may not act as a representative or accredited legal representative;

(b)   bring to an end a representative's or accredited legal representative's appointment;

(c)   appoint a new representative or accredited legal representative in place of an existing one; or

(d)   vary the terms of a representative's or accredited legal representative's appointment.

(2) If an application for an order under paragraph (1) is based on the conduct of the representative or accredited legal representative, it must be supported by evidence.

(3) The court may not appoint a representative or accredited legal representative under this rule unless it is satisfied that the person to be appointed satisfies the conditions in rule 147.

(4) The appointment of a representative or accredited legal representative continues until brought to an end by court order.

(5) The court must bring to an end the appointment of a representative or an accredited legal representative if P has capacity to appoint such a representative and does not wish the appointment by the court to continue.

Appointment of rule 3A representative by court order – supplementary

148C The applicant must serve a copy of an application for an order under rule 148 or rule 148B on –

   (a)   the person on whom an application form is to be served in accordance with rule 32 (service on children and protected parties);

   (b)   every other person who is a party to the proceedings;

   (c)   any person who is the representative, or accredited legal representative, purporting to act as such representative, when the application is made; and

   (d)   unless that person is the applicant, the person who it is proposed should be the representative or accredited legal representative,

as soon as practicable and in any event within 14 days of the date on which the application was issued.

Practice direction in relation to rule 3A representatives

149 A practice direction may make additional or supplementary provision in relation to representatives or accredited legal representatives.

APPENDIX 3

PRACTICE DIRECTIONS RELATING TO DEPRIVATION OF LIBERTY

Practice Direction 10A – Applications Within Proceedings

This practice direction supplements Part 10 of the Court of Protection Rules 2007

PRACTICE DIRECTION A – APPLICATIONS WITHIN PROCEEDINGS

Application notice

1. Rule 77 provides that an applicant may use the Part 10 procedure if the application is made:

  (a) in the course of existing proceedings; or
  (b) as provided for in a rule or relevant practice direction.

2. An application under Part 10 must be made by filing an application notice using form COP9.

3. An application notice must, in addition to the matters set out in rule 79, be signed and include (unless an order to the contrary pursuant to rule 19 has been made):

  (a) the name of the person to whom the application relates (P);
  (b) the case number (if available);
  (c) the full name of the applicant;
  (d) where the applicant is not already a party, his address; and
  (e) a draft of the order sought.

4. If the order sought is unusually long or complex, a disk containing the draft order sought should be made available to the court in a format compatible with the word processing software used by the court. (Queries in relation to software should be directed to a court officer.)

5. The application notice must be supported by evidence set out in either:

  (a) a witness statement; or
  (b) the application notice provided that it is verified by a statement of truth.

6. For the purposes of rules 90 to 92, a statement of truth in an application notice may be made by a person who is not a party.[1]

7. The evidence must set out the facts on which the applicant relies for the application, and all material facts known to the applicant of which the court should be made aware.

8. A copy of the application notice and evidence in support must be served by the person making the application as soon as practicable and in any event within 21 days of the application notice being issued.

9. An application may be made without service of an application notice only:

(a)   where there is exceptional urgency;
(b)   where the overriding objective is best furthered by doing so;
(c)   by consent of all parties;
(d)   with the permission of the court; or
(e)   where a rule or other practice direction permits.

    (Practice direction B accompanying Part 10 sets out more detailed requirements for urgent applications.)

10. Where an application is made without service on the respondent, the evidence in support of the application must also set out why service was not effected.

11. The court may decide, upon considering the application, that other persons ought to be served with or notified of it and have the opportunity of responding. In such a case, the court will give directions as to who should be served with or notified of the application.

12. On receipt of an application notice, the court will issue the application notice and, if there is to be a hearing, give notice of the date on which the matter is to be heard by the court.

13. Notice will be given to:

(a)   the applicant;
(b)   anyone who is named as a respondent in the application notice (if not otherwise a party to the proceedings);
(c)   every other party to the proceedings; and
(d)   any other person, as the court may direct.

14. Any directions given by the court may specify the form that the evidence is to take and when it is to be served.

15. Applications should wherever possible be made so that they can be considered at a directions hearing or other hearing for which a date has already been fixed or for which a date is about to be fixed.

16. Where a date for a hearing has been fixed and a party wishes to make an application at that hearing but does not have sufficient time to file an application notice, he should inform the court (if possible in writing) and, if

---

[1]   See rule 11(6)(a).

possible, the other parties as soon as he can of the nature of the application and the reason for it. He should then make the application orally at the hearing.

Type of case may be indicated in the application notice

17. The applicant may indicated in the application notice that the application:

  (a)   is urgent;
  (b)   should be dealt with by a particular judge or level of judge within the court;
  (c)   requires a hearing; or
  (d)   any combination of the above.

Telephone hearings

18. The court may direct that an application or part of an application will be dealt with by a telephone hearing.

19. The applicant should indicate in his application notice if he seeks a direction pursuant to paragraph 17. Where he has not done so but nevertheless wishes to seek such a direction the request should be made as early as possible.

20. A direction under paragraph 17 will not normally be given unless every party entitled to be given notice of the application and to be heard at the hearing has consented to the direction.

Video conferencing

21. Where the parties to a matter wish to use video conferencing facilities, and those facilities are available, they should apply to the court for such a direction.

  (Practice direction A accompanying Part 14 contains guidance on the use of video conferencing.)

Consent orders

22. The parties to an application for a consent order must ensure that they provide the court with any material it needs to be satisfied that it is appropriate to make the order. Subject to any rule or practice direction, a letter signed by all parties will generally be acceptable for this purpose.

23. Where an order has been agreed in relation to an application for which a hearing date has been fixed, the parties must inform the court immediately.

Practice Direction 10AA – Deprivation of Liberty

This practice direction supplements Part 10A of the Court of Protection Rules 2007

PRACTICE DIRECTION A – DEPRIVATION OF LIBERTY APPLICATIONS

Introduction

1. This Practice Direction is in three parts. Part 1 addresses the procedure to be followed in applications to the court for orders under section 21A of the Mental Capacity Act 2005 relating to a standard or urgent authorisation under Schedule A1 of that Act to deprive a person of his or her liberty; or proceedings (for example, relating to costs or appeals) connected with or consequent upon such applications. Part 2 addresses the procedure to be followed in applications under s 16(2)(a) of that Act to authorise deprivation of liberty under section 4A(3) and (4) pursuant to a streamlined procedure. Part 3 makes provision common to applications under both Parts 1 and 2.

PART 1 – APPLICATIONS UNDER SECTION 21A RELATING TO A STANDARD OR URGENT AUTHORISATION UNDER SCHEDULE A1

2. This Part sets out the procedure to be followed in applications to the court for orders under section 21A of the Mental Capacity Act 2005 relating to a standard or urgent authorisation under Schedule A1 of that Act to deprive a person of his or her liberty. By their nature, such applications are of special urgency and therefore will be dealt with by the court according to the special procedure described here. Other applications may, while not being DoL applications within the meaning of the term explained above, raise issues relating to deprivation of liberty and require similarly urgent attention; and while the special DoL procedure will not apply to such applications, they should be raised with the DoL team at the earliest possible stage so that they can be handled appropriately. The key features of the special DoL procedure are:

   (a)   special DoL court forms ensure that DoL court papers stand out as such and receive special handling by the court office;

   (b)   the application is placed before a judge of the court as soon as possible – if necessary, before issue of the application – for judicial directions to be given as to the steps to be taken in the application, and who is to take each step and by when;

   (c)   the usual Court of Protection Rules (for example, as to method and timing of service of the application) will apply only so far as consistent with the judicial directions given for the particular case;

   (d)   a dedicated team in the court office ("the DoL team") will deal with DoL applications at all stages, including liaison with would-be applicants/other parties;

(e)   the progress of each DoL case will be monitored by a judge assigned to that case, assisted by the DoL team.

Before issuing an application

3. Potential applicants should contact the DoL team at the earliest possible stage before issuing a DoL application. Where this is not possible, the applicant should liaise with the DoL team at the same time as, or as soon as possible after, lodging the application. The DoL team can be contacted by telephone in the first instance and by fax.

4. The information that the DoL team needs, with as much advance warning as possible, is (1) that a DoL application is to be made; (2) how urgent the application is (ie by when should the Court's decision, or interim decision, on the merits be given); and (3) when the Court will receive the application papers. In extremely urgent cases, the DoL team can arrange for a telephone application to be made to the judge for directions and/or an interim order even before the application has been issued. Further brief details should be given which may include:

(a)   the parties' details
(b)   where the parties live
(c)   the issue to be decided
(d)   the date of urgent or standard authorisation
(e)   the date of effective detention
(f)   the parties' legal representatives
(g)   any family members or others who are involved
(h)   whether there have been any other court proceedings involving the parties and if so, where.

5. Contact details for the DoL team are:

PO Box 70185
First Avenue House
42-49 High Holborn
London
WC1A 9 JA
DX: 160013 Kingsway 7
Enquiries: 0300 456 4600

6. The public counter is open between 9.30 a.m. to 4.30 p.m. on working days. The DoL team can receive telephone calls and faxes between 9.00 a.m. and 5.00 pm. Faxes transmitted after 4.30 p.m. will be dealt with the next working day.

7. When in an emergency it is necessary to make a telephone application to a judge outside normal court hours, the security office at the Royal Courts of Justice should be contacted on 020 7947 6000. The security officer should be informed of the nature of the case. In the Family Division, the out-of-hours application procedure involves the judge being contacted through a Family Division duty officer, and the RCJ security officer will need to contact the duty officer and not the judge's clerk or the judge.

8. Intending applicants/other parties may find it helpful to refer to:

(a)   the Code of Practice Deprivation of Liberty Safeguards (June 2008), ISBN 978-0113228157, supplementing the main Mental Capacity Act 2005 Code of Practice: in particular Chapter 10, What is the Court of Protection and who can apply to it?; and

(b)   the judgment of Mr Justice Munby in *Salford City Council v GJ, NJ and BJ (Incapacitated Adults)* [2008] EWHC 1097 (Fam); [2008] 2 FLR 1295. Although this case was decided before the coming into force of the DoL amendments to the Mental Capacity Act 2005, it sets out helpful guidance on the appropriate court procedures for cases relating to the deprivation of liberty of adults.

9. The DoL team will be pleased to explain the court's procedures for handling DoL cases. Please note that the team (as with all court staff) is not permitted to give advice on matters of law. Please do not contact the DoL team unless your inquiry concerns a deprivation of liberty question (whether relating to a potential application, or a case which is already lodged with the Court).

DoL court forms

10. The special DoL court forms are as follows:

(a)   DLA: Deprivation of Liberty Application Form: to be used for all DoL applications;

(b)   DLB: Deprivation of Liberty Request for Urgent Consideration: this short form allows applicants to set out the reasons why the case is urgent, the timetable they wish the case to follow, and any interim relief sought. A draft of any order sought should be attached. Ideally, the DLB (plus any draft order) should be placed at the top of the draft application and both issued and served together;

(c)   DLD: Deprivation of Liberty Certificate of Service/non-service and Certificate of notification/non-notification;

(d)   DLE: Deprivation of Liberty Acknowledgement of service/notification.

These forms can be obtained from the Court of Protection office or downloaded from the court's website: http://hmctsformfinder.justice.gov.uk/HMCTS/GetForms.do?court_forms_category=court_of_protection.

11. To ensure that papers relating to DoL applications are promptly directed to the DoL team at the court, it is essential that the appropriate DoL court forms are used.

12. The DoL court forms should be used for, and only for, DoL applications. If in such a case it is anticipated that other issues may arise, the DoL forms should identify and describe briefly those issues and any relief which may be sought in respect of them: sections 3.5 and 5 of form DLA, the Deprivation of Liberty Application Form, offer an opportunity to do this. "Other issues" are perhaps most likely to arise in the event that the court decides the DoL application in the applicant's favour. In such a case, if the applicant has already identified the

"other issues" in his/her form DLA, the court will be able to address these, either by dealing with them immediately or by giving directions for their future handling.

13. Accordingly, unless the court expressly directs, applicants should not issue a second and separate application (using the standard court forms) relating to any "other issues".

14. Where an application seeks relief concerning a deprivation of P's liberty other than under section 21A in respect of a standard or urgent authorisation (for example, where the application is for an order under section 16(2)(a)), the dedicated DoL court forms should not be used. Rather the standard court forms should be used for such an application, but it should be made clear on them that relief relating to a deprivation of P's liberty is being sought, and the proposed applicant should contact the DoL team to discuss handling at the earliest possible stage before issuing the application.

How to issue a DoL application

15. To issue a DoL application, the following forms should be filed at court:

    (a)   form DLA
    (b)   form DLB (plus draft order)
    (c)   the appropriate court fee.

Where a draft order is lodged with the court, it would be helpful – although not compulsory – if an electronic version of the order could also be lodged on disc, if possible.

16. In cases of extreme emergency or where it is not possible to attend at the court office, for example during weekends, the court will expect an applicant to undertake to file form DLA and to pay the court fee unless an exemption applies.

Inviting the court to make judicial directions for the handling of the application

17. The following is a sample list of possible issues which the court is likely to wish to consider in judicial directions in a DoL case. It is intended as a prompt, not as a definitive list of the issues that may need to be covered:

    (a)   upon whom, by when and how service of the application should be effected;
    (b)   dispensing with acknowledgement of service of the application or allowing a short period of time for so doing, which in some cases may amount to a few hours only;
    (c)   whether further lay or expert evidence should be obtained;
    (d)   whether P/the detained person should be a party and represented by the Official Solicitor and whether any other person should be a party;
    (e)   whether any family members should be formally notified of the application and of any hearing and joined as parties;
    (f)   fixing a date for a First Hearing and giving a time estimate;

(g) fixing a trial window for any final hearing and giving a time estimate;
(h) the level of judge appropriate to hear the case;
(i) whether the case is such that it should be immediately transferred to the High Court for a High Court Judge to give directions;
(j) provision for a bundle for the judge at the First Hearing.

18. If you are an applicant without legal representation, and you are not sure exactly what directions you should ask for, you may prefer simply to invite the judge to make appropriate directions in light of the nature and urgency of the case as you have explained it on the DLB form. In exceptionally urgent cases, there may not be time to formulate draft directions: the court will understand if applicants in such cases (whether or not legally represented) simply ask the judge for appropriate directions.

After issue of the application

19. The DoL team will immediately take steps to ensure that the application is placed before a judge nominated to hear Court of Protection cases and DoL applications.

20. As soon as the court office is put on notice of a DoL application, the DoL team will notify a judge to put the judge on stand-by to deal with the application. The judge will consider the application on the papers and make a first order.

Steps after the judge's first order

21. The DoL team will:

(a) action every point in the judge's note or instruction;
(b) refer any query that arises to the judge immediately or, if not available, to another judge;
(c) make all arrangements for any transfer of the case to another court and/or for a hearing.

22. The applicant or his/her legal representative should follow all steps in the judge's order and:

(a) form DLD should be filed with the court if appropriate; and
(b) form DLE should be included in any documents served unless ordered otherwise.

The First Hearing

23. The First Hearing will be listed for the court to fix a date for any subsequent hearing(s), give directions and/or to make an interim or final order if appropriate. The court will make such orders and give such directions as are appropriate in the case.

24. The court will aim to have the First Hearing before a judge of every DoL application within 5 working days of the date of issue of the application.

25. Applicants can indicate on the DLB form if they think that the application needs to be considered within a shorter timetable, and set out proposals for such a timetable. On the first paper consideration the court will consider when the First Hearing should be listed.

26. If time allows and no specific direction has been made by the court, an indexed and paginated bundle should be prepared for the judge and any skeleton arguments and draft orders given to the court as soon as they are available. A copy of the index should be provided to all parties and, where another party appears in person, a copy of the bundle should be provided.

PART 2 – APPLICATIONS UNDER SECTION 16(2)(a) FOR AN ORDER AUTHORISING DEPRIVATION OF LIBERTY UNDER SECTION 4A(3) AND (4) PURSUANT TO A STREAMLINED PROCEDURE

27. This Part sets out the procedure to be followed in applications to the court under section 16(2)(a) to authorise deprivation of liberty under section 4A(3) of the Act pursuant to a streamlined procedure and applies only to such applications. Reference should be made generally to the decision of the Supreme Court in *P (by his litigation friend the Official Solicitor) v Cheshire West and Chester Council and another; P and Q (by their litigation friend the Official Solicitor) v Surrey County Council* [2014] UKSC 19, and in relation to the procedure in these cases, to the judgments of the President of the Court of Protection in *Re X and others (Deprivation of Liberty)* [2014] EWCOP 25 and in *Re X and others (Deprivation of Liberty) (Number 2)* [2014] EWCOP 37.

Making the application

28. To bring proceedings, the applicant must file an application using form COPDOL 10, verified by a statement of truth and accompanied by all attachments and evidence required by that form and its annexes.

29. The application form and accompanying annexes and attachments are specifically designed to ensure that the applicant provides the court with essential information and evidence as to the proposed measures, on the basis of which the court may adjudicate as to the appropriateness of authorising a deprivation of liberty, and in particular to identify whether a case is suitable for consideration without an oral hearing. The use of the form and its annexes is mandatory and they must be provided fully completed and verified by the required statements of truth.

30. The applicant must ensure that the evidence in the application form, accompanying annexes and attachments is succinct and focussed.

31. A separate application must be made for every individual for whom the applicant requests an authorisation of deprivation of liberty. However, where there are matters in relation to which the facts are identical for a number of individuals, such as common care arrangements, the applicant may, in addition

to addressing the specific issues relating to each individual, attach a generic statement dealing with the common care arrangements or other matters common to those individuals.

Deponent

32. The applicant must consider carefully who should complete the form and each annex with regard to the nature of the evidence required by each. There is no requirement that the same individual should complete and verify by statement of truth the form and each annex and indeed it might be inappropriate for this to be the case, where different people are best placed to provide evidence on different matters.

Applicant's duty of full and frank disclosure

33. The applicant has a duty of full and frank disclosure to the court of all facts and matters that may have an impact on the court's decision whether to authorise the deprivation of liberty. The applicant should therefore scrutinise the circumstances of the case and clearly identify in the evidence in support (in Annex A to form COPDOL 10) factors –

    (a)   needing particular judicial scrutiny;
    (b)   suggesting that the arrangements in relation to which authorisation is sought may not in fact be in the best interests of the person the application is about, or the least restrictive option; or
    (c)   otherwise tending to indicate that the order should not be made.

Pursuant to this duty, the applicant should also identify those persons, not consulted by the applicant, who are in the same category under paragraph 39 as persons with whom the applicant has consulted. Those persons must be listed in Annex B to form COPDOL 10 together with an explanation in that Annex of why they have not been consulted.

Draft order

34. The application must be accompanied by a draft of the order which the applicant seeks, including the duration of the authorisation sought, appropriate directions for review, and liberty to apply for its reconsideration.

Consultation with the person the application is about

35. Consultation with the person the application is about must take place before the application form is lodged with the court. The applicant must arrange for that person to be informed of the following matters –

    (a)   that the applicant is making an application to court;
    (b)   that the application is to consider whether the person lacks capacity to make decisions in relation to his or her residence and care, and whether to authorise a deprivation of their liberty in connection with the arrangements set out in the care plan;
    (c)   what the proposed arrangements under the order sought are;

(d)   that the person is entitled to express his or her views, wishes and feelings in relation to the proposed arrangements and the application, and that the person undertaking the consultation will ensure that these are communicated to the court;

(e)   that the person is entitled to seek to take part in the proceedings by being joined as a party or otherwise, what that means, and that the person undertaking the consultation will ensure that any such request is communicated to the court;

(f)   that the person undertaking the consultation can help him or her to obtain advice and assistance if he or she does not agree with the proposed arrangements in the application.

36. The person undertaking the consultation must complete Annex C to form COPDOL 10.

37. The applicant must confirm that the person the application is about has been supported and assisted to express his or her views, wishes and feelings in relation to the application and the arrangements proposed in it, and encouraged to take part in the proceedings to the extent that he or she wishes, in accordance with section 4(4) of the Act.

Consultation with other persons regarding the making of the application

38. The consultation required by paragraph 39 below must take place before the application is lodged with the court.

39. The applicant must ensure that the following people are consulted about the intention to make the application –

(a)   any donee of a lasting power of attorney granted by the person;
(b)   any deputy appointed for the person by the court;

together with, if possible, at least three people in the following categories —

(c)   anyone named by the person the application is about as someone to be consulted on the matters raised by the application; and
(d)   anyone engaged in caring for the person or interested in his or her welfare.

40. When consulting such people, the applicant must inform them of the following matters –

(a)   that the applicant is making an application to court;
(b)   that the application is to consider whether the person the application is about lacks capacity to make decisions in relation to his or her residence and care and whether he or she should be deprived of liberty in connection with the arrangements set out in the care plan;
(c)   what the proposed arrangements under the order are; and

(d)   that the applicant is under an obligation to inform the person the application is about of the matters listed in paragraph 35 above, unless in the circumstances it is inappropriate for the applicant to give that person such information.

Dispensing with notification or service of the application form

41. Provided that the court is satisfied as to the adequacy of consultation with the person the application is about in accordance with paragraphs 35 to 37, and with other persons with whom consultation should take place in accordance with paragraphs 38 to 40, the court may dispense with notification of the issue of the application under rules 42, 69 and 70.

Court fees

42. An application fee is payable for all applications, and if the court decides to hold a hearing before making a decision, a hearing fee will be payable.

43. If an application is received without a fee it will be treated as incomplete and returned.

Applications suitable for the streamlined procedure

44. As soon as practicable after receipt the court officers will consider the suitability of the application to be the subject of paper determination, or to be considered at an oral hearing.

45. All applications considered suitable for the streamlined procedure will be referred to a judge for consideration without an oral hearing, as soon as practicable after receipt.

Applications not suitable for the streamlined procedure

46. If the judge considers that the application is not suitable for the streamlined process, case management directions shall be given.

Applicant to supply a copy of the order to each person consulted

47. The applicant must provide all persons consulted, including the person the application is about, with a copy of the order made pursuant to the streamlined procedure granting or refusing the authorisation of the deprivation of liberty.

Review of the authorisation

48. An application for a review of the authorisation of the deprivation of liberty must be made in accordance with the terms of the order.

PART 3 – PROVISIONS COMMON TO APPLICATIONS UNDER PART 1 AND PART 2

Hearing in private

49. Part 13 of the Court of Protection Rules 2007 provides at rule 90, as supplemented by Practice Direction A to Part 13, that the general rule is that a hearing is held in private. Rule 92 allows the court to order that a hearing be in public if the criteria in rule 93 apply.

Costs

50. The general rule, in rule 157 of the Court of Protection Rules 2007, is that in a health and welfare case there will be no order as to costs of the proceedings.

The general rule applies to DoL applications.

Appeals

51. Part 20 of the Court of Protection Rules 2007 applies to appeals. Permission is required to appeal (rules 171B and 172) and this will only be granted where the court considers that the appeal would have a real prospect of success or there is some other compelling reason why the appeal should be heard (rule 173).

Practice Direction 10B – Urgent and Interim Applications

This practice direction supplements Part 10 of the Court of Protection Rules 2007

PRACTICE DIRECTION B – URGENT AND INTERIM APPLICATIONS

Urgent applications and applications without notice

1. These fall into two categories:

    (a)   applications where an application form has already been issued; and
    (b)   applications where an application form has not yet been issued,

and, in both cases, where notice of the application has not been given to the respondent(s).

2. Wherever possible, urgent applications should be made within court hours. These applications will normally be dealt with at court but cases of extreme urgency may be dealt with by telephone. Telephone contact may be made with the court during business hours on 0300 456 4600.

3. When it is not possible to apply within court hours, contact should be made with the security office at the Royal Courts of Justice on 020 7947 6000. The security officer should be informed of the nature of the case.

4. In some cases, urgent applications arise because applications to the court have not been pursued sufficiently promptly. This is undesirable, and should be avoided. A judge who has concerns that the facility for urgent applications may have been abused may require the applicant or the applicant's representative to attend at a subsequent hearing to provide an explanation for the delay.

Applications without notice

5. The applicant should take steps to advise the respondent(s) by telephone or in writing of the application, unless justice would be defeated if notice were given.

6. If an order is made without notice to any other party, the order will ordinarily contain:

    (a)   an undertaking by the applicant to the court to serve the application notice, evidence in support and any order made on the respondent and any other person the court may direct as soon as practicable or as ordered by the court; and
    (b)   a return date for a further hearing at which the other parties can be present.

Applications where an application form has already been issued

7. An application notice using form COP9, evidence in support and a draft order should be filed with the court in advance of the hearing wherever possible. If the order sought is unusually long or complex, a disk containing the draft order sought should be made available to the court in a format compatible with the word processing software used by the court. (Queries in relation to software should be directed to a court officer.)

(Practice direction A accompanying Part 10 sets out more detailed requirements in relation to an application notice.)

8. If an application is made before the application notice has been filed, a draft order should be provided at the hearing, and the application notice and evidence in support must be filed with the court on the next working day or as ordered by the court.

Applications made before the issue of an application form

9. Where the exceptional urgency of the matter requires, an application may be started without filing an application form if the court allows it (but where time permits an application should be made in writing). In such a case, an application may be made to the court orally. The court will require an undertaking that the application form in the terms of the oral application be filed on the next working day, or as required by the court.

10. An order made before the issue of the application form should state in the title after the names of the applicant and the respondent, "the Applicant and Respondent in an Intended Application".

Applications made by telephone

11. Where it is not possible to file an application form or notice, applications can be made by telephone in accordance with the contact details set out in paragraphs 2 and 3 of this practice direction.

Hearings conducted by telephone

12. When a hearing is to take place by telephone, if practical it should be conducted by tape-recorded conference call, and arranged (and paid for in the first instance) by the applicant. All parties and the judge should be informed that the call is being recorded by the service provider. The applicant should order a transcript of the hearing from the service provider.

Type of case may be indicated in the application notice

13. The applicant may indicate in the application notice that the application:

    (a)   is urgent;
    (b)   should be dealt with by a particular judge or level of judge within the court;
    (c)   requires a hearing; or

(d)   any combination of the above.

Urgent cases in relation to serious medical treatment

14. Practice direction E accompanying Part 9 sets out the procedure in relation to applications relating to serious medical treatment. Practice direction A accompanying Part 12 sets out the manner in which those cases are to be allocated.

Interim injunction applications

15. Rule 82 enables the court to grant an interim injunction.

16. Any judge of the court may vary or discharge an interim injunction granted by any judge of the court.

17. Any order for an interim injunction must set out clearly what the respondent or any other person must or must not do. The order may contain an undertaking by the applicant to pay any damages which the respondent(s) sustains which the court considers the applicant should pay.

APPENDIX 4

MENTAL CAPACITY (DEPRIVATION OF LIBERTY: STANDARD AUTHORISATIONS, ASSESSMENTS AND ORDINARY RESIDENCE) REGULATIONS 2008, SI 2008/1858

PART 1
PRELIMINARY

1 Citation, commencement and application

(1) These Regulations may be cited as the Mental Capacity (Deprivation of Liberty: Standard Authorisations, Assessments and Ordinary Residence) Regulations 2008 and shall come into force on 3 November 2008.

(2) These Regulations apply in relation to England only.

2 Interpretation

In these Regulations –

'approved mental health professional' means a person approved under
section 114(1) of the Mental Health Act 1983 to act as an approved
mental health professional for the purposes of that Act;
'best interests assessor' means a person selected to carry out a best interests
assessment under paragraph 38 of Schedule A1 to the Act;
'the Act' means the Mental Capacity Act 2005.

Amendments—SI 2012/1479.

PART 2
ELIGIBILITY TO CARRY OUT ASSESSMENTS

3 Eligibility – general

(1) In addition to any requirement in regulations 4 to 9, a person is eligible to carry out an assessment where paragraphs (2) to (4) are met.

(2) The person must satisfy the supervisory body that there is in force in relation to that person an adequate and appropriate indemnity arrangement which provides cover in respect of any liabilities that might arise in connection with carrying out the assessment.

(2A) For the purposes of this regulation, an 'indemnity arrangement' may comprise –

(a)   a policy of insurance;

(b)   an arrangement made for the purposes of indemnifying a person; or

(c)   a combination of a policy of insurance and an arrangement made for the purposes of indemnifying a person.

(3) The supervisory body must be satisfied that the person has the skills and experience appropriate to the assessment to be carried out which must include, but are not limited to, the following –

(a)   an applied knowledge of the Mental Capacity Act 2005 and related Code of Practice; and

(b)   the ability to keep appropriate records and to provide clear and reasoned reports in accordance with legal requirements and good practice.

(4) The supervisory body must be satisfied that there is in respect of the person –

(a)   an enhanced criminal record certificate issued under section 113B of the Police Act 1997 (enhanced criminal record certificates); or

(b)   if the purpose for which the certificate is required is not one prescribed under subsection (2) of that section, a criminal record certificate issued pursuant to section 113A of that Act (criminal record certificates).

Amendments—SI 2009/827.

4 Eligibility to carry out a mental health assessment

(1) A person is eligible to carry out a mental health assessment if paragraphs (2) and (3) are met.

(2) The person must be –

(a)   approved under section 12 of the Mental Health Act 1983; or

(b)   a registered medical practitioner who the supervisory body is satisfied has at least three years post registration experience in the diagnosis or treatment of mental disorder.

(3) The supervisory body must be satisfied that the person has successfully completed the Deprivation of Liberty Safeguards Mental Health Assessors training programme made available by the Royal College of Psychiatrists.

(4) Except in the 12 month period beginning with the date the person has successfully completed the programme referred to in paragraph (3), the supervisory body must be satisfied that the person has, in the 12 months prior to selection, completed further training relevant to their role as a mental health assessor.

5 Eligibility to carry out a best interests assessment

(1) A person is eligible to carry out a best interests assessment if paragraphs (2) and (3) are met.

(2) The person must be one of the following –

    (a)   an approved mental health professional;

    (b)   (*revoked*)

    (c)   a first level nurse, registered in Sub-Part 1 of the Nurses' Part of the Register maintained under article 5 of the Nursing and Midwifery Order 2001;

    (d)   an occupational therapist registered in Part 6, or a social worker registered in Part 16, of the register maintained under article 5 of the Health and Social Work Professions Order 2001; or

    (e)   a chartered psychologist who is listed in the British Psychological Society's Register of Chartered Psychologists and who holds a relevant practising certificate issued by that Society.

(3) The supervisory body must be satisfied that the person –

    (a)   is not suspended from the register or list relevant to the person's profession mentioned in paragraph (2);

    (b)   has at least two years post registration experience in one of the professions mentioned in paragraph (2);

    (c)   has successfully completed training that has been approved by the Secretary of State to be a best interests assessor;

    (d)   except in the 12 month period beginning with the date the person has successfully completed the training referred to in sub-paragraph (c), the supervisory body must be satisfied that the person has, in the 12 months prior to selection, completed further training relevant to their role as a best interests assessor; and

    (e)   has the skills necessary to obtain, evaluate and analyse complex evidence and differing views and to weigh them appropriately in decision making.

Amendments—SI 2012/1479.

6 Eligibility to carry out a mental capacity assessment

A person is eligible to carry out a mental capacity assessment if that person is eligible to carry out –

    (a)   a mental health assessment; or

    (b)   a best interests assessment.

7 Eligibility to carry out an eligibility assessment

A person is eligible to carry out an eligibility assessment if that person is –

    (a)   approved under section 12 of the Mental Health Act 1983 and is eligible to carry out a mental health assessment; or

    (b)   an approved mental health professional and is eligible to carry out a best interests assessment.

8 Eligibility to carry out an age assessment

A person is eligible to carry out an age assessment if that person is eligible to carry out a best interests assessment.

9 Eligibility to carry out a no refusals assessment

A person is eligible to carry out a no refusals assessment if that person is eligible to carry out a best interests assessment.

PART 3
SELECTION OF ASSESSORS

10 Selection of assessors – relatives

(1) A supervisory body must not select a person to carry out an assessment if the person is –

    (a)   a relative of the relevant person; or

    (b)   a relative of a person who is financially interested in the care of the relevant person.

(2) For the purposes of this regulation a 'relative' means –

    (a)   a spouse, ex-spouse, civil partner or ex-civil partner;

    (b)   a person living with the relevant person as if they were a spouse or a civil partner;

    (c)   a parent or child;

    (d)   a brother or sister;

    (e)   a child of a person falling within sub-paragraphs (a), (b) or (d);

    (f)   a grandparent or grandchild;

    (g)   a grandparent-in-law or grandchild-in-law;

    (h)   an uncle or aunt;

    (i)   a brother-in-law or sister-in-law;

    (j)   a son-in-law or daughter-in-law;

    (k)   a first cousin; or

    (l)   a half-brother or half-sister.

(3) For the purposes of this regulation –

    (a)   the relationships in paragraph (2)(c) to (k) include step relationships;

    (b)   references to step relationships and in-laws in paragraph (2) are to be read in accordance with section 246 of the Civil Partnership Act 2004; and

    (c)   financial interest has the meaning given in regulation 11.

11 Selection of assessors – financial interest

(1) A supervisory body must not select a person to carry out an assessment where the person has a financial interest in the case.

(2) A person has a financial interest in a case where –

    (a)   that person is a partner, director, other office-holder or major shareholder of the managing authority that has made the application for a standard authorisation; and

    (b)   the managing authority is a care home or independent hospital.

(3) A major shareholder means –

    (a)   any person holding one tenth or more of the issued shares in the managing authority, where the managing authority is a company limited by shares; and

    (b)   in all other cases, any of the owners of the managing authority.

12 Selection of best interests assessors

(1) A supervisory body must not select a person to carry out a best interests assessment if that person is involved in the care, or making decisions about the care, of the relevant person.

(2) Where the managing authority and supervisory body are both the same body, the supervisory body must not select a person to carry out a best interests assessment who is employed by it or who is providing services to it.

PART 4
ASSESSMENTS

13 Time frame for assessments

(1) Except as provided in paragraph (2), all assessments required for a standard authorisation must be completed within the period of 21 days beginning with the date that the supervisory body receives a request for such an authorisation.

(2) Where a supervisory body receives a request for a standard authorisation and the managing authority has given an urgent authorisation under paragraph 76 of Schedule A1 to the Act, the assessments required for that standard authorisation must be completed within the period during which the urgent authorisation is in force.

14 Time limit for carrying out an assessment to decide whether or not there is an unauthorised deprivation of liberty

Subject to paragraph 69(3) to (5) of Schedule A1 to the Act, an assessment required under that paragraph must be completed within the period of 7 days beginning with the date that the supervisory body receives the request from an eligible person.

15 Relevant eligibility information

(1) This regulation applies where an individual is being assessed and the eligibility assessor and the best interests assessor are not the same person.

(2) The eligibility assessor must request that the best interests assessor provides any relevant eligibility information that the best interests assessor may have.

(3) The best interests assessor must comply with any request made under this regulation.

(4) In this regulation 'eligibility assessor' means a person selected to carry out the eligibility assessment under paragraph 46 of Schedule A1 to the Act.

PART 5
REQUESTS FOR A STANDARD AUTHORISATION

16 Information to be provided in a request for a standard authorisation

(1) A request for a standard authorisation must include the following information –

(a)   the name and gender of the relevant person;

(b)   the age of the relevant person or, where this is not known, whether the managing authority believes that the relevant person is aged 18 years or older;

(c)   the address and telephone number where the relevant person is currently located;

(d)   the name, address and telephone number of the managing authority and the name of the person within the managing authority who is dealing with the request;

(e)   the purpose for which the authorisation is requested;

(f)   the date from which the standard authorisation is sought; and

(g)   whether the managing authority has given an urgent authorisation under paragraph 76 of Schedule A1 to the Act and, if so, the date on which it expires.

(2) Except as provided for in paragraph (3), a request for a standard authorisation must include the following information if it is available or could reasonably be obtained by the managing authority –

(a)   any medical information relating to the relevant person's health that the managing authority considers to be relevant to the proposed restrictions to the relevant person's liberty;

(b)   the diagnosis of the mental disorder (within the meaning of the Mental Health Act 1983 but disregarding any exclusion for persons with learning disability) that the relevant person is suffering from;

(c)   any relevant care plans and relevant needs assessments;

(d)   the racial, ethnic or national origins of the relevant person;

(e)   whether the relevant person has any special communication needs;

(f)   details of the proposed restrictions on the relevant person's liberty;

(g)   whether section 39A of the Act (person becomes subject to Schedule A1) applies;

(h)   where the purpose of the proposed restrictions to the relevant person's liberty is to give treatment, whether the relevant person has made an advance decision that may be valid and applicable to some or all of that treatment;

(i)   whether the relevant person is subject to –
  (i)   the hospital treatment regime,
  (ii) the community treatment regime, or
  (iii) the guardianship regime;

(j)   the name, address and telephone number of –
  (i)   anyone named by the relevant person as someone to be consulted about his welfare,
  (ii)   anyone engaged in caring for the person or interested in his welfare,
  (iii) any donee of a lasting power of attorney granted by the person,
  (iv)   any deputy appointed for the person by the court, and
  (v)   any independent mental capacity advocate appointed in accordance with sections 37 to 39D of the Act; and

(k)   whether there is an existing authorisation in relation to the detention of the relevant person and, if so, the date of the expiry of that authorisation.

(3) Where –

(a)   there is an existing authorisation in force in relation to the detention of the relevant person; and

(b)   the managing authority makes a request in accordance with paragraph 30 of Schedule A1 to the Act for a further standard authorisation in relation to the same relevant person,

the request need not include any of the information mentioned in paragraph (2)(a) to (j) if that information remains the same as that supplied in relation to the request for the existing authorisation.

(4) In this regulation 'existing authorisation' has the same meaning as in paragraph 29 of Schedule A1 to the Act.

PART 6
SUPERVISORY BODIES: CARE HOMES AND HOSPITALS

Disputes about the Place of Ordinary Residence

17 Application and Interpretation of Part 6

(1) This Part applies where –

(a)   a local authority ('local authority A') receives a request from –
  (i)   a care home or hospital for a standard authorisation under paragraph 24, 25 or 30 of Schedule A1 to the Act, or

    (ii)   an eligible person to decide whether or not there is an unauthorised deprivation of liberty in a care home or hospital under paragraph 68 of Schedule A1 to the Act;

  (b)   local authority A wishes to dispute that it is the supervisory body; and

  (c)   a question as to the ordinary residence of the relevant person is to be determined by the Secretary of State under paragraph 183 of Schedule A1 to the Act.

(2) In this Part –

  (a)   'local authority A' has the meaning given in paragraph (1); and

  (b)   'local authority C' has the meaning given in regulation 18(2).

Amendments—SI 2013/235.

Note—These Regulations were amended with effect from 1 April 2013 to provide for amendments consequential to the coming into force of the provisions of the Health and Social Act 2012, which abolished Primary Care Trusts in England and necessitated the transfer of supervisory body responsibilities in England to local authorities for deprivations of liberty occurring in hospitals.

18 Arrangements where there is a question as to the ordinary residence

(1) Local authority A must act as supervisory body in relation to a request mentioned in regulation 17(1)(a) until the determination of the question as to the ordinary residence of the relevant person.

(2) But where another local authority ('local authority C') agrees to act as the supervisory body in place of local authority A, that local authority shall become the supervisory body until the determination of the question as to the ordinary residence of the relevant person.

(3) When the question about the ordinary residence of the relevant person has been determined, the local authority which has been identified as the supervisory body shall become the supervisory body.

19 Effect of change in supervisory body following determination of any question about ordinary residence

(1) Where the question of ordinary residence of the relevant person is determined in accordance with paragraph 183(3) of Schedule A1 to the Act, and another local authority ('local authority B') becomes the supervisory body in place of local authority A or local authority C, as the case may be, paragraphs (3) to (6A) shall apply.

(2) Where the question of ordinary residence of the relevant person is determined in accordance with paragraph 183(3) of Schedule A1 to the Act and local authority C remains the supervisory body, paragraphs (7) to (10) shall apply.

(3) Local authority B shall be treated as the supervisory body that received the request mentioned in regulation 17(1)(a) and must comply with the time limits specified in –

(a) regulation 13 for carrying out the assessments required for a standard authorisation; or

(b) regulation 14 for carrying out an assessment required under paragraph 69 of Schedule A1 to the Act,

as the case may be, where the assessments have still to be completed.

(4) Anything done by or in relation to local authority A or local authority C in connection with the authorisation or request, as the case may be, has effect, so far as is necessary for continuing its effect after the change, as if done by or in relation to local authority B.

(5) Anything which relates to the authorisation or request and which is in the process of being done by or in relation to local authority A or local authority C at the time of the change may be continued by or in relation to local authority B.

(6) But –

(a) local authority A or local authority C does not, by virtue of this regulation, cease to be liable for anything done by it in connection with the authorisation or request before the change; and

(b) local authority B does not, by virtue of this regulation, become liable for any such thing.

(6A) Local authority A or local authority C shall be entitled to recover from local authority B expenditure incurred in exercising functions as the supervisory body.

(7) Local authority C shall be treated as the supervisory body that received the request mentioned in regulation 17(1)(a) and must comply with the time limits specified in –

(a) regulation 13 for carrying out the assessments required for a standard authorisation; or

(b) regulation 14 for carrying out an assessment required under paragraph 69 of Schedule A1 to the Act,

as the case may be, where the assessments have still to be completed.

(8) Anything done by or in relation to local authority A in connection with the authorisation or request, as the case may be, has effect, so far as is necessary for continuing its effect after the change, as if done by or in relation to local authority C.

(9) Anything which relates to the authorisation or request and which is in the process of being done by or in relation to local authority A at the time of the change may be continued by or in relation to local authority C.

(10) But –

(a) local authority A does not, by virtue of this regulation, cease to be liable for anything done by it in connection with the authorisation or request before the change; and

(b) local authority C does not, by virtue of this regulation, become liable for any such thing.

APPENDIX 5

MENTAL CAPACITY (DEPRIVATION OF LIBERTY: APPOINTMENT OF RELEVANT PERSON'S REPRESENTATIVE) REGULATIONS 2008, SI 2008/1315

1 Citation, commencement and application

(1) These Regulations may be cited as the Mental Capacity (Deprivation of Liberty: Appointment of Relevant Person's Representative) Regulations 2008 and shall come into force on 3 November 2008.

(2) These Regulations apply in relation to England only.

2 Interpretation

In these Regulations –

'best interests assessor' means a person selected to carry out a best interests assessment under paragraph 38 of Schedule A1 to the Act;

'donee' is a person who has a lasting power of attorney conferred on them by the relevant person, giving that donee the authority to make decisions about the relevant person's personal welfare;

'the Act' means the Mental Capacity Act 2005; and

'the relevant person's managing authority' means the managing authority that has made the application for a standard authorisation in respect of the relevant person.

PART 1
SELECTION OF REPRESENTATIVES

3 Selection of a person to be a representative – general

(1) In addition to any requirements in regulations 6 to 9 and 11, a person can only be selected to be a representative if they are –

(a) 18 years of age or over;
(b) able to keep in contact with the relevant person;
(c) willing to be the relevant person's representative;
(d) not financially interested in the relevant person's managing authority;
(e) not a relative of a person who is financially interested in the managing authority;
(f) not employed by, or providing services to, the relevant person's managing authority, where the relevant person's managing authority is a care home;

(g)   not employed to work in the relevant person's managing authority in a role that is, or could be, related to the relevant person's case, where the relevant person's managing authority is a hospital; and

(h)   not employed to work in the supervisory body that is appointing the representative in a role that is, or could be, related to the relevant person's case.

(2) For the purposes of this regulation a 'relative' means –

(a)   a spouse, ex-spouse, civil partner or ex-civil partner;

(b)   a person living with the relevant person as if they were a spouse or a civil partner;

(c)   a parent or child;

(d)   a brother or sister;

(e)   a child of a person falling within sub-paragraphs (a), (b) or (d);

(f)   a grandparent or grandchild;

(g)   a grandparent-in-law or grandchild-in-law;

(h)   an uncle or aunt;

(i)   a brother-in-law or sister-in-law;

(j)   a son-in-law or daughter-in-law;

(k)   a first cousin; or

(l)   a half-brother or half-sister.

(3) For the purposes of this regulation –

(a)   the relationships in paragraph (2)(c) to (k) include step relationships;

(b)   references to step relationships and in-laws in paragraph (2) are to be read in accordance with section 246 of the Civil Partnership Act 2004;

(c)   a person has a financial interest in a managing authority where –

    (i)   that person is a partner, director, other office-holder or major shareholder of the managing authority that has made the application for a standard authorisation, and

    (ii)   the managing authority is a care home or independent hospital; and

(d)   a major shareholder means –

    (i)   any person holding one tenth or more of the issued shares in the managing authority, where the managing authority is a company limited by shares, and

    (ii)   in all other cases, any of the owners of the managing authority.

4 Determination of capacity

The best interests assessor must determine whether the relevant person has capacity to select a representative.

5 Selection by the relevant person

(1) Where the best interests assessor determines that the relevant person has capacity, the relevant person may select a family member, friend or carer.

(2) Where the relevant person does not wish to make a selection under paragraph (1), regulation 8 applies.

6 Selection by a donee or deputy

(1) Where –

    (a)   the best interests assessor determines that the relevant person lacks capacity to select a representative; and

    (b)   the relevant person has a donee or deputy and the donee's or deputy's scope of authority permits the selection of a family member, friend or carer of the relevant person,

the donee or deputy may select such a person.

(2) A donee or deputy may select himself or herself to be the relevant person's representative.

(3) Where a donee or deputy does not wish to make a selection under paragraph (1) or (2), regulation 8 applies.

7 Confirmation of eligibility of family member, friend or carer and recommendation to the supervisory body

(1) The best interests assessor must confirm that a person selected under regulation 5(1) or 6(1) or (2) is eligible to be a representative.

(2) Where the best interests assessor confirms the selected person's eligibility under paragraph (1), the assessor must recommend the appointment of that person as a representative to the supervisory body.

(3) Where the best interests assessor is unable to confirm the selected person's eligibility under paragraph (1), the assessor must –

    (a)   advise the person who made the selection of that decision and give the reasons for it; and

    (b)   invite them to make a further selection.

8 Selection by the best interests assessor

(1) The best interests assessor may select a family member, friend or carer as a representative where paragraph (2) applies.

(2) The best interests assessor may make a selection where –

    (a)   the relevant person has the capacity to make a selection under regulation 5(1) but does not wish to do so;

    (b)   the relevant person's donee or deputy does not wish to make a selection under regulation 6(1) or (2); or

    (c)   the relevant person lacks the capacity to make a selection and –

        (i)   does not have a donee or deputy, or

        (ii)   has a donee or deputy but the donee's or deputy's scope of authority does not permit the selection of a representative.

(3) Where the best interests assessor selects a person in accordance with paragraph (2), the assessor must recommend that person for appointment as a representative to the supervisory body.

(4) But the best interests assessor must not select a person under paragraph (2) where the relevant person, donee or deputy objects to that selection.

(5) The best interests assessor must notify the supervisory body if they do not select a person who is eligible to be a representative.

9 Selection by the supervisory body

(1) Where a supervisory body is given notice under regulation 8(5), it may select a person to be the representative, who –

(a) would be performing the role in a professional capacity;
(b) has satisfactory skills and experience to perform the role;
(c) is not a family member, friend or carer of the relevant person;
(d) is not employed by, or providing services to, the relevant person's managing authority, where the relevant person's managing authority is a care home;
(e) is not employed to work in the relevant person's managing authority in a role that is, or could be, related to the relevant person's case, where the relevant person's managing authority is a hospital; and
(f) is not employed by the supervisory body.

(2) The supervisory body must be satisfied that there is in respect of the person –

(a) an enhanced criminal record certificate issued pursuant to section 113B of the Police Act 1997 (enhanced criminal record certificates); or
(b) if the purpose for which the certificate is required is not one prescribed under subsection (2) of that section, a criminal record certificate issued pursuant to section 113A of that Act (criminal record certificates).

Amendments—SI 2008/2368.

PART 2
APPOINTMENT OF REPRESENTATIVES

10 Commencement of appointment procedure

The procedure for appointing a representative must begin as soon as –

(a) a best interests assessor is selected by the supervisory body for the purposes of a request for a standard authorisation; or
(b) a relevant person's representative's appointment terminates, or is to be terminated, under regulation 14 and the relevant person remains subject to a standard authorisation.

11 Appointment of representative

Except where regulation 9 applies, a supervisory body may not appoint a representative unless the person is recommended to it under regulations 7 or 8.

12 Formalities of appointing a representative

(1) The offer of an appointment to a representative must be made in writing and state –

   (a)   the duties of a representative to –
      (i)   maintain contact with the relevant person,
      (ii)   represent the relevant person in matters relating to, or connected with, the deprivation of liberty, and
      (iii)   support the relevant person in matters relating to, or connected with, the deprivation of liberty; and

   (b)   the length of the period of the appointment.

(2) The representative must inform the supervisory body in writing that they are willing to accept the appointment and that they have understood the duties set out in sub-paragraph (1)(a).

(3) The appointment must be made for the period of the standard authorisation.

(4) The supervisory body must send copies of the written appointment to –

   (a)   the appointed person;
   (b)   the relevant person;
   (c)   the relevant person's managing authority;
   (d)   any donee or deputy of the relevant person;
   (e)   any independent mental capacity advocate appointed in accordance with sections 37 to 39D of the Act, involved in the relevant person's case; and
   (f)   every interested person named by the best interests assessor in their report as somebody the assessor has consulted in carrying out the assessment.

13 Termination of representative's appointment

A person ceases to be a representative if –

   (a)   the person dies;
   (b)   the person informs the supervisory body that they are no longer willing to continue as representative;
   (c)   the period of the appointment ends;
   (d)   a relevant person who has selected a family member, friend or carer under regulation 5(1) who has been appointed as their representative informs the supervisory body that they object to the person continuing to be a representative;
   (e)   a donee or deputy who has selected a family member, friend or carer of the relevant person under regulation 6(1) who has been appointed as a

representative informs the supervisory body that they object to the person continuing to be a representative;

(f)   the supervisory body terminates the appointment because it is satisfied that the representative is not maintaining sufficient contact with the relevant person in order to support and represent them;

(g)   the supervisory body terminates the appointment because it is satisfied that the representative is not acting in the best interests of the relevant person; or

(h)   the supervisory body terminates the appointment because it is satisfied that the person is no longer eligible or was not eligible at the time of appointment, to be a representative.

14 Formalities of termination of representative's appointment

(1) Where a representative's appointment is to be terminated for a reason specified in paragraphs (c) to (h) of regulation 13, the supervisory body must inform the representative of –

(a)   the pending termination of the appointment;
(b)   the reasons for the termination of the appointment; and
(c)   the date on which the appointment terminates.

(2) The supervisory body must send copies of the termination of the appointment to –

(a)   the relevant person;
(b)   the relevant person's managing authority;
(c)   any donee or deputy of the relevant person;
(d)   any independent mental capacity advocate appointed in accordance with sections 37 to 39D of the Act, involved in the relevant person's case; and
(e)   every interested person named by the best interests assessor in their report as somebody the assessor has consulted in carrying out the assessment.

15 Payment to a representative

A supervisory body may make payments to a representative appointed following a selection under regulation 9.

APPENDIX 6

MENTAL CAPACITY ACT 2005 (INDEPENDENT MENTAL CAPACITY ADVOCATES) (GENERAL) REGULATIONS 2006, SI 2006/1832

1 Citation, commencement and extent

(1) These Regulations may be cited as the Mental Capacity Act 2005 (Independent Mental Capacity Advocates) (General) Regulations 2006.

(2) These Regulations shall come into force –

    (a)   for the purpose of enabling the Secretary of State to make arrangements under section 35 of the Act, and for the purpose of enabling local authorities to approve IMCAs, on 1 November 2006, and

    (b)   for all other purposes, on 1 April 2007.

(3) These Regulations apply in relation to England only.

2 Interpretation

(1) In these Regulations –

    'the Act' means the Mental Capacity Act 2005; and
    'IMCA' means an independent mental capacity advocate.

(2) In these Regulations, references to instructions given to a person to act as an IMCA are to instructions given under sections 37 to 39 of the Act or under regulations made by virtue of section 41 of the Act.

3 Meaning of NHS Body

(1) For the purposes of sections 37 and 38 of the Act, 'NHS body' means a body in England which is –

    (a)   … ;
    (b)   an NHS foundation trust;
    (ba)   a clinical commissioning group
    (bb)   the National Health Service Commissioning Board
    (bc)   a local authority (within the meaning of section 2B of the National Health Service Act 2006) acting in the exercise of public health functions (within the meaning of that Act)
    (c)   … ;
    (d)   an NHS Trust; or
    (e)   a Care Trust.

(2) In this regulation –

'Care Trust' means a body designated as a Care Trust under section 45 of the Health and Social Care Act 2001;

'clinical commissioning group' means a body established under section 14D of the National Health Service Act 2006;

'NHS foundation trust' has the meaning given in section 1 of the Health and Social Care (Community Health and Standards) Act 2003;

'NHS trust' means a body established under section 5 of the National Health Service and Community Care Act 1990;

Amendments—SI 2013/235.

4 Meaning of serious medical treatment

(1) This regulation defines serious medical treatment for the purposes of section 37 of the Act.

(2) Serious medical treatment is treatment which involves providing, withdrawing or withholding treatment in circumstances where –

(a)   in a case where a single treatment is being proposed, there is a fine balance between its benefits to the patient and the burdens and risks it is likely to entail for him,

(b)   in a case where there is a choice of treatments, a decision as to which one to use is finely balanced, or

(c)   what is proposed would be likely to involve serious consequences for the patient.

5 Appointment of independent mental capacity advocates

(1) No person may be appointed to act as an IMCA for the purposes of sections 37 to 39 of the Act, or regulations made by virtue of section 41 of the Act, unless –

(a)   he is for the time being approved by a local authority on the grounds that he satisfies the appointment requirements, or

(b)   he belongs to a class of persons which is for the time being approved by a local authority on the grounds that all persons in that class satisfy the appointment requirements.

(2) The appointment requirements, in relation to a person appointed to act as an IMCA, are that –

(a)   he has appropriate experience or training or an appropriate combination of experience and training;

(b)   he is a person of integrity and good character; and

(c)   he is able to act independently of any person who instructs him.

(3) Before a determination is made in relation to any person for the purposes of paragraph (2)(b), there must be obtained, in respect of that person, an enhanced criminal record certificate issued pursuant to section 113B of the Police Act 1997 which includes –

(a) where the determination is in respect of a person's appointment as an IMCA for a person who has not attained the age of 18, suitability information relating to children (within the meaning of section 113BA of the Police Act 1997);

(b) where the determination is in respect of a person's appointment as an IMCA for a person who has attained the age of 18, suitability information relating to vulnerable adults (within the meaning of section 113BB of that Act).]

Amendments—SI 2009/2376.

6 Functions of an independent mental capacity advocate

(1) This regulation applies where an IMCA has been instructed by an authorised person to represent a person ('P').

(2) 'Authorised person' means a person who is required or enabled to instruct an IMCA under sections 37 to 39 of the Act or under regulations made by virtue of section 41of the Act.

(3) The IMCA must determine in all the circumstances how best to represent and support P.

(4) In particular, the IMCA must –

(a) verify that the instructions were issued by an authorised person;

(b) to the extent that it is practicable and appropriate to do so –
   (i) interview P, and
   (ii) examine the records relevant to P to which the IMCA has access under section 35(6) of the Act;

(c) to the extent that it is practicable and appropriate to do so, consult –
   (i) persons engaged in providing care or treatment for P in a professional capacity or for remuneration, and
   (ii) other persons who may be in a position to comment on P's wishes, feelings, beliefs or values; and

(d) take all practicable steps to obtain such other information about P, or the act or decision that is proposed in relation to P, as the IMCA considers necessary.

(5) The IMCA must evaluate all the information he has obtained for the purpose of –

(a) ascertaining the extent of the support provided to P to enable him to participate in making any decision about the matter in relation to which the IMCA has been instructed;

(b) ascertaining what P's wishes and feelings would be likely to be, and the beliefs and values that would be likely to influence P, if he had capacity in relation to the proposed act or decision;

(c) ascertaining what alternative courses of action are available in relation to P;

(d) where medical treatment is proposed for P, ascertaining whether he would be likely to benefit from a further medical opinion.

(6) The IMCA must prepare a report for the authorised person who instructed him.

(7) The IMCA may include in the report such submissions as he considers appropriate in relation to P and the act or decision which is proposed in relation to him.

7 Challenges to decisions affecting persons who lack capacity

(1) This regulation applies where –

    (a)   an IMCA has been instructed to represent a person ('P') in relation to any matter, and

    (b)   a decision affecting P (including a decision as to his capacity) is made in that matter.

(2) The IMCA has the same rights to challenge the decision as he would have if he were a person (other than an IMCA) engaged in caring for P or interested in his welfare.

APPENDIX 7

FORMS

COPDLA – Application Form

Print form Reset form

Court of Protection

Deprivation of liberty

Application form

For urgent consideration

Case no.	
Date of application	
Date of issue	

This form should only be used for applications to vary or terminate a standard or urgent authorisation made by a supervisory body under Schedule A1 of the Mental Capacity Act 2005.

Full name of person to whom the application relates including their date of birth
(this is the name of the person who lacks, or is alleged to lack, capacity)

Date of birth [ ] / [ ] / [   ]

Date of urgent/
standard authorisation [ ] / [ ] / [   ]   Date of effective detention [ ] / [ ] / [   ]

Section 1 – Contact details

Applicant

Name

Address

Telephone no.

Mobile no.

Postcode

Email

What is the applicant's relationship to the
relevant person? (This is the person that the
application is about)

Applicant's solicitor or representatives

Name

Address

Telephone no.

Mobile no.

Fax no.

Postcode

Email

1

© Crown copyright 2015

Relevant person's details if not applicant

Name

Address

Telephone no.

Mobile no.

Fax no.

Postcode

Email

Supervisory body PCT/LA

Name

Address

Telephone no.

Mobile no.

Fax no.

Postcode

Email

Managing Authority/Hospital/Care Home

Name

Address

Telephone no.

Mobile no.

Fax no.

Postcode

Email

2

IMCA

Name	

Address		Telephone no.	
		Mobile no.	
		Fax no.	

Postcode

Email

Relevant person's representative

Name	

Address		Telephone no.	
		Mobile no.	
		Fax no.	

Postcode

Email

3

Section 2 – Details of other interested parties

Name

Address

Telephone no.

Fax no.

DX no.

Postcode

Email

Name

Address

Telephone no.

Fax no.

DX no.

Postcode

Email

Section 3 – Details of issue to be challenged

3.1 Date of decision

3.2 Where an **urgent** authorisation has been given, the court may determine any question relating to any of the following matters:

☐ whether the urgent authorisation should have been given

☐ the period during which the urgent authorisation is to be in force

☐ the purpose for which the urgent authorisation is given

☐ other

4

3.3 Where a **standard** authorisation has been given, the court may determine any question relating to any of the following matters:

☐ whether the relevant person meets one or more of the qualifying requirements

☐ the period during which the standard authorisation is to be in force

☐ the purpose for which the standard authorisation is given

☐ the conditions subject to which the standard authorisation is given

☐ other

3.4 Other issues that may arise

Are you making an interim application?	☐ Yes	☐ No
Do you intend to bring other applications if this application succeds in whole or in part?	☐ Yes	☐ No
Do you intend to bring other applications if this application fails?	☐ Yes	☐ No

Section 4 – Detailed statement of grounds

☐ Set out below   ☐ Attached

Section 5 – Other issues of the case

5.1   Are there other issues that will arise for determination in respect of the relevant person and any applications that you have made or intend to make in respect of them?   ☐Yes   ☐No

If Yes, please give details below

Section 6 – Other applications

6.1   Are you aware of any previous application(s) to the Court of Protection regarding   ☐ Yes   ☐ No
       the person to whom this application relates?

       If Yes, please give as much of the following information as you can. If there has
       been more than one previous application please attach the information about
       other previous applications on a separate sheet of paper.

       The name of the applicant

       _____

       The date of the order

       ☐☐ / ☐☐ / ☐☐☐☐

       Case number

       _____

       Please attach a copy of the order(s), if available.

           ☐ Copy attached   ☐ Not available

Section 7 - Attending court hearings

7.1   If the court requires you to attend a hearing do you need any special   ☐ Yes   ☐ No
       assistance or facilities?

       If Yes, please say what your requirements are. If necessary,
       court staff may contact you about your requirements.

Section 8 – Statement of facts relied on

Section 9 - Statement of truth

The statement of truth is to be signed by you, your solicitor or your litigation friend.

*(I believe) (The applicant believes) that the facts stated in this application form and its annex(es) are true.

Signed

Date

Name

Name of firm

Position or office held

8

Section 10 - Supporting documents

10.1   Which of the following documents are you filing with this application and any you will be filing later?

☐ Standard authorisation   ☐ Best interests assessment

☐ Urgent authorisation   ☐ Form COP DLB Declaration of
                                                exceptional urgency

☐ Age assessment   ☐ Form COP 24 Witness Statement

☐ No refusals assessment   ☐ A copy of the Legal Aid or CSLF certificate
                                                (if legally represented)

☐ Mental capacity assessment   ☐ Copies of any relevant statutory material

☐ Mental health assessment   ☐ Draft Order or Directions

☐ Eligibility assessment

10.2   The following documents not being in my possession. I request   the Supervisory Body/
        Managing Authority, to file copies of the following documents with their acknowledgment of service

☐ Standard authorisation   ☐ Mental health assessment

☐ Urgent authorisation   ☐ Eligibility assessment

☐ Age assessment   ☐ Best interests assessment

☐ No refusals assessment   ☐ Care plan

☐ Mental capacity assessment

10.3   Please explain why you have not supplied a document and a date when you expect it to be available:

Signed ....   Applicant's Solicitor ....

Print form   Reset form

COPDLB – Declaration of Exceptional Emergency

	Print form	Reset form

COP DLB 07.15 Court of Protection

Deprivation of liberty

Declaration of
exceptional urgency

Case no.	
Date of application	
Date of issue	

This form should only be used for applications to vary or terminate a standard or urgent authorisation made by a supervisory body under Schedule A1 of the Mental Capacity Act 2005.

Full name of person to whom the application relates
(this is the name of the person who is deprived/will be deprived of their liberty)

Date of urgent/
standard authorisation [ ] / [ ] / [   ]   Date of effective detention [ ] / [ ] / [   ]

Section 1 - Reasons for urgency

1.1   Please give reasons for the urgency

1.2   Please state what interim relief is sought and why?

Signed [   ]   Dated [ ] / [ ] / [   ]

Section 2 - Proposed timetable

2.1   Please tick the boxes that apply

☐ The application for interim relief should be
considered within

[   ] ☐ hours
☐ days

☐ Abridgement of time is sought for the lodging of
acknowledgments of service

1

© Crown Copyright 2015

Section 3 – Service

3.1   On whom have you served a copy of this form?

☐ **Relevant person**

Date served
☐ ☐ / ☐ ☐ / ☐ ☐ ☐ ☐

☐ by fax machine
Fax no.
[   ]
Time sent
[   ]

☐ by handing it to or leaving it with
Name
[   ]

☐ by e-mail (please give address below)
[   ]

☐ **Managing Authority**

Date served
☐ ☐ / ☐ ☐ / ☐ ☐ ☐ ☐

☐ by fax machine
Fax no.
[   ]
Time sent
[   ]

☐ by handing it to or leaving it with
Name
[   ]

☐ by e-mail (please give address below)
[   ]

☐ **Supervisory Body**

Date served
☐ ☐ / ☐ ☐ / ☐ ☐ ☐ ☐

☐ by fax machine
Fax no.
[   ]
Time sent
[   ]

☐ by handing it to or leaving it with
Name
[   ]

☐ by e-mail (please give address below)
[   ]

☐ **IMCA**

Date served
☐ ☐ / ☐ ☐ / ☐ ☐ ☐ ☐

☐ by fax machine
Fax no.
[   ]
Time sent
[   ]

☐ by handing it to or leaving it with
Name
[   ]

☐ by e-mail (please give address below)
[   ]

☐ **Relevant persons representative**

Date served
☐ ☐ / ☐ ☐ / ☐ ☐ ☐ ☐

☐ by fax machine
Fax no.
[   ]
Time sent
[   ]

☐ by handing it to or leaving it with
Name
[   ]

☐ by e-mail (please give address below)
[   ]

☐ **Interested parties**

Date served
☐ ☐ / ☐ ☐ / ☐ ☐ ☐ ☐

☐ by fax machine
Fax no.
[   ]
Time sent
[   ]

☐ by handing it to or leaving it with
Name
[   ]

☐ by e-mail (please give address below)
[   ]

Print form | Reset form

COPDLD – Certificate of Service/Non-Service

Print form   Reset form

Court of Protection

Deprivation of liberty

**Certificate of service/
non-service**

**Certificate of notification/
non-notification**

Case no.	
Name of applicant	
Name of respondent	
Filed by	
Date	

This form should only be used for applications to vary or terminate a standard or urgent authorisation made by a supervisory body under Schedule A1 of the Mental Capacity Act 2005.

Full name of person to whom the application relates
(this is the person who is deprived/will be deprived of their liberty)

Section 1 – Details of the person served/notified

1.1   Name of the person(s) served/notified:

Name ....

Date served/notified
☐☐/☐☐/☐☐☐☐

Name ....

Date served/notified
☐☐/☐☐/☐☐☐☐

Name ....

Date served/notified
☐☐/☐☐/☐☐☐☐

Name ....

Date served/notified
☐☐/☐☐/☐☐☐☐

Section 2 – Document served

2.1   Title or description of the document (tick only **one** box)

☐ application form

☐ other (please give details)

1

© Crown Copyright 2015

Section 3 – Person(s) not served or notified

3.1   Name of the person(s) who have not been served/notified:

Name

Reason

Name

Reason

Name

Reason

Name

Reason

Section 4 – Statement of truth

The statement of truth must be signed by the person who served/provided notification.

I believe that the facts stated in this certificate are true.

Signed

Date

Name

Name of firm

Position or office held

▶ Print form   ▶ Reset form

COPDLE – Acknowledgment of Service/Notification

| Print form | Reset form |

Court of Protection

Deprivation of liberty

Acknowledgment of service/notification

Case no.	
Name of applicant	
Name of respondent	
Name of party acknowledging	
Date	

This form should only be used for applications to vary or terminate a standard or urgent authorisation made by a supervisory body under Schedule A1 of the Mental Capacity Act 2005.

Full name of person to whom the application relates
(this is the name of the person who is deprived/will be deprived of their liberty)

Section 1 - The person served/notified

1.1   Your details   ☐ Mr.   ☐ Mrs.   ☐ Miss   ☐ Ms.   ☐ Other _____

     First name

     Last name

1.2   Address (including postcode)   Telephone no.

     E-mail address

1.3   Is a solicitor representing you?   ☐ Yes   ☐ No

     If Yes, please give the solicitor's details.

     Name

     Address (including postcode)   Telephone no.

     Fax no.

     DX no.

     E-mail address

1

1.4   Which address should official documentation be sent to?

☐ Your address

☐ Solicitor's address

☐ Other address (please provide details)

Section 2 – Attending court hearings

2.1   If the court requires you to attend a hearing do you need any special
assistance or facilities?   ☐ Yes   ☐ No

If Yes, please say what your requirements are. If necessary, court staff may
contact you about your requirements.

Section 3 – Signature

Signed

Date served/notified

Person served/notified ('s solicitor) ('s litigation friend)

Name

Name of firm

Position or office held

Section 4 – Supervisory Body or Managing Authority only

4.1   I am serving and filing the following documents:

1.

2.

3.

4.

Signed

Date

Print form   Reset form

COPDOL10 – Application to Authorise a Deprivation of Liberty

**COP
DOL10
10.14** Court of Protection

Application to authorise
a deprivation of liberty

(section 4A(3) and 16(2)(a) of the
Mental Capacity Act 2005)

A streamlined procedure pursuant to Re X and Ors (Deprivation
of Liberty) [2014] EWCOP 25 and Re X and Ors (Deprivation of
Liberty)(Number 2) Re [2014] EWCOP 37

> Print form   Reset form

For office use only
Date received
Case no.
Date issued

Before completing this form please read the guidance leaflet attached. You can
download forms and leaflets at hmctsformfinder.justice.gov.uk. Search for form
type: 'Court of Protection'.

SEAL

Please give the full name of the person to whom the application is about

1. Statement of reasons for urgency

Any factors that ought to be brought specifically to the court's attention
(the applicant being under a specific duty to make full and frank
disclosure to the court of all facts and matters that might have an
impact upon the court's decision).

2. Order sought

Please specify the nature of the order you seek and attach a draft.

Duration of the Order sought

If granted the deprivation of liberty will be reviewed by the court at least annually. Do you consider that the authorisation will require a shorter review period? ☐ Yes ☐ No

If Yes, please provide details

3. Your details (the applicant)

☐ Mr. ☐ Mrs. ☐ Miss ☐ Ms. ☐ Other _____

Full name

Post held/Job title

Name of organisation

Address

DX number

Telephone

Email

4. Permission

Are you applying for permission to make this application? ☐ Yes

5. The person the application is about

(a) Personal details

☐ Mr. ☐ Mrs. ☐ Miss ☐ Ms. ☐ Other _____

First name

Middle name(s)

Last name

Maiden name
(if applicable)

Date of birth | D | D | M | M | Y | Y | Y | Y |

Is the person:

☐ Married or in a civil partnership

☐ In a relationship with a person who is not a spouse or civil partner

☐ Separated

☐ Divorced (give date)

☐ Widowed (give date of death of spouse or civil partner)

☐ Single

Full address including postcode

What type of accommodation is this?
eg. supported living arrangement, shared lives, own home, other

Name of local authority or NHS body responsible for the care placement

3

Is the person the application about subject to

☐ Detention under the Mental Health Act 1983

☐ A Community Treatment Order

☐ Guardianship

Will the proposed deprivation of liberty conflict with any such treatment or measure?   ☐ Yes   ☐ No

If Yes, please give details

[blank box]

(b) Decisions already made

Has the person the application is about made a relevant advance decision?   ☐ Yes   ☐ No

If Yes, please provide details and set out whether the decision made conflicts with the order sought in this application.

[blank box]

Has the person the application is about made a lasting power of attorney?   ☐ Yes   ☐ No

If Yes, please provide details and set out whether any relevant decision(s) made by the attorney(s) conflicts with the order sought in this application.

[blank box]

Has the court made an order appointing a deputy? ☐ Yes ☐ No

If Yes, please provide details of the deputy(s) and set out whether any relevant decision(s) made by the deputy(s) conflict with the order sought in this application

Are you aware of any previous application to the court regarding the person the application is about? ☐ Yes ☐ No

If Yes, please provide details.

I enclose a copy of the

☐ advance decision

☐ LPA

☐ relevant court order

6. Statement of truth

I believe the facts stated in this application form are true.

Signed

*Applicant ('s solicitor)

Name

Date

Name of organisation

Position or office held

* Please delete the options in brackets that do not apply.

Annex A: Evidence in support of an application to authorise a deprivation of liberty

(Section 4A(3) and 16(2)(a) of the Mental Capacity Act 2005)

Please give the full name of the person the application is about

☐

1. Assessment of capacity

☐ I confirm that the person the application is about has been assessed as having an impairment or disturbance in the functioning of the mind or brain and lacks capacity to consent to the measures proposed and the deprivation of liberty which is identified within the application.

☐ I attach form COP3 or other evidence of capacity

2. Mental Health Assessment - Unsoundness of mind

☐ I confirm that the person has been medically diagnosed as being of "unsound mind" and I attach written evidence from a medical practitioner

If your assessment of capacity on form COP3 has not been completed by a registered medical practitioner, you must also attach written evidence from a registered medical practitioner containing a diagnosis that the person this application is about suffers from a diagnosis of 'unsoundness of mind'.

☐ I am submitting the mental health assessment and assessment of capacity as a single document

☐ COP3 completed by a medical practitioner

3. Deprivation of liberty

Describe the factual circumstances relating to the deprivation of liberty with particular reference to whether the person the application is about is free to leave their residence and what type of supervision arrangements are in place.

(a) Is the person free to leave? ☐ Yes ☐ No

If No, please give details

[blank box]

(b) Is the person under constant supervision and control? ☐ Yes ☐ No

If Yes, please give details

[blank box]

(c) Is the person under physical restraint? ☐ Yes ☐ No

(d) Is sedation being used? ☐ Yes ☐ No

If you have answered Yes to either question above, please give details

[blank box]

(e) Is the person prevented from having contact with others? ☐ Yes ☐ No

If Yes, please give details

(f) What restrictions if any are imposed or measures used which affect the person's access to the community?

Please give details

(g) Are there any other relevant factors that relate to the deprivation of liberty? ☐ Yes ☐ No

If Yes, please give details

(h) Please explain why the proposed deprivation of liberty
is thought to be imputable to the state

In the light of the responses to the questions under
this heading, do you consider that the arrangements
represent a deprivation of liberty?

☐ Yes ☐ No

4. Statement of best interests

State why the arrangements for which the authorisation as a deprivation of liberty is sought are necessary in
the best interests of the person the application is about.

State what harm may occur or what the risks would be if the person were not deprived of their liberty.
Provide detail of what the harm would be, how serious it would be and how likely it is to arise.

State why the deprivation of liberty is proportionate

Explain why it is considered that the risk of harm and the seriousness of harm justifies the restrictions amounting to a deprivation of liberty.

What less restrictive options have been tried or considered?

Explain why the option you propose is the least restrictive option and is in the best interests of the person.

☐ I attach the care plan

☐ I attach a copy of the best interests assessment relating to the placement

5. Other information

Provide any other information you think may be relevant in helping the court reach a decision

6. Statement of truth

I believe the facts stated in this annex are true.

Signed

Name

Date

Name of organisation

Position or office held

Annex B: Consultation with people with an interest in an application to authorise a deprivation of liberty

(Section 4A(3) and 16(2)(a) of the Mental Capacity Act 2005)

Please give the full name of the person the application is about

Section 4(7) of the Mental Capacity Act places a duty on a decision maker to take into account the views of other people who have an interest in the person's personal welfare.

You should consult with:

(a) any donee of a lasting power of attorney granted by the person;

(b) any deputy appointed for the person by the court;

and, if possible, with at least three people from the following categories:

(c) anyone named by the person to whom the application is about as someone to be consulted on the matters raised by the application; and

(d) anyone engaged in caring for the person or interested in their welfare

You must inform the people consulted with of the information contained in section 40 of the Practice Direction 10AA and provide details, including attaching statements.

1. People who have been consulted and who fall within the categories (a) - (d) above

Name	Address	Connection to the person	Date consulted	Please state whether they support or object to the proposed arrangements and provide details of any views expressed. If none, insert 'none'.

2. People who have not been consulted within the categories (a) - (d) above

Name	Address	Reason why they were not consulted	Connection to the person

3. Litigation friend

If required, please list who would be prepared to act as Litigation Friend

Name	Address

4. Statement of truth

I believe the facts stated in this annex are true.

Signed

Name

Date

Name of organisation

Position or office held

Annex C: Consultation with the person the application is about in support of an application to authorise a deprivation of liberty

(Section 4A(3) and 16(2)(a) of the Mental Capacity Act 2005)

Please give the full name of the person the application is about

_____

Notes:
The person this application is about must be consulted about the application and the person undertaking this consultation must take all reasonable steps to assist the person to make a decision. If the person the application is about does not have capacity to consent to being deprived of their liberty, they must be given the opportunity to be involved in the proceedings, and to express their wishes and views, to help the court reach a decision about whether the proposed deprivation of liberty would be in their best interests.

Chapter 3 of the Mental Capacity Act Code of Practice contains practical guidance about consulting and encouraging participation.

The person undertaking the consultation should be someone who knows the person the application is about, and who is best placed to express their wishes and views. It could be a relative or close friend, or someone who the person has previously chosen to act on their behalf (for example an attorney). If no suitable person is available, then an IMCA (Independent Mental Capacity Advocate) or another similar or independent advocate should be appointed to perform the role.

1. Details of the person undertaking the consultation

☐ Mr.   ☐ Mrs.   ☐ Miss   ☐ Ms.   ☐ Other _____

First name _____

Middle name(s) _____

Last name _____

2. Statement by the person undertaking the consultation

Describe your relationship to the person

How long have you known them?

Date of consultation

D	D	M	M	Y	Y	Y	Y

(a) Confirm that you explained to the person the application is about:

(i) that the applicant is making an application to court;

(ii) that the application is to consider whether the person lacks capacity to make decisions in relation to their residence and care, and whether to authorise a deprivation of their liberty in connection with the arrangements set out in the care plan;

(iii) what the proposed arrangements under the order sought are;

(iv) that the person is entitled to express their views, wishes and feelings in relation to the proposed arrangements and the application, and that the person undertaking the consultation will ensure that these are communicated to the court;

(v) that the person is entitled to seek to take part in the proceedings by being joined as a party or otherwise, what that means, and that the person undertaking the consultation will ensure that any such request is communicated to the court;

(vi) that the person undertaking the consultation can help them to obtain advice and assistance if they do not agree with the proposed arrangements in the application.

Please give details

(b) Did the person this application is about express any views, wishes or feelings in relation to the application and the proposed/actual deprivation of liberty? ☐ Yes ☐ No

If Yes, please give details and the manner of expressing those views if appropriate

(c) Does the person wish to take part in the proceedings? ☐ Yes ☐ No

If Yes, please explain how

(d) Are you aware of any present or past wishes, feelings or beliefs (including religious, cultural and moral beliefs of the person this application is about) and values that must be taken into account before the court authorises a deprivation of liberty? ☐ Yes ☐ No

If Yes, please give details; include in particular any relevant oral or written statements made or views expressed when they had capacity. Set out any beliefs and values which might influence the decision if they had capacity and any other factors that they would be likely to consider were they able to do so.

(e) Provide any other information that you consider to be relevant to the court

3. Statement of truth

I believe the facts stated in this annex are true.

Signed

Name

Date

Name of organisation

Position or office held

Checklist for completing form
COPDL10 for a Court authorised deprivation of liberty.

Every question on the forms should be completed, or stated that information is not available. Failure to provide the information required by the court could lead to unnecessary delays to proceedings.

A separate application must be made for each individual for whom an authorisation of a deprivation of liberty is sought.

Please ensure that the following forms have been completed:

☐ **COPDL10** Application under section 4A(3) and 16(2)(a) of the Mental Capacity Act 2005 to authorise a deprivation of liberty

☐ **Annex A** Evidence in support of an application under section 4A(3) and 16(2)(a) of the Mental Capacity Act 2005 to authorise a deprivation of liberty

☐ **Annex B** Consultation with people with an interest in an application under section 4A(3) and 16(2)(a) of the Mental Capacity Act 2005 to authorise a deprivation of liberty

☐ **Annex C** Consultation with the person the application is about for an application under section 4A(3) and 16(2)(a) of the Mental Capacity Act 2005 to authorise a deprivation of liberty.

You must also supply:

☐ COP3 Evidence of capacity

☐ Mental Health Assessment

☐ a copy of any Advance Decision

☐ a copy of any Lasting Power of Attorney (LPA)

☐ any relevant Court orders

☐ Care Plan

☐ Best Interest Assessment

☐ the application fee

General information for completing form
COPDL10 for a Court authorised deprivation of liberty.

These forms should be used to make applications to the Court of Protection for the court to authorise a deprivation of liberty for people who are receiving care in domestic settings such as shared lives and supported living. The forms should not be used for applications to vary or terminate a standard or urgent authorisation made by a supervisory body under Schedule A1 of the Mental Capacity Act.

1. COPDL10 — The Application Form

- Order sought – you must specify in the box the nature of the order you seek, i.e a declaration that the person the application is about lacks capacity to make decisions relating to their care and residence or an order that it is in the best interests of the person the application is about to deprive that person of their liberty.

- Explain why the proposed deprivation of liberty is thought to be imputable to the state. Are the care arrangements which give rise to the deprivation of liberty being made either by a local authority or the NHS?

- Permission. These applications fall under the personal welfare jurisdiction of the Court therefore permission is required in all cases.

- Date of Birth – Proof that the person the application is about is 16 years old or over.

2. Annex A — Evidence in Support of Application

In most cases the allocated social worker with the relevant skill and knowledge, involved with the care arrangements may complete the form. However, if one or more of the trigger factors apply, someone independent (who may still be employed by the applicant public authority) to the allocated social worker should provide the evidence.

- The purpose of the mental health assessment is to establish that the person the application is about has been diagnosed as being of 'unsound mind', and therefore comes within the scope of article 5 of the European Convention on Human Rights.

- The evidence may be provided by a registered medical practitioner or psychiatrist, evidence from a social worker or other non-medical practitioner listed in the notes to form COP3 will not be accepted.

- The mental health assessment may take the form of a letter setting out the diagnosis, the name of the practitioner and their qualifications. If it is not possible to provide the original letter, a copy certified by the applicant as a true copy of the original will be acceptable. The evidence should not be more than 12 months old and should also make reference to the person's eligibility to be deprived of their liberty.

- In cases where suitable mental health evidence is not readily available, then it would be acceptable to provide the assessment of capacity and mental health assessment as a single document using form COP3, but the combined evidence must be provided by a registered medical practitioner or psychiatrist.

- Is the person the application is about free to leave? This does not relate to the ability of the person to express a desire to leave but on what those with control over their care arrangements would do if they attempted to leave.

- Is the person the application is about under constant supervision and control? Provide details of the number of hours of supervision and under what situations. Provide details of the type of control exercised by staff/carers other than physical restraint.

- Is the person the application is about under physical restraint/is sedation being used? You should describe the situations when physical restraint is used. The type of restraint the frequency and duration. If sedation is used please describe the type of sedation administered.

- Is the person the application is about prevented from having contact with others? Authorisations for deprivation of liberty cannot be used to regulate or restrict contact between the person for whom the authorisation is sought and others –this includes family members or others who share living arrangements with the person the application is about.
- Statement of Best Interests You may find it helpful to refer to paragraph 5.13 in the Mental Capacity Act Code of Practice.

3. Annex B — Consultation with People with an interest in an application to authorise a deprivation of liberty.

Section 4(7) of the Mental Capacity Act places a duty on a decision maker to consult with other people who have an interest in the person's personal welfare.

You should consult with:

(a) any donee of a lasting power of attorney granted by the person;

(b any deputy appointed for the person by the court;

together with, if possible, at least three people in the following categories:

(c) anyone named by the person the application is about as someone to be consulted on the matters raised by the application; and

(d) anyone engaged in caring for the person or interested in their welfare

You must tell the people you consult with that

(a) that the applicant is making an application to court;

(b) that the application is to consider whether the person the application is about lacks capacity to make decisions in relation to his or her residence and care and whether they should be deprived of their liberty in connection with the arrangements set out in the care plan;

(c) what the proposed arrangements under the order sought are.

and that you are under an obligation to tell the person the application is about:

(d) that they are entitled to express their views, wishes and feelings in relation to the proposed arrangements and the application and that the person undertaking the consultation with them will ensure that these are communicated to the court;

(e) that they are entitled to seek to take part in the proceedings by being joined as a party or otherwise, what that means, and that the person consulting with them will ensure that any such request is communicated to the court;

(f) that the person consulting them can help them to obtain advice and assistance if they do not agree with the proposed arrangements in the application.

If the people you consult with express any views about the application or the proposed deprivation of liberty you should provide details, including attaching statements.

4. Annex C

Annex C Consultation with the person the application is about is used to inform the court that the person the application is about has been consulted about the application.

The person undertaking the consultation should be someone who knows the person the application is about, and who is best placed to express their wishes and views. It could be a relative or close friend, or someone who the person has previously chosen to act on their behalf (for example an attorney).

If no one is available, then the allocated social worker may undertake the consultation and complete the form, but where appropriate, an IMCA (Independent Mental Capacity Advocate) or another independent advocate should be appointed to assist.

The person the application is about must be consulted regarding the application and the person undertaking the consultation must take all reasonable steps to assist the person to make a decision. If the person the application is about does not have capacity to consent to being deprived of their liberty, they must be given the opportunity to be involved in the proceedings, and to express their wishes and views, to help the court reach a decision about whether the detention would be in their best interests.

Chapter 3 of the Mental Capacity Act Code of Practice contains practical guidance about consulting and encouraging participation.

Application to authorise a deprivation of liberty
(section 4A(3) and 16(2)(a) of the Mental Capacity Act 2005)

Your application must answer the following matters, either in the body of the application form or in attached documents.

Failure to provide the information required may result in the case not being suitable for the application to be dealt with under the streamlined process for an authorisation to deprive a person of their liberty under existing or continuing care arrangements.

Information required:

1.	Are there any reasons for particular **urgency** in determining the application?	☐ Yes	☐ No
2.	Have you confirmed that 'P' (the person the application is about) is 16 years old or more and is not ineligible to be deprived of liberty under the 2005 Act?	☐ Yes	☐ No
3.	Have you attached the relevant medical evidence stating the basis upon which it is said that 'P' suffers from unsoundness of mind?	☐ Yes	☐ No
4.	Have you attached the relevant medical evidence stating the basis upon which it is said that 'P' lacks the capacity to consent to the care arrangements?	☐ Yes	☐ No
5.	Have you attached a copy of 'P's' care plan?	☐ Yes	☐ No
6.	Does the care plan state the nature of 'P's' care arrangements and why it is said that they do or may amount to a deprivation of liberty?	☐ Yes	☐ No
7.	Have you stated the basis upon which it is said that the arrangements are or may be imputable to the state?	☐ Yes	☐ No
8.	Have you attached a best interests assessment?	☐ Yes	☐ No
9.	Have steps been taken to consult 'P' and all other relevant people in 'P's' life (who should be identified) of the application and to canvass their wishes, feelings and views?	☐ Yes	☐ No
10.	Have you recorded in Annex B any relevant wishes and feelings expressed by 'P' and any views expressed by any relevant person?	☐ Yes	☐ No
11.	Have you provided details of any relevant advance decision by 'P' and any relevant decisions under a lasting power of attorney or by 'P's' deputy (who should be identified)?	☐ Yes	☐ No
12.	Have you identified anyone who might act as a litigation friend for the person to whom the application relates?	☐ Yes	☐ No
13.	Have you listed any factors that ought to be brought specifically to the court's attention (the applicant being under a specific duty to make full and frank disclosure to the court of all facts and matters that might impact upon the court's decision), being factors: a) needing particular judicial scrutiny; or b) suggesting that the arrangements may not in fact be in 'P's' best interests or be the least restrictive option; or c) otherwise indicating that the order sought should not be made.	☐ Yes	☐ No
14.	Have you enclosed the fee?	☐ Yes	☐ No

The following triggers may indicate that your application is not suitable to be made under the streamlined process and that an oral hearing may be required in the first instance:

1. Any contest by the person the application is about or by anyone else to any of the matters listed at 2 – 8 above

2. Any failure to comply with any of the requirements referred in 9 above.

3. Any concerns arising out of information supplied in accordance with 10, 12 and 13 above.

4. Any objection by the person this application is about.

5. Any potential conflict with any decision of the kind referred to in 11 above.

6. If for any other reason the court thinks that an oral hearing is necessary or appropriate

▶ Print form   ▶ Reset form

APPENDIX 8

USEFUL WEB LINKS

Re X (Court of Protection Practice) [2015] EWCA Civ 599

http://www.bailii.org/ew/cases/EWCA/Civ/2015/599.html

P v Cheshire West and Chester Council and another; P and Q v Surrey County Council [2014] UKSC 14

http://www.bailii.org/uk/cases/UKSC/2014/19.html

Re NRA & Others [2015] EWCOP 59

http://www.bailii.org/ew/cases/EWCOP/2015/59.html

Re AJ (Deprivation of Liberty) [2015] EWCOP 5

http://www.bailii.org/ew/cases/EWCOP/2015/5.html

Mental Capacity and Deprivation of Liberty; A Consultation Paper (Law Commission, No 122, 2015)

http://www.lawcom.gov.uk/wp-content/uploads/2015/07/cp222_mental_capacity.pdf

Mental Capacity Act 2005: post-legislative scrutiny (Select Committee on the Mental Capacity Act 2005, Report of Session 2013-2014

http://www.publications.parliament.uk/pa/ld201314/ldselect/ldmentalcap/139/139.pdf

INDEX

References are to paragraph numbers.